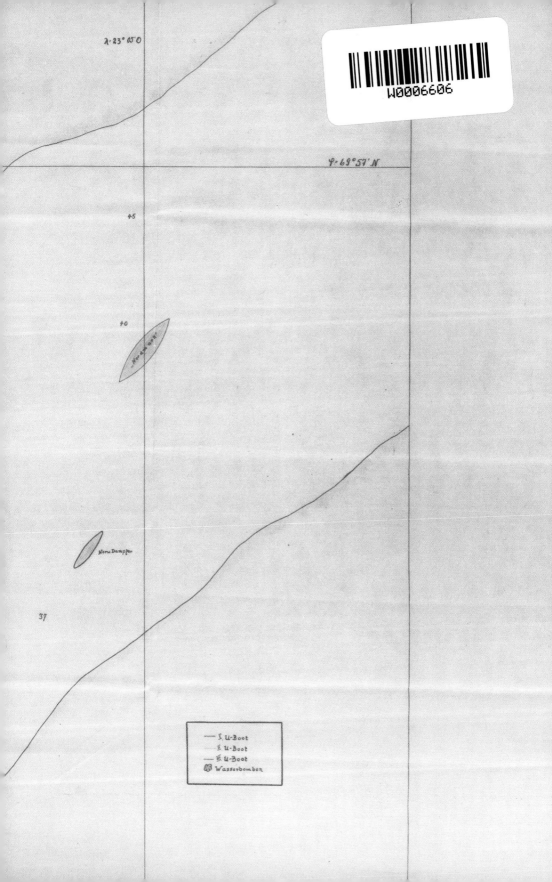

λ = 23° 05' O

φ = 69° 57' N

45

40

37

— I. U-Boot
— II. U-Boot
— III. U-Boot
🔴 Wasserbomben

X-CRAFT VERSUS TIRPITZ

THE MYSTERY OF THE MISSING X5

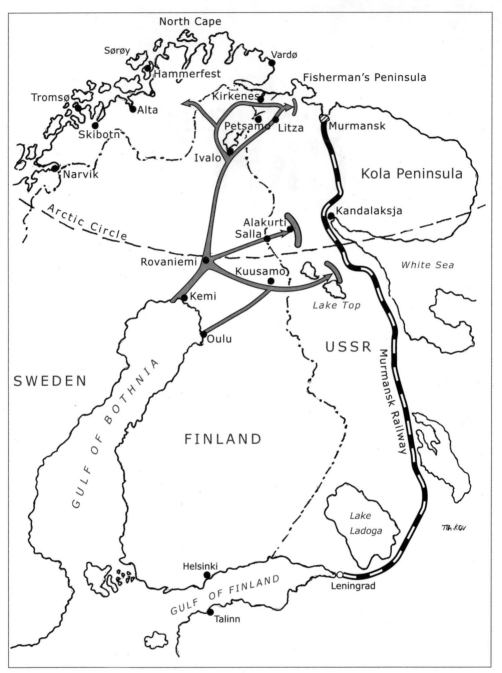

Map showing the northern theatre of war, where General Eduard Dietl's Mountain Army was halted and held on the Litza front (far north), and the courses taken by the attacks directed at Kandalaksja and the White Sea further south. The aim was to cut the Murmansk Railway, a task which proved beyond the capabilities of the German and Finnish troops involved.

X-CRAFT VERSUS
TIRPITZ
THE MYSTERY OF THE MISSING X5

ALF R. JACOBSEN

Translated from the Norwegian
by J. Basil Cowlishaw

SUTTON PUBLISHING

First published as *Banesår* in 2003 by H. Aschehoug & Co. (W. Nygaard), Oslo.

First published in English in 2006 by
Sutton Publishing Limited · Phoenix Mill
Thrupp · Stroud · Gloucestershire · GL5 2BU

Translated from the Norwegian by J. Basil Cowlishaw. This translation has been published with the financial support of NORLA (Norwegian Literature Abroad, Fiction and Non-Fiction).

British Library Cataloguing in Publication Data
A catalogue record for this book is available from the British Library.

ISBN 0-7509-4112-X

Typeset in 11/14 Garamond 3.
Typesetting and origination by
Sutton Publishing Limited.
Printed and bound in England by
J.H. Haynes & Co. Ltd, Sparkford.

Contents

Table of Equivalent Ranks

German Navy	**Royal Navy**
Grossadmiral	Admiral of the Fleet
Generaladmiral	No equivalent
Admiral	Admiral
Vize-Admiral	Vice-Admiral
Konter-Admiral	Rear-Admiral
Kommodore	Commodore (2nd class)
Kapitän-zur-See	Captain
Fregattenkapitän	Commander
Korvettenkapitän	Lieutenant-Commander
Kapitänleutnant	Lieutenant
Oberleutnant-zur-See	Sub-Lieutenant
Leutnant-zur-See	Junior Sub-Lieutenant
Oberfänrich-zur-See	Midshipman
Fänrich-zur-See	Junior Midshipman

Luftwaffe	**Royal Air Force**
Reichsmarschall	No equivalent
Generalfeldmarschall	Marshal of the RAF
Generaloberst	Air Chief Marshal
General der Flieger	Air Marshal
Generalleutnant	Air Vice Marshal
Generalmajor	Air Commodore
Oberst	Group Captain
Oberstleutnant	Wing Commander
Major	Squadron Leader
Hauptmann	Flight Lieutenant
Oberleutnant	Flying Officer
Leutnant	Pilot Officer

PART I

CHAPTER ONE

The Mystery of X5

THE KÅ FJORD, WEDNESDAY 22 SEPTEMBER 1943

The third midget submarine was sighted 700 metres north-east of the *Tirpitz*. In the shadow cast by Mount Sakkobadne it looked remarkably like the gleaming back of a killer whale that had briefly broken the surface of the water. It came and went so quickly that many of the men on board the battleship were left wondering what it really was that they had seen. A steel ring-bolt that had suddenly cut across the ripples? A gleaming eye that could have been the lens of a periscope? Only half an hour had elapsed since a violent explosion had rent the water beneath the ship. They couldn't afford to take any chances. On the anti-aircraft gun control platform 40 metres above the main deck the battleship's Third Gunnery Officer, *Leutnant-zur-See* Hein Hellendoorn, was still bleeding from a cut above his eye after having been thrown against a bulkhead when the mines went off. But this was not the time to call for help.

Made of Krupp Wotan C steel, the armoured plating of the battleship's hull was strong enough to withstand all known conventional weapons. The glass in the range-finders had been ground by expert craftsmen at the Carl Zeiss factory in Jena. And in the computing rooms amidship were installed electromechanical computers capable of converting, in a matter of seconds, visual observations into accurate firing data. The best of all that Nazi Germany's top arms factories could produce was installed on board the *Kriegsmarine*'s most fearsome battleship. This made her what was probably the most advanced military machine of her time. It also explained the shock and desperation felt by the men who manned her. Miracle of high technology though she was, the *Tirpitz* was now a stricken giant, listing to starboard and with heavy fuel oil flooding out in a violet fan towards the mouth of the fjord from her gashed tanks. Says Hellendoorn:

We had no idea of what we were up against. With my own eyes I had seen one of the midget U-boats trying to force its way over the net like some strange monster of the deep. We ourselves had nothing similar. We didn't know how many of them there were, or what they were armed with, not to mention for how long they could remain submerged. The only thing we did know was that the situation was critical. We had to defend ourselves with every means at our disposal.

Below deck, chaos reigned. Most of the battleship's generators had been put out of action, depriving the ship of its power supply and leaving it in darkness. The loudspeakers had been smashed to pieces and the telephone lines were a tangle of broken wires. Hellendoorn had to shout to make himself heard. But the gun crews were well trained and knew their emergency drill by heart. They sprang to their wheels and levers, and it didn't take long before such light and medium guns as had not been blown out of kilter had been manhandled round and brought to bear on the spot where the last midget submarine had been seen. The depressed barrels belched smoke and flame as a hail of shells and bullets churned up the sea. Every spout of water was greeted with a triumphant shout by men who were following the action through powerful binoculars. Like Hellendoorn, they knew that the *Tirpitz* had been damaged. They also knew that she was far from being defeated.

'At such moments time ceases to exist. I can still picture the situation, though I can no longer remember the details. We were firing at short range. Our 3.7cm guns weren't fully automatic, but their penetrating power was tremendous. The midget U-boats weren't armoured, so they hadn't much of a chance if they were hit.'

Many of the men threw themselves down on to the deck to avoid being hit by splinters and ricochets as salvo after salvo shattered the calm of the fjord. But John Lorimer and Richard Kendall from the midget submarine *X6* remained standing, unable to wrest their gaze from the drama unfolding before their eyes. The two young men were in what seemed to them a surreal situation. Only an hour earlier they had released the two delayed-action charges suspended like giant saddlebags on either side of their frail craft, allowing the two steel canisters, which together held 4 tons of Amatex high explosive, to sink slowly into the mud of the seabed below the battleship's keel. They had then opened the vents and the submarine's commander, Lieutenant Donald Cameron, had thrust open the hatch cover and waved a white jersey. Manned by gaping German seamen, a launch from the *Tirpitz* drew alongside, enabling them to clamber dryshod into it from the sinking submarine.

'Sorry, lads, there's nothing else for it. We shall have to surrender,' Cameron had said as he jumped on to the grating of the gangway.

On board the *Tirpitz* all was confusion. On the battleship's clean-scrubbed teak deck stood four young Britons in dirty sweaters and leather jackets, looking for all the world as though they were paying a courtesy visit. They caused a sensation. Most of the Germans had never seen a live representative of their implacable enemy. In all probability the submariners were the first Britons to set foot on the ship since her launch at Kiel on 1 April 1939 in the presence of Adolf Hitler himself.

News of the prisoners' presence spread through the lower deck like wildfire.

'Another rating came rushing in. "Have you ever seen an Englishman?", he asked, "because there are four standing outside the Regulating Office at the moment,"' recalls Max Krause, an Ordinary Seaman from Berlin, who was then, at the age of twenty-one, serving on the staff of the officer commanding the 1st Battle Group, *Admiral* Oskar Kummetz. Krause immediately dropped what he was doing and bounded up the ladder. 'They were husky fellows,' he said, 'with full beards, wearing leather jackets with no visible signs of rank.' He noticed that they kept peering at their watches.

Confusion soon gave way to anger and frustration. Many of the men crowding the rail had seen the black, 15-metre-long steel cylinder that had now disappeared from view directly beneath the battleship's bow. The officers, at least, knew that its mission had most certainly not been a peaceful one. A submarine normally carried only one kind of cargo, and that was high explosive. In all probability the *Tirpitz* was in deadly peril.

Richard Kendall, a Londoner, had volunteered to serve as a naval diver. At the age of twenty he was unprepared for what had happened. Before he knew it, he had found himself on board the battleship he had come to destroy. 'The mood changed quickly,' he says. 'When I was taken below deck, an officer slipped the safety catch off his pistol and yelled: "I'll give you one minute to tell me everything, otherwise you'll be shot!"'

Kendall and his companions knew that they had to disregard all such threats and abuse. They had given themselves up just after nine o'clock in the morning. The mines were due to go off in an hour's time, which meant that, if all went well, their nightmare would be over shortly after ten, and with any luck the *Tirpitz* would sink at her moorings. If they survived the explosion, the Germans would have something else to think about than what to do with a handful of prisoners.

'The second hand seemed to stand still. But we had to steel ourselves and try to ignore all thought of what the result of the explosion might be. We had come to destroy the battleship. That was what we had been trained for. Nothing else mattered.'

There was another reason why they had to withstand the pressure for a few more minutes. With the discovery of X6, the element of surprise had been lost. From the outset the operation had been considered bold in the extreme. The waters round about teemed with destroyers and guardships, all equipped with hydrophones and depth charges. If the alarm were raised the attack might all too easily prove suicidal – for the others involved. For X6 was by no means alone.

Two days earlier four midget submarines had set out on the long voyage from Lopphavet, a notably treacherous stretch of the Arctic Ocean, where they had slipped their tows, on through Stjerne Sound and into Nazi Germany's most heavily guarded naval base. Crowded together, hunched over their instruments, in each thin steel cylinder were four men. They were barely able to stand upright and beads of water continually dripped from the inside walls of the casing. Hot meals were mostly nothing but a dream, and getting to the heads was a difficult procedure indeed. Put-putting away aft was a 42hp Gardner diesel engine of the kind that powered London's red double-decker buses. On the surface, it drove the submarines forward at a speed of 6 knots; an electric motor took over when they were submerged. Ingenious though they were for their time, these frail craft offered little protection against shellfire or armour-piercing bullets. Midget submarines of this kind had never before been tested in war. Churchill's latest and most secret weapon, they were built with one objective: to destroy the world's most formidable and best-protected battleship, the *Tirpitz*, the steel giant anchored within the confines of a triple anti-torpedo net at the head of the narrow Kå fjord in northern Norway.

The German officers were all at sixes and sevens. The attack had come as a complete surprise to them. We let them go on shouting their heads off until they started getting divers ready. They were going to send them down to dispose of any mines we might have laid. But we knew it was only a few minutes before the explosion would come. We told them not to do it, as it was too late. There was simply no point.

The four prisoners were conducted along a passageway behind 'C' turret and divided into two pairs. The Germans had just begun to interrogate Donald Cameron and John Lorimer when the charges went off. The time was exactly 10.12.

'The German officer behaved correctly, but spoke only broken English. "You was born, was you?", he said. I assumed that he wanted to know when I was born. I was just about to answer when the deck suddenly heaved. We were all slammed hard against a bulkhead.'

Max Krause, his curiosity satisfied, was back in the Admiral's office when the charges went off. The whole conning tower swayed and the top of the mast broke off and toppled sternwards:

It was a tremendous explosion. The ship was blown a metre out of the water and fell back with a list. All the lights went out, doors were jammed and there were bits of equipment strewn everywhere. All who happened to be standing up were thrown off balance and many men fell, striking their heads against the deck. The whole ship was in turmoil. There were men running about all over the place with blood streaming from cuts in their faces. No one knew either what had happened or what to do.

In the bowels of the ship, thirty-year-old Werner Brand from Hamburg had just come on watch. An Engine Room Artificer, he was responsible for no. 6 boiler room. 'The hull bent and buckled throughout its length. I think I was thrown right up to the ceiling before finding myself on the deck. Suddenly we were in complete darkness. Steel gratings were slung all over the place. I was in a daze, but unhurt. When we got the lights going we saw that water had poured into section eight, almost directly below "C" turret.'

From 10.15 onwards a stream of damage reports reached the bridge: leaks in the engine-room aft, power failures, hydrophones unserviceable, radio station off the air, two of the three float-planes damaged, rangefinders smashed. To the Commanding Officer, 44-year-old *Kapitän-zur-See* Hans Karl Meyer, the situation seemed truly menacing. Bruised, bleeding and badly concussed, his First Officer, Wolf Junge, had been taken to the sickbay on a stretcher. A *Kriegsmarine* veteran, Meyer had won his spurs at a critical time in Germany's history. While serving with the *Freikorps von Löwenfeld* he had lost his left arm in the street-fighting that ensued in the wake of the First World War. In command, Meyer usually exuded an air of aloofness and authority, and rarely betrayed signs of emotion. But when the charges went off and blew 50,000 tons of steel out of the sea, he appears to have momentarily lost his composure. Max Krause was a witness. 'Up on the bridge, the Captain flew into a rage and ordered the four Englishmen to be shot at once as saboteurs, only to change his mind when it was pointed out to him that they were only soldiers doing their duty.'

*

A bare two weeks had passed since Meyer had taken the *Tirpitz* to Spitsbergen and back at the head of a force comprising the battlecruiser *Scharnhorst*, nine destroyers and a battalion of soldiers from Pioneer Regiment 349, which was stationed in nearby Talvik. For the first time for eighteen long months the battleship's 38cm heavy guns had been fired in anger. Coal depots and military installations in Longyearbyen and Barentsburg had been left a heap of ashes and smoking ruins. In Berlin, Hitler himself had expressed his satisfaction with the raid, and in the communiqués issued afterwards the Battle Group had been lavishly praised.

A report issued by German Naval High Command declared: 'The operation was carried out with vigour, resourcefulness and efficiency.' In his war diary the Commander-in-Chief of the 1st Battle Group, *Admiral* Oskar Kummetz, noted that the raid had been a success and expressed a wish for more of the same. 'A Battle Group lying idle at its base grows lethargic and incapable of rising to major challenges,' he wrote.

Those taking part in the operation had received their reward during the afternoon of Monday 20 September. At an impressive ceremony Kummetz and Meyer had presented more than 400 Iron Crosses (2nd class) to members of the ship's company. Meyer was a captain of the old school and a strict disciplinarian. Nonetheless, the successful sortie to Spitsbergen had to be properly celebrated, so for a brief period the men had been allowed to relax. A large store of Russian cigarettes, chocolate and other goodies had been found at Barentsburg and seized as spoils of war. Some of the men fetched bottles of what was popularly referred to as a *Polarzulage* (Polar Perk), a gift from *Reichkommissar* Josef Terboven personally. No one was quite sure what the liquid in the bottles really was, but whatever it was, it had a kick like a mule. Accordions were produced and large sums of money changed hands in the card schools that were soon under way. Autumn had come to the Kå fjord and the valleys and lower slopes of Mount Haldde were ablaze with the purple, red and gold of heather and dwarf birch. Many of the 2,300 men on board the *Tirpitz* had been without leave for more than a year and homesickness was rife. However, that particular evening had been different, and for a few precious hours the *Tirpitz* had seemed to be a happy ship.

The attack, which had caught the battleship completely unawares, had ruined everything. In the course of only a few minutes, what had been a peaceful Wednesday morning had turned into a nightmare. From the moment the first midget submarine was sighted, just after nine, until the devastating explosion an hour later, the *Tirpitz* had been reduced from a disciplined, smoothly functioning, battle-ready unit to a crippled hulk. The external damage was not all that serious – steel plating could be welded and replaced – but Meyer feared the worst. The problem was the many sensitive electrical, optical and mechanical instruments that together constituted the very nerve-centre of the battleship. The nearest repair shop was some 2,000 kilometres distant, so if the fire control or other vital systems had been adversely affected, the ship was in a bad way. Worse still, neither he nor his officers knew whether the attack was over. The first midget submarine had been scuttled by its crew on the port side of the battleship's bow; minutes later, a second submarine had broken the surface of the fjord 100 metres dead ahead of the *Tirpitz*. It had immediately come under a murderous fusillade of small-arms fire. The submarine had disappeared, but not before one member of its crew had leaped from it on to a practice target moored nearby.

On board the SS *Stamsund*, which lay at anchor some 400 metres from the *Tirpitz*, Captain Sven Hertzberg watched the surreal scene unfold. 'Bullets were flying all about him [the survivor], but he didn't appear to have been hit. When the firing died away, he lit a cigarette and began to pace to and fro on the raft until a launch came and took him prisoner.'

The man who had so miraculously escaped the fusillade was Lieutenant Godfrey Place, commander of the midget submarine X7. Without being detected, he had crept into the netted enclosure at the same time as X6 and deposited his mines, with their 4 tons of amatol, beneath the battleship's keel. This meant that, in all, 8 tons of high explosive detonated at 10.12, to blow the *Tirpitz* out of the water. However, X7 was herself badly damaged. Place had made his escape at the very last moment. The submarine sank to the bottom, taking with her the three remaining members of the crew. One of them, Robert Aitken, a diver, managed to reach the surface three hours later and, almost at the end of his tether, was taken on board the *Tirpitz*. His two companions perished when their oxygen gave out.

John Lorimer was standing on the main deck under strong guard when Place was brought on board. 'He came lumbering up to us wearing outsize seaboots, trousers and a sweater. He was soaking wet, but he was a cheering sight, standing there in the lee of the gun turret. It was a pity that the *Tirpitz* was still afloat. We had done our best and hoped that she would sink inside the nets. We felt bitter at not having succeeded.'

The morning dragged slowly on towards eleven o'clock. The thick film of heavy oil continued to spread across the fjord. On board the battleship an ugly atmosphere prevailed. The battered guards had released the safety catches on their guns. For a moment Lorimer and the rest of the captives feared that it was all up with them, that they were destined to end their lives in a pool of blood on the *Tirpitz*'s quarterdeck. But suddenly there was a cry from one of the lookouts: a third midget submarine had been sighted a few hundred metres away from the battleship, this time to starboard. Says Lorimer:

> Our guards forgot that we were standing there. The sea was as calm as a millpond. I could clearly see the periscope moving from east to west. It could have been only one sub, *X5* under the command of Lieutenant Henty-Creer, as *X10* had been damaged and had aborted. I offered up a silent prayer that they would manage to escape. But the guns opened up and spouts of water shot up all round the little craft. It was a heartbreaking moment for us, helpless bystanders as we were.

A launch manned by men from the destroyer *Z29* had that same morning been on a routine errand to the *Tirpitz*. The moment the alarm sounded, they cast off and sped at top speed to the nearest destroyer, where they took on board ten depth charges. *Leutnant-zur-See* Eberhard Schmölder and his three-man crew then set about hunting the small, black steel cylinders that kept appearing at different places in the fjord. In a report he made the next day Schmölder wrote:

> After about half an hour, getting on for eleven o'clock, I saw that the *Tirpitz* was firing at something to starboard. Looking across, I again saw a U-boat appear (U-boat C), though I was unable to determine the direction in which it was travelling. I could not observe hits from the 15cm, 10.5cm, 3.7cm and 2.0cm guns because spouts of water obscured the target. The U-boat dived and firing ceased. I immediately made for the spot and dropped a series of five depth charges at about 30-metre intervals.

From the battleship's quarterdeck Lorimer and Kendall watched with sinking hearts as the periscope of their comrades' craft disappeared in a shower of spray. 'I saw *X5* hit and go down. I don't think the men on board had a chance to save themselves,' John Lorimer says.

Richard Kendall remembers: 'There was at least one gun of large calibre on the starboard side firing. The guncrew grew more jubilant every time they thought they'd scored a hit. We had some nasty moments. I can still see in my mind's eye the cascades of water thrown up on the far side of the fjord.'

When firing ceased, Schmölder and his men spent about an hour sailing backwards and forwards across the spot where the submarine had last been seen. In his report he wrote: 'The next-to-last depth charge left behind an extra-strong eddy and oil welled to the surface. The oil spread out to form a large slick on the surface of the sea. The U-boat had undoubtedly been badly damaged and put out of action.'

As commander of the launch, Schmölder had been able to follow the drama from minute to minute at close quarters. His conclusion left no room for doubt. 'In the light of my observations I consider it certain that a total of three U-boats have been destroyed, the last two by depth charges,' he wrote.

With the depth charging of X5 shortly before eleven o'clock on the morning of Wednesday 22 September 1943, the British attack was in reality at an end, though Captain Meyer and his superiors in Berlin were later to spend many hours and days going over the course of events to determine what had actually happened. The six exhausted British survivors were taken to Germany, where they were made prisoners of war. No one yet realised that the attack would go down in the annals of war as one of the boldest and most successful operations ever, planned and carried out as it was with incredible coolness by a handful of men against a superior enemy.

One of those who did have an idea of the courage displayed by the submarines' crews was the Flag Officer Submarines, Rear-Admiral Claud Barry. The first reports that the *Tirpitz* would be out of action for several months had reached London when, in a memorandum dated 14 October 1943, he wrote:

There is no doubt in my mind that these three craft pressed home their attack to the full. In doing so they accepted all the dangers which human ingenuity could devise for the protection in harbour of vitally important fleet units.

The courage and utter contempt for danger and the qualities of inspiring leadership under these conditions of hardship and extreme hazards displayed by these officers are emphasised in the fact that none of them returned from their successful enterprise.

I consider that they all three merit the award of the highest decoration and I trust that the award of the Victoria Cross in each case will not be considered inappropriate.

Barry was wrong on one count only: not all three Commanding Officers were dead. Both the commander of X6, Donald Cameron, and the commander of X7,

Godfrey Place, survived, to return home to a hero's welcome. Both were awarded the Victoria Cross.

Lieutenant Henty Henty-Creer, commanding X5, was also recommended for a Victoria Cross, but in the event all he received was a Mention in Despatches, which resulted in a laudatory article in the *The Times* but nothing more. The explanation was that the Admiralty had discovered that there was no 'positive proof' that Henty-Creer and X5 had completed their attack. Or, as the summary report put it in 1945:

> It remains to be recorded that at 0843 [10.43 local time] a third X-craft was sighted some 500 yards outside the nets. *Tirpitz* opened fire and claims to have hit and sunk this X-craft. Depth charges were also dropped in the position in which the craft disappeared. This was X5 (Lieutenant Henty-Creer, RNVR) which had last been seen off Sørøy on 21st September by X7.
>
> Nothing is known of her movements, nor was any member of her crew saved.

This about-turn caused lasting bitterness in Henty-Creer's family and much dissatisfaction among other Royal Navy personnel. They felt that the young Australian had deserved more than a few words of praise in a newspaper. The problem was that X5 had disappeared, seemingly without trace.

In his report, Z29's torpedo officer, Eberhard Schmölder, had proposed that X5 be salvaged. 'U-boat C may be partially intact. The spot where it is lying is marked on the attached sketch. To speed matters up it would probably pay to drag the seabed with a hawser suspended between two tugs.'

As long as the weather permitted, the Germans made repeated efforts to locate the midget submarine with the aid of divers, but to no avail. After the war, further attempts were made, but again without success; there was no trace of X5. The submarine had disappeared, with the result that rumours began to circulate. Henty-Creer was reported to have been seen in a prison camp. He and his companions had managed to reach the shore and had disappeared somewhere in the trackless wastes of the north; there was even a whisper of Siberia. Others believed that he had lost his memory and was living as a nomad among the Sámi. Newspaper articles were written and expeditions equipped and despatched to the Kå fjord. No one came close to solving the mystery. The last man to see the midget submarine was Torpedo Officer Eberhard Schmölder. Since then, there had been no sign of the submarine or of the men who manned it.

*

For many years after the war the fate of X5 was the subject of much controversy. It was also one of the great unsolved mysteries of the Second World War. I personally was naïve enough to believe that, more than sixty years after the attack, the story had been forgotten – until, one spring day in 2003, an unexpected telephone call forced me to change my mind.

CHAPTER TWO

The Wreckage in the Kå Fjord

OSLO AND ALTA, MARCH 2003

The phone call was from my friend Ulf Dahlslett, a television film cameraman and teacher from Alta. He wanted to know whether I was still interested in unsolved mysteries of the Second World War.

'I'd be lying if I said no,' I told him.

'Some divers from Alta have found pieces of wreckage at the bottom of the Kå fjord. They think they may be from *X5*.'

Ulf had accompanied me on my search for the wreck of the *Scharnhorst*, so he had first-hand experience of what was involved. He never expressed his views unless sure of his facts. My pulse quickened. 'It'll cause an international sensation if it is,' I said.

A few days later I found myself, together with Ulf, in the home of Jon Røkenes, watching the first pictures from the site flicker across a television screen. Jon, a burly, good-humoured 49-year-old, was a navy diver. For many years he had worked in the North Sea offshore oil industry, before returning to his home town of Alta to start his own business, which specialised in underwater welding and similar operations. In his spare time he was a stalwart of the Alta Diving Club, which used the Kå fjord for training purposes.

'The fjord's an underwater graveyard,' he said. 'The sea floor's covered with wrecks and scrap metal. We've surveyed a lot of them, but sometimes it's hard to see what you're doing. We need to get ashore and study the pictures at leisure to identify some of the wrecks. There isn't a diver who doesn't know about *X5*, and not a few of us have dreamed of finding it one day. We'd known about this particular wreck for a long time, but we'd never associated it with the sub. It was only when we began to scrutinise the films that it occurred to us that we might be on to something. We're still not sure, though – the wreck's too badly damaged for that.'

I knew what Jon meant. The pictures had been taken at a depth of 40 metres close to the spot where *Leutnant-zur-See* Schmölder, the last man to do so, had seen *X5* disappear beneath the waves. The films were of excellent quality and revealed parts of a narrow steel craft of some kind covered in barnacles and marine growth. It was lying on its side, partly buried in the grey mud of the seabed. The sharp bow was intact, but the stern had been blown off: where the propeller and rudder had once been, there was nothing but a gaping hole. Amidships was an open hatch cover, suggesting that someone had made a last-minute attempt to escape. There was no sign of a periscope, aerial or air intake. The whole of the superstructure seemed to have been peeled away. The bottom of the fjord close by was strewn with twisted pieces of metal. The hull – about 10 metres of which was visible – appeared to have imploded. *X5* had been cylindrical and looked like a fat cigar, whereas this particular craft, whatever it was, had been ripped apart and crushed like an empty beer can.

'We're a bit disheartened at the moment,' Jon said with a wry smile. 'We've spent hours studying the pictures, but we still can't identify the wreck for certain. Some details seem to fit, others don't. What we need are the original drawings, but in 1943 the operation was top secret, so it's by no means certain that there are any.'

I was inclined to agree with him. The six 15.7-metre-long midget submarines with which it was planned to attack the *Tirpitz* in her lair were built at the Vickers yard in Barrow-in-Furness between September 1942 and January 1943. The secrecy surrounding them was total. The workshop was partitioned off, and when the hulls were taken out they were hidden from view beneath tarpaulins. Only a select few knew what the steel cylinders would eventually be used for. To make matters worse, the designs had been continually modified as work progressed, so even if blueprints did exist, it was by no means certain that they were in accordance with the final version.

'Well, at least we know that it's a vessel of some kind,' I said. 'And it does look to me like a midget submarine because of the vents and hatch. It looks about the right size, too. It's not very likely that there'd be another wrecked midget sub just there, right where *X5* went down.'

Jon smiled. 'That's what we think too. There are lots of things in favour, including the spot where we found it, but we daren't breathe a word until we're absolutely sure.'

I agreed. There wasn't a trace on the film of the characteristic side-charges, each of which had been packed with 2 tons of amatol. They'd gone, at least the one on the upper side of the wreck had. That meant that they'd either exploded when *X5* was hit by a shell from the *Tirpitz* or that Lieutenant Henty-Creer and his crew had succeeded in releasing them beneath the battleship *before* the submarine was sunk.

'I don't think they could have detonated when she sank,' Jon said. 'For one thing, there'd have been such a powerful explosion that the boats on the surface would have felt it. What's more, it would have blown the sub to smithereens. No, if it really is *X5*, then the charges have gone. That may mean that Henty-Creer did what he came to do and was on his way out when he was spotted. If that's the case, the British will have to reassess the whole operation and give him the credit he deserves.'

As though determined to add to the mystery, Jon then showed me another shot. This showed that about 500 metres away from the wreck, close to the spot where the *Tirpitz* had lain at anchor, there was another large metal object half-buried in the sludge of the seabed. Rectangular – near-oval – in shape, it looked concave on one side, as though designed to fit snugly against a rounded hull. It perfectly matched one of the side-charges carried by the midget submarines that had attacked the *Tirpitz*.

'We think it's an unexploded side-charge,' Jon said. 'You can see the fastenings that held such charges to the submarine's hull and the remains of something that looks like a timer mechanism. The question is, which of the midget submarines was it that transported it to the target? If we can prove that it really is an intact side-charge and that it was one of those carried by *X5*, it would mean that Henty-Creer did, in fact, complete his attack. That would justify a reassessment of his part in the operation.'

I knew that the controversy surrounding *X5* had given rise to much bitterness in Britain and Australia. The Henty-Creer family was very close-knit, although Henty's parents were divorced. During the war his father, Reginald, an officer in the Royal Australian Navy, spent four years in Manila as a prisoner of the Japanese. His mother, Eulalia, was living in England at the time and had been very proud of the fact that her 23-year-old son was an officer in the Royal Navy and had been chosen to command a submarine. She had, in fact, been so keen to follow his career that she had moved to Scotland, together with her two daughters, Deirdre and Pamela, to be near her son during the last three months of his rigorous training.

Deirdre Henty-Creer, an artist, who is now in her eighties, harbours fond memories of her brother. 'He was good-looking and daring. We were very fond of him. Before he left, he said that he had no intention of surrendering. He planned to return home and was intent on winning a Victoria Cross. It was a terrible blow to Mother when he was lost.'

In 1944 Rear-Admiral Barry wrote a personal letter to Henty-Creer's mother in which he said that her son had died a hero's death. But Eulalia was in deep mourning at the time. She was also both angry and disappointed at the way the Admiralty had treated her son. In August 1944 she wrote in reply:

After your kind letters about Henty, I find it impossible to believe that his part in the *Tirpitz* exploit should have been so lightly assessed that his name appears under a 'mention' in *The Times*.

Those three boats took equal risks and had an equal part to play in the attack and even if it were possible to say what explosion maimed *Tirpitz*, the honours should surely have been equally divided, as were all the hazards over a long and terrible period. Cameron, Henty-Creer and Place shared in the exploit from beginning to end and I can only suspect some very queer influences and cross-currents have been allowed to cloud the issue if that inadequate mention in despatches is your final word. . . .

I have noted in various naval lists how everyone who had any part in the planning of the attack and all those who participated in any way, as well as those who were merely on the fringe of the affair, have been suitably decorated. No-one would question the rightness of those awards, but no-one will fail to ask why Henty-Creer, as a midget commander who had been presumed to have died in the face of the enemy and what you yourself described in a letter to me as the bravest deed in history, should not only have been denied his rightful honour but cruelly passed over as expendable. . . .

Had your son been in Henty-Creer's shoes, I feel sure you would have felt as I do and I write to ask that the subject be reviewed and the dead given equal honours with the living. Alive or dead, he did not do less than Cameron or Place.

But the Admiralty had closed ranks. Barry's reply was firm and to the point:

The facts of the case are these. There is positive evidence that Cameron and Place completed their attacks and caused all the damage. There is no [underlined] evidence that Henty-Creer did, although we know he did all he could possibly do. But it is only [underlined] on positive deeds that it is possible to give the highest award and so I fear it is really impossible in your son's case.

Eulalia Henty-Creer's protests were in vain. The admirals had made up their minds and were not to be moved.

CHAPTER THREE

From Forgotten Outpost to Theatre of War

FINNMARK, 1940-42

When, in July 1940, the Führer personally awarded his favourite soldier, Eduard Dietl, the Iron Cross with Oak Leaves and at the same time appointed him Germany's first General of Mountain Troops, he was rewarding one of his oldest comrades-in-arms. Dietl, the ascetic 'hero of Narvik', was a fanatical National Socialist and had joined the Nazi Party in 1919, as early as Hitler himself. He had been a soldier all his life, fighting first in the mud and trenches of Flanders and then in the streets and beer cellars of Bavaria. The bloody clashes in the mountains surrounding Narvik in the spring of 1940 had been his hardest-fought battle ever. Both he and the men of *Gebirgskorps Norwegen*, the mountain troops he commanded, needed to rest. This they were able to do in northern Norway, which, following Norway's capitulation on 10 June 1940, evolved into a peaceful and demilitarised zone on the fringe of Europe. There was only one drawback: Hitler had something quite different in mind. He set out to make Dietl a German Cock o' the North, the all-conquering 'hero' not only of Narvik but of the whole of the Arctic.

The *Wehrmacht*'s more traditional generals followed the meteoric rise of Hitler's old ally with a blend of envy and concern. This was true both of the Chief of the General Staff, Franz Halder, and of Dietl's immediate superior, the autocratic *Generaloberst* Nicolaus von Falkenhorst, who had been in overall command of the campaign in Norway. But in the summer of 1940 Adolf Hitler ruled supreme. '*I* decide who are to be popular heroes,' he growled. 'They are the two I have chosen, Dietl and Rommel.'

Only a few weeks later, on 15 August 1940, Dietl was summoned to the Royal Hotel in Trondheim, where von Falkenhorst held court. The two top generals in Norway were poles apart. Von Falkenhorst, thickset and stockily built, was a scion of an old family of Polish nobles. He was the epitome of a Prussian General Staff officer, well educated, aloof and possessed of a razor-sharp intellect. Dietl, tall and lean, was the son of a bank employee from Bad Aibling. A man of the people, quick and birdlike in his movements, he was a charismatic personality. He had fought with the Brownshirts and despised the snobbishness of the military upper class. The two hated each other like poison.

Von Falkenhorst made it very clear that the time for celebration of Germany's overwhelming victories in Scandinavia and on the continent had passed. Berlin was already planning further conquests, and preparations for what was to come had to be made, also in the remote regions north of the Arctic Circle. There would be need for a man of Dietl's calibre.

'Northern Scandinavia is an irreplaceable source of the raw materials Germany needs, especially iron and nickel ore,' von Falkenhorst declared when he issued Dietl with his new orders. Thanks to the Ribbentrop–Molotov pact, Stalin was already busy turning the Baltic countries and eastern Poland into vassal states and might be tempted to move in now that Germany had done the spadework. Von Falkenhorst continued:

> The province of Finnmark is practically unoccupied, which will make it a magnet to all the warring powers. . . . Because of Germany's inferiority at sea and the tremendous distances involved, we cannot rule out an Allied landing in the north, a landing that we are in no position to repulse at the moment. . . . Whoever gets there first will have won the war in this region. That means we have to be the first to occupy Finnmark.

The period of relaxation was at an end. Starting on 17 August, detachments of Dietl's main body of troops, the 2nd and 3rd Mountain Divisions, embarked on 53 cargo vessels and sailed northwards. The two divisions, which each comprised 12,600 highly trained and seasoned soldiers, took with them rations for 30 days, together with some 1,000 motor vehicles, artillery and 1,200 horses. Accompanied by a handful of his staff, General Dietl himself set out on a long and gruelling reconnaissance trip by air, road, on foot and on skis that took them through the whole of the counties of Finnmark and Troms. The two mountain divisions were dispersed over an expanse of more than 1,000 kilometres, from Narvik in the south to Kirkenes in the north-east. They found themselves in a harsh, trackless and sparsely populated wasteland utterly devoid of railways and airfields. A gravel road, National Highway 50, wound its way across the Finnmark plateau, but it was open to vehicular traffic only in summer. The problems of supply and command appeared to be insuperable.

'How are we expected to maintain a whole staff, complete with supporting personnel and equipment, in a tiny fishing village?' complained Dietl's adjutant, *Oberleutnant* Herrmann.

Someone, somewhere, came up with a bright idea: a floating HQ. Dietl gave the scheme his blessing, and a few days later two brand-new combined cargo and passenger vessels that had been laid up near Trondheim, the Fred. Olsen Line's 5,000-ton liners *Black Watch* and *Black Prince*, had been commandeered. In peacetime they had operated a regular service between Bergen and Newcastle, but had been seized by the Germans when they attacked Norway in April. The *Black Watch* was quickly camouflaged with a coat of grey paint, adorned with the mountain troops' pale-yellow edelweiss emblem and renamed *Büffel* (Buffalo). On 17 September 1940 she dropped anchor in the Kå fjord, off Alta, and this picturesque and well-sheltered fjord was pressed into service as one of wartime Germany's most advanced bases.

It wasn't the first time international interest had focused on the Kå fjord, however. Ever since 1826 the rich deposits of copper in the mountains around it had been mined with the aid of British capital and workers from Finland, Sweden and the UK. When mining operations were at their peak, more than a thousand men had transformed the sleepy little fjordside settlement into a thriving community. In 1899 a large observatory was built on the summit of 900-metre-high Mount Haldde to study the Northern Lights, bringing scientists to Alta from all over the world. But the wheel of history had turned again: the mines had been worked out, the Alten Copper Works had been closed down and the scientists had moved elsewhere. When General Dietl and his staff arrived there in the autumn of 1940, all that remained to remind them of the settlement's heyday were a few slagheaps on the western shore of the fjord. The square granite buildings atop windswept Mount Haldde stood gaunt and deserted; the few people left eked out a living from farming and fishing.

From his headquarters in the well-appointed lounges of the *Black Watch* Dietl not only regrouped his mountain troops but also took time to relax. For anyone as fond of hunting and fishing as he was, the area surrounding the Kå fjord had much to offer. In the south, the River Mattis flowed into a sheltered lagoon teeming with salmon and trout, and the birchwoods were full of elk, lynx and ptarmigan. Further out, the fjord was well stocked with cod, halibut and coalfish.

'He enjoyed himself in the company of the local Norwegian sea captains and ships' officers, and most of all when he was able to indulge his greatest passion and fish with rod and line from an old launch,' his family remembers.

The Germans were able to complete the occupation of Finnmark at their leisure and without any trouble, chiefly because the fragile alliance between Hitler and Stalin, dating from 1939, still held. To all intents and purposes relations between Moscow and Berlin were amicable and peaceful. In the north, German ships were allowed to put into Murmansk in case of need, and well into the autumn of 1940 diplomatic negotiations were in progress with a view to establishing a permanent base for the *Kriegsmarine* at a deepwater anchorage in the Motovsky fjord south of the Fisherman's Peninsula.

It was the calm before the storm. Hitler's plan for a devastating attack on the Soviet Union was already taking shape. Shortly before Christmas 1940 von Falkenhorst and Dietl were informed by the *Führer* himself of his intention to mount Operation Barbarossa. Three months later his plans were complete. In the north, provision was made for an advance by nine German and Finnish divisions along three axes running eastwards from Kirkenes in Norway and Rovaniemi and Kuusamo in northern Finland. In a boldly envisaged manoeuvre, a combined force of some 200,000 men was to be charged with the task of advancing to the White Sea, isolating Murmansk and cutting the vital railway link between the ice-free ports of the Kola Peninsula and the central regions of the Soviet Union.

This plan completely transformed the strategic picture. From being no more than a remote arctic outpost, northern Norway had been turned into an important combat zone, with Lapland as its central base and concentration area. For General Dietl, the winter of 1941 was a hectic one indeed: he was to command the northern axis and discharge two important tasks. To start with, his Mountain Corps would occupy the Finnish region of Petsamo and secure the Canadian-owned nickel mines at Kolosjoki. After that, the Soviet troops stationed between the Titovka and Litza rivers were to be annihilated, to open the way to the Kola fjord. It looked easy on the map: it was a mere 50 kilometres from Kirkenes to Petsamo, and only another 100 to Murmansk. When Dietl visited the Reich Chancellery in Berlin on 21 April, after having attended the celebrations to mark the *Führer*'s birthday, a jovial Hitler tapped the table with his finger and said: 'You and your mountain troops must put these piffling 100 kilometres between Petsamo and Murmansk behind you and lay the ghost for good and all!'

But Dietl had already spent a winter in Finnmark and he was very well aware that these trackless arctic wastes were no laughing matter. He set out to convince Hitler of the difficulties involved:

Mein Führer, up there on the tundra around Murmansk it's like Earth just after the Creation. There are no trees, no bushes, no signs of human habitation. There are no roads, either, not even tracks – only rocks and gravel. It's a maze of lakes, streams and rivers full of rapids and waterfalls. In summer it's bogland, in winter there's nothing but snow and ice, and temperatures fall to 50 to 60 degrees below zero. Violent storms rage all through the eight months of the polar night. The tundra is a wasteland. It rings Murmansk like an armoured belt a hundred kilometres across. It will be virtually impassable for my troops. If we're going to keep our soldiers and horses alive, we shall need to build roads, and for that I shall need a lot of men.

Hitler was impressed. He made no promises, but said that he would give serious thought to his general's objections. In the meantime, however, preparations would need to go ahead in order to maintain the timetable. Combat-ready regiments from *Gebirgskorps Norwegen* and the *SS* went into hiding between the Tana and Pasvik rivers. They were reinforced by machine-gun battalions, bicycle companies, military police, artillery, Labour Corps (*Organisation* Todt) detachments, Pioneers and signals personnel. Air support was provided by the *Luftwaffe* in the shape of 112 bombers, fighters and reconnaissance aircraft. The troops were transported northwards by sea in convoy after convoy, all bound for the Varanger fjord. The ships also carried valuable cargoes of ammunition, motor vehicles, provisions, oil and equipment. From the port of Tromsø the convoys were escorted by destroyers, minesweepers and armed trawlers. Bases and fortifications were built to protect the heavily laden cargo vessels from attack by British planes and submarines. The raid on the Lofotens in March 1941 by British and Norwegian Commandos had strengthened Hitler's fear of an Allied landing in the north. A further 165 batteries were allocated to the coastal artillery: the Norwegian coast was to be an integral part of the Atlantic Wall.

From the autumn of 1940 to the spring of 1941 the number of German troops stationed on the north-eastern border rose to more than 50,000. They were housed in barracks, schools, churches, meeting halls and requisitioned private homes. Pressure on the civilian population dramatically increased.

Many people watched the Germans' preparations with misgiving, especially those who, before the war, had been politically active on the Left. In August 1940 the Norwegian Communist Party had been banned, and shortly afterwards the first arrests were made. Some people elected not to wait for the *Gestapo*'s knock at the door. This was especially true of the population of the tiny fishing village of Kiberg on the tip of the Varanger Peninsula, who, in the autumn, fled almost en masse to the Soviet Union. The first forty-eight to leave set out in thick fog on 25 September. As Christmas approached they were followed by many more until, in the end, close on one hundred Norwegian men, women and children had crossed the Varanger fjord and sought refuge in the Soviet Union. Many of them looked upon Stalin's Russia as the Promised Land. It therefore came as a great shock when the men were thrown into prison and threatened with five years' hard labour for having illegally crossed the border.

'We landed on the Fisherman's Peninsula, and were taken from there to Murmansk by a warship. The women and children were sent on to Belokamika [a collective farm]; the men spent three months in prison in Murmansk. We were interrogated more or less daily about our lives and how things were in Norway,' one of the more prominent refugees, Åge Halvari, a 48-year-old fisherman and veteran member of the Norwegian Communist Party, said when he was interrogated later.

Despite the friendship pact, the Russians viewed with increasing suspicion the German build-up in the north, prompting, in November 1940, a KGB major by the name of Berkowitz to persuade an initial party of six men to return to Norway to determine whether the Germans were preparing to invade. In return, they would not be punished for violating Soviet law by entering the workers' paradise without proper papers. 'On our return to Murmansk [after a fairly successful trip] Major Berkowitz plied us with food and drink. The whole thing turned into a wild party. He then asked us if we were willing to go back to Norway for a second time as spies. I don't know how the others responded, but I personally said no, as my wife was already in Russia,' said Halvari, a member of the reconnaissance group.

Most of the Norwegians spent the winter of 1941 on a collective farm outside the mining town of Apatity. When bombs began to fall on the towns of the Kola Peninsula in June, the time of waiting was at an end. Some fifty of the Norwegians were conscripted for military service and stationed in a camp near Lavna; the women were sent to a fruit farm in Siberia.

'In Lavna we were given military training by the KGB. We learned to handle rifles and pistols, to throw hand grenades and to parachute. We wore KGB uniforms. Our training lasted for about four months. We were told that we would be fighting alongside Russians, as partisans in Norway or Finland,' recalled Halvari, who became a submarine pilot and during the next two years took part in the landing of ten partisan groups behind the German lines. Some of the men who were rowed ashore at lonely spots along the coast had undergone additional training as wireless operators. One such was Leif Falk Utne, a seventeen-year-old boy who had accompanied his uncle and grandmother when they fled Kiberg for the USSR.

In the meantime, in Norway work on building up *Festung* Kirkenes proceeded apace. As soon as the snow melted, Pioneers (in German, *Pioniere* – engineer troops who were also highly trained infantrymen) set to work clearing a mountain plateau a few kilometres south of the town. The intention was to build two kilometre-long runways to make Høybuktmoen the *Luftwaffe*'s most forward airfield for the attack on the Soviet Union and the headquarters of *Die Eismeerjäger* (Arctic Fighters), the renowned and feared *Jagdgeschwader 5* (*JG 5*), whose pilots in the course of the next four years claimed to have shot down more than 3,000 Russian aircraft.

'There was nothing there when we arrived, just a wasteland of rocks and stones. But the engineers did a wonderful job. Within only a few weeks the airfield was operational,' says Hans Moos, a signaller, who for the next three and a half years was to help man the wireless station on Hill 212.

Some days later, on the night before Sunday 22 June, the first German vehicles rolled over the Norwegian–Finnish frontier and into the Petsamo region. A specialist detachment made up of men from the *SS* Infantry Regiment 'Kirkenes', personnel from the military intelligence service, *Abwehr*, and Norwegian Nazis stormed the Soviet consulate in Parkkina with machine pistols. The staff, who were engaged in burning papers and files, were taken completely by surprise. Thirty Russians were taken prisoner and large numbers of documents and codebooks seized. Both Kirkenes and Rovaniemi subsequently became important centres of espionage and wireless intelligence. The *Luftwaffe*'s 5th Signals Regiment established one of its most valuable listening posts in Varanger, while the *Kriegsmarine*'s direction-finding (D/F) station *Marine-Peilhauptstelle* (MPHS) Kirkenes became part of a chain extending from Sicily to the Arctic. This enabled the Germans to obtain accurate cross-bearings on, and thus pinpoint, enemy transmitters, even on board a ship at sea or in an aircraft in flight. Many of Germany's and Finland's crack codebreakers were stationed in Kirkenes and Rovaniemi, where *Meldekopf* Nordland, helped initially by the material seized in Petsamo, became adept at reading encrypted Soviet wireless traffic.

In central Europe, German panzer divisions pressed on towards Moscow and Leningrad at great speed, but in the north the Finns still dragged their feet. It was not until the Russians bombed Helsinki and other Finnish towns on 25 June that Marshal Mannerheim declared war on the Soviet Union. In the early morning of Sunday 29 June Dietl's advance units crossed the Soviet border in dense fog, one week behind schedule in relation to the attack on the continent. That same day Messerschmitt fighters flew their first sorties from the makeshift runways at Høybuktmoen. Supplies and spare parts had still not been unpacked, and many of the installations on the ground were only half-finished. But the young pilots were in high spirits:

'I hardly had time to start getting the squadron properly organised, as we were in the air all the time. The campaign had been in progress for three days and we were convinced that it would be over before very long, within three weeks at the most. But if we were to emerge victorious, even aircraft that were only partly combat-ready had to be thrown into the battle,' noted one of the group leaders, *Major* von Lojewski, early in June.

Despite his worries about the terrain, Dietl, like most of his staff, believed in an early victory. Behind the front, preparations were well in hand for a ceremonial parade through the streets of Murmansk as early as 20 July, and invitations to the evening's celebratory banquet at the Artika Hotel had already been printed. And true enough, to begin with things looked bright. Despite determined resistance by General Frolov's 14th Soviet Army the bunkers guarding the frontier were quickly overrun, and one week later, after a succession of bloody battles, German spearheads reached the River Litza. The river was only 60 kilometres from Murmansk and debouched into the Motovsky fjord, which, as irony would have it, only a few months earlier Hitler had wanted to lease as a naval base. But the Russians' aggressive spirit grew ever stronger and by this time the German supply lines were over 100 kilometres in length. The last stretch leading to Murmansk took them through a roadless wilderness, which meant that every shell, every kettle of soup, had to be hauled by horses, and finally carried to the front line by hand; the wounded were taken back on the return journey.

Leutnant Stenzel of 112 Mountain Artillery Regiment wrote:

We follow the débris of battle: dead horses, shattered guns. The corpses stink to high heaven. . . . Before long the road comes to an end and we find ourselves in open country. The wheels of the gun limbers sink to their axles in the soft ground. But the horses go on straining and pulling, they have to. Every kilometre takes hours. . . . Not until late in the afternoon do we permit ourselves a break. It takes many hours for the last batteries to catch up. Men sink to the ground, exhausted. But we all know that we have to get our howitzers through to the front. At seven we set off again, but then . . .

marshes. Everyone is slipping and slithering and pulling with all their might, men and horses alike. We have to get out of these bogs! Suddenly the alarm is given. Aircraft! We all fall flat, trying to worm our way to the shelter of a boulder. By some miracle no one is hit and we carry on to the next kilometre-wide bog. It takes us four hours to cross it. The ammunition has to be carried by hand, shell by shell. Again we have to rest. But we are determined to keep going. We know they need us at the front.

In one furious attack after another, from mid-July to the end of September 1941, the Mountain Corps made desperate attempts to force a breakthrough. Bridgeheads were established on the far bank, but each time the Russians counter-attacked and threw the Germans back. On more than one occasion the German troops were compelled by a shortage of food and ammunition to give up hard-won ground. Both sides suffered heavy losses. In August a deeply dejected Dietl was forced to acknowledge that he could go no further. His 2nd Mountain Division alone had lost 3,000 men killed, wounded and missing; this was 35 per cent of the division's strength. The *SS* 'Kirkenes' regiment had suffered equally heavy losses. The men who remained were worn out and demoralised. The Mountain Corps seemed doomed to bleed to death on the banks of the Litza.

One of the *SS* soldiers who had fought his way to the river, metre by metre, across incredibly difficult ground, was a young *Untersturmführer* from Berlin by the name of Marten Nissen. On 6 September he wrote to his family from a position just behind the front line:

My dear parents and brothers and sisters!
   I spent my birthday in the tent, as it was raining. The occasion was marked by organ music from our own and the enemy's artillery. In other respects I'm fine. I was very happy to be able to talk to you. . . . Everyone here hopes that the rain will soon stop . . .

It was to be Marten's last birthday. Two days later he was among the men who set out to take Hill 371.3 near the Litza when they were caught by a sudden rain of shells from the Russian guns. Marten was hit, and died in the arms of the regimental commander, *Obersturmbannführer* Ernst Deutsch, who, with his neatly trimmed moustache and white silk scarf, was a familiar figure at the front. Only four days later, on 12 September 1941, Deutsch wrote a personal letter to Nissen's family in Berlin:

It is my duty to inform you that your son fell under enemy artillery fire in the afternoon of 8 September. His life, which was full of promise, thus came to an end in performance of his duty. It falls to me to express the whole regiment's sympathy with your family. With your son I myself lost a highly conscientious and gifted leader and comrade.

This was only one of many such letters that reached Germany from the northern front that bloody autumn of 1941. By the time the fighting died down towards the end of September the Germans had suffered more than 12,000 casualties. Many units were down to only a few men and owing to lack of supplies were compelled to ration every round. Winter was fast approaching and the attempt to take Murmansk had to be given up, at least for the time being. The campaign developed into static trench warfare that was to last for more than three years – until the autumn of 1944. The 'hero of Narvik' who, on Hitler's orders, had set out to take National Socialism to the desolate wastes of the Arctic, was helplessly bogged down.

Further south, before Leningrad and Moscow, the situation was still critical for the Russians. Dietl had been brought to a temporary halt 50 kilometres from Murmansk, but Hitler's armoured columns continued their forward drive with seemingly irresistible force. From Moscow, Stalin despatched increasingly urgent appeals for assistance to Great Britain and the USA. Soviet losses in the first months of the war had been appalling: more than one million soldiers had been killed, wounded or taken prisoner and thousands of aircraft and armoured vehicles destroyed. These losses had to be replaced if the Soviet Union were not to go under.

It only needed a glance at a map to realise that the shortest supply route from the Allies in the west to the Soviet Union in the east was through the Barents Sea, to the ice-free ports of the Kola Peninsula. As long as the Arctic front held and the railway from Murmansk to the interior remained in operation, it would be possible to transport these vital supplies to the most endangered sectors in the south. For this reason Stalin needed two things: immediate shipments of weapons and other matériel, along with Allied intervention to disrupt the German convoys that sustained Dietl's divisions on the Kola Peninsula. That Stalin should feel impelled to plead for Allied assistance further underlined the strategic importance of the confrontation in the far north. If the Mountain Corps clinging to the rocky slopes above the River Litza were cut off, the railway line running south from Murmansk could be kept open. This would enable urgently needed weapons of war to reach the central sectors of the front, where the German invaders were thrusting towards Moscow. What happened in the Arctic would help determine the outcome of what had by this time grown into a world war.

'But the opening of the Russian campaign had other and, in the long run, still more far-reaching consequences on our maritime strategy, for it gradually shifted the focus of the Home Fleet's responsibilities from the passages between Scotland and Greenland to the north-east, and in particular to the waters between northern Norway and the varying limits imposed by the Arctic ice,' wrote S.W. Roskill in his two-volume work *The War at Sea*. He continued: 'The first signs of this change came in July, when the Russians began to press for attacks to be made on the enemy's traffic moving between such ports as Kirkenes in north Norway and the formerly Finnish port of Petsamo, now in German hands.'

Although the resources of the British Home Fleet were strained almost to breaking point, two aircraft carriers, *Victorious* and *Furious*, were immediately despatched to the Barents Sea. This was a political gesture. From a military point of view it was a wasted effort, as the force of torpedo-bombers that attacked Petsamo found no ships in harbour. What was worse, over Varanger the aircraft were intercepted by German fighters and half of them were shot down.

Despite this setback, new operations were mounted in August. Two submarines, *Tigress* and *Trident*, combed the sea between Tromsø and the North Cape, while two cruisers, *Nigeria* and *Aurora*, acting as escorts for a fleet of transports, evacuated the Norwegian and Russian settlements on Spitsbergen. While this was taking place, the *Argus*, an old aircraft carrier, and a merchantman were sent eastwards with forty-eight Hurricane fighters on board. The merchantman discharged her cargo in Archangel, whence the Hurricanes were flown to the airfield at Vaenga, where they were immediately thrown into the battle for the Kola Peninsula.

At about the same time several German convoys were on their way northwards with reinforcements for Dietl's badly depleted forces. They included *Generalleutnant* Ferdinand Schörner's 6th Mountain Division, which had been resting in Germany after its successes in Greece. The division was now earmarked for the Arctic front, to enable Dietl to break through to Murmansk in one great autumn offensive. But the ships were detected by the *Trident*. The submarine's first torpedo struck the 6,000-ton *Donau* amidships. Only six minutes later her boilers exploded, causing the ship to rear into the air and sink like a stone, stern first.

We were standing by the field kitchen when the torpedo hit. From our position on board the troopship *Bahia Laura* we watched the *Donau*'s stern go under as men were flung overboard. Then, a short time afterwards, a tremor went through our own ship and a tongue of flame leaped up just in front of the bridge. I assumed that the petrol tank in Hold no. 3 had been hit by a torpedo. A quarter of an hour later we were forced to jump into the ice-cold water.

Thus Johan Schlemmer, an infantryman from *Marsch-Bataillon* Salzburg after having been picked up and taken to Hammerfest. Some horrific scenes ensued when the two transports went down. Between them they were carrying more than 1,600 men, including a veterinary company with over a hundred horses that were tethered below deck. By the time lifeboats and a number of local vessels reached them in the evening, more than 600 soldiers and all the horses had drowned.

Only a week later the cruisers *Nigeria* and *Aurora* approached the coast of Finnmark on their way back from Spitsbergen. Near the North Cape they ran into the German auxiliary cruiser *Bremse*, which was escorting two more troopships, the *Trautenfels* and *Barcelona*, with, between them, 1,500 men of the 6th Mountain Division on board. In a brave endeavour to save the transports, the *Bremse* sacrificed herself and was sent to the bottom after putting up heroic resistance. The scene of the battle was shrouded in dense fog, with the result that while the British were busy engaging the ancient cruiser, the two troopships slipped into a nearby fjord. The troops they were carrying were saved, but the two attacks were to have far-reaching consequences. The German Naval High Command refused to let the ships continue. Instead, the troops were put ashore and forced to make their way to the front, 700 kilometres distant, on foot. The following convoys were ordered to return to Trondheim, whence the rest of the division entrained for Oslo. From the capital, it continued by sea through the Baltic to Finland. Only after several weeks of travel and hard marching in freezing cold and driving snowstorms did the 6th Mountain Division reach the front and bring the corps up to strength. By then it was too late. The lengthy period spent on the move had taken its toll of the soldiers and their massed attack ground to a halt on the stony wastes bordering the Litza.

While Dietl's troops were withdrawing to winter positions and preparing to go on the defensive, the *Luftwaffe* continued its unrelenting assault on Murmansk. Day after day, all through the autumn of 1941 and the winter of 1942, Stuka and Heinkel bombers continued their attempts to cut the railway line over which so many vital supplies were being transported south – but in vain. The bombers were protected by what had by that time become the legendary *Jagdgeschwader* 5 (*JG* 5), which in Kirkenes and Petsamo could call upon some fifty Messerschmitt Bf 109 and Bf 110 fighters. Opposing them were several hundred Soviet fighters, which were soon reinforced by the addition of British Hurricanes and American Curtiss P-40s. 'Measured against the Soviet superiority [in numbers] in the air, our relatively light losses are ascribable solely to the skill of our pilots,' claimed the unofficial history of *JG* 5.

One fighter pilot who quickly made a name for himself in the skies above the Kola Peninsula was a dark-haired lieutenant, Heinrich Ehrler; a carpenter's son, he was twenty-four years of age and came from Oberbalbach in Bavaria. On leaving elementary school Ehrler was apprenticed to a butcher until, in 1935, he enlisted in the new *Wehrmacht* that Hitler was busy building up. Overwhelmingly ambitious, highly intelligent and blessed with lightning reactions, he was a born fighter pilot. Five years after leaving the butcher's, he had become an officer in the *Luftwaffe*.

'He was clever, brave and a first-class pilot, and tremendously popular with the men,' says Hans Moos, who maintained daily wireless contact with the pilots when they were in the air. Kurt Schultze, a former major, who was for a time Ehrler's adjutant, adds: 'No one taught me more about flying than Heinrich. He was a natural, and absolutely fearless in the air.'

When Ehrler's score of shot-down Soviet aircraft topped the forty mark, he was awarded the Knight's Cross of the Iron Cross, one of the very first such awards to be made in the Northern theatre. Like General Dietl, he thus became a member of an elite band who, in the interests of wartime propaganda, were lauded as Arctic heroes. Heinrich Ehrler was well on the way to becoming one of the Commander-in-Chief of the *Luftwaffe*, Hermann Göring's most vaunted fighter aces. The road to the top seemed short, although he was as yet unaware of it. But fate had something different in store for him, and Ehrler's name was to be for ever linked with the *Tirpitz*, which in the summer of 1942, for the first time, dropped anchor in the Kå fjord. On board was another young lieutenant, Hein Hellendoorn, who was in charge of the battleship's anti-aircraft guns.

CHAPTER FOUR

The Journey to Finnmark

LONDON, SUMMER 2003

The first thing to greet a visitor in the entrance hall of Deirdre Henty-Creer's flat in Kensington is an impressive painting of a Sámi encampment not far from Alta. With bold, vivid strokes of the brush she has captured camp life as she saw it one summer day midway through the twentieth century: men fishing for salmon, children playing, women at work plaiting sedge and preparing reindeer hides.

'They are members of the Bongo family, whom I met in the summer of 1950. They were most hospitable. I am still grateful for having been allowed to paint them,' said the 83-year-old painter the first time I was invited to her home, together with my wife, in July 2003. The walls of the flat were hung with more canvases testifying to the family's lifelong love of Norway's northernmost county, landscapes picturing waterfalls and the endless moors of Finnmark's mountain plateau. There was also a view of the Kå fjord, with the precipitous slopes of Mount Sakkobadne looming large and ominously in mid-picture. 'You see, Henty was not just our only brother,' Deirdre Henty-Creer explained, 'he had taken on the role of father. When he went missing, we lost both our friend and our guardian.'

Talented and strong-willed, Eulalia Henty-Creer, the matriarch, was a remarkable woman by any standards. She resolutely refused to rest content with Rear-Admiral Barry's conclusion – so much so that in June 1950 she had her Hillman Minx hoisted on board ship at Newcastle and, together with Deirdre, the elder of her two daughters, set off for Bergen and the north of Norway. She was determined to find out what had happened to X5 and her son Henty. Deirdre has vivid recollections of their journey:

In Bergen we boarded the coastal-express steamer and sailed northwards. We had a most enjoyable trip up the coast, disembarking in Hammerfest five days later. Chief Constable Wallerud and Sergeant Johnsen of the local police force had been notified of our coming and made us very welcome. But it was a cold summer and I shall never forget that first night. The accommodation was wretched. We were lodged in a room in a barrack hut, but it was impossible to sleep in it. The bedclothes were clammy from the damp that seeped through the walls. We had brought nothing with us but a tent, a mosquito net and a sheet of plastic from a barrage balloon in case of rain.

I was born in Hammerfest in February 1950 and was only four months old when Eulalia and Deirdre arrived in search of their son and brother. I have no recollection of the first years of my life, but from photographs and what I have heard and read I know that at that time Hammerfest was still dominated by barracks and makeshift homes. It had not yet been rebuilt after having been destroyed by the retreating German troops five years earlier. When I told her of this, Deirdre produced a photograph of Police Sergeant Johnsen and herself on the deck of the police launch *Broder*. The launch was moored at a wharf known locally as the Iron Curtain. The photograph had clearly been taken on a typical Arctic summer morning, just like those I remembered from the 1950s. The light fell softly across the harbour, where purse-seiners and other fishing boats lay at anchor, gulls wheeling above their mast-tops; I could see that some of the boats had their engines running. As I studied the photograph, I felt that I could hear again the sounds of my childhood: the plaintive cries of seagulls, intermingled with the put-put of newly fired cylinders, slow and lingering, like the pulsing of an artery. The dainty little auburn-haired painter was smiling at the photographer, but it was plain that there was no heat in the sun and that it was still cold. For this reason Deirdre was sensibly dressed in a tweed jacket and windproof trousers, and she was wearing gloves.

'My mother was a strong personality,' she said. 'She wanted answers to her questions and she was determined to find them herself. The police were outstandingly helpful. They took us to all the nearby islands, and the launch went into the fjords that Henty himself might have entered. It was a strenuous, but inspiring, trip.'

With her soft skin and auburn hair, Deirdre Henty-Creer was still very much an English rose. It felt strange to be sitting among the antique furniture of her West End flat, listening as she reeled off names familiar to me from my childhood. My father's family came from one of the lovely fjords that Deirdre visited. My mother was born on a small farm overlooking the mouth of the Kå fjord; she was only four years old when her own mother bled to death in childbed. She was sent away, to grow up with foster parents on a smallholding in the lean years following the First World War. It was a tiny farm, and hay for the family's few cows had to be cut and dried on the far side of the sound, in the shadow of the lofty Seiland mountains. Like the rest of the family, my mother was a big-boned and physically strong woman, frugal and of amazing stamina. She had a good head on her shoulders, but bore in her heart a secret sorrow that remained with her all her life. When I was born, a late-comer, the last of four children, my mother was thirty-two years old. Although I have suppressed a great deal, I seem still to feel her sadness deep within me. She never said anything, as, secure in her faith, she believed it was ordained by God that one should not complain, but humbly accept life's trials and tribulations. It was only late in her life, when we had both begun to reconcile ourselves to one another, that she let me into her secret. She said that in her mind's eye she could still see her mother dying in a welter of blood. She had been sent away and had never been able to get rid of her sense of guilt, as though she herself had been responsible for the tragedy. It was an absurd idea, the product of a child's sense of loss, sorrow and yearning for love – all the complex emotions that accompany us through life. I looked at Deirdre's paintings. They depicted my mother's landscape, a landscape that was also my own. I can't say that I completely understood, but I did sense a little of what impelled the two to set out on the long, exhausting journey north to the shores of the Arctic Ocean.

When they reached Hammerfest, Eulalia mobilised the local press in her quest to uncover the truth of her son's disappearance. The first article that resulted appeared in the *Vestfinnmark Arbeiderblad* on Monday 3 July 1950 and bore the headline: 'What happened in the Kå fjord on 26 [*sic*] September 1943?' It continued:

The mother of the commander of the third submarine has not given up hope of finding her son alive. Since the war she has busied herself compiling information on the operation, to try to ascertain more about her son's fate. She has now come here in person to talk with anyone who may have witnessed the attack and who can tell her what they saw. . . . She believes that it is possible that the submarine was damaged and that the men on board made it to the shore. If they did, she thinks they would have tried to make their way across the frontier to Murmansk. To have done so they would have donned civilian clothes and, in all probability, come into contact with

Norwegians. Her son may also have undergone some experience that caused him to lose his memory or impaired his faculties in some other way. We urge anyone with information on these matters to get into touch with Mrs Henty-Creer at the Bossekop Gjestgiveri [an inn].

I could not help but admire the two intrepid ladies who had travelled more than 2,000 kilometres to find answers to the questions that the Royal Navy declined to pursue further. In 1950 Europe was still a continent in which millions of people were missing after the bloodiest conflict in history. In thousands of homes everywhere, widows and orphans refused to relinquish the hope that their loved ones would one day return. Only a very few possessed the courage and resources required to institute a search themselves. Eulalia Henty-Creer's journey was exceptional in this regard – and it was undertaken by an exceptional woman. Deidre said:

My mother was most certainly not rich, anything but. She had divorced Father when he found himself another woman and had to manage alone. But she had will-power and loved Henty deeply. She was fearless, too, and had travelled the world with three small children. She was inspired by what had happened to Father. He had been in command of a naval base in Hong Kong when the Japanese attacked in December 1941. When the settlement fell early in the New Year, he was taken prisoner. But the ship taking him into captivity was torpedoed in the South China Sea. Father was rescued after six hours and taken to the Philippines. Nothing was heard from him for more than four years, when he was found ill and starving in a camp outside Manila. They were divorced, but had remained in touch. If Father could turn up many years after he had been given up for lost and forgotten by most people, why shouldn't the same be true of Henty? That was the way Mother thought, and that was why she wished to see and experience for herself the moorland wastes of the Arctic. She knew that they were wide and desolate. She wanted to assure herself that Henty wasn't wandering aimlessly about somewhere, not knowing that the war was over.

After spending the night in Hammerfest, Eulalia slipped behind the wheel of her trusty Hillman Minx and drove the 150 kilometres to Alta along the unmetalled road that *Organisation* Todt had built together with the Norwegian Highways Authority. It was along this road that Dietl's Mountain Corps had both advanced and, some years later, retreated. Many of the snowscreens that lined the road had been dismantled in 1943 and 1944 when attacks on the *Tirpitz* heightened in intensity; their timbers were needed to make coffins for the many who were killed.

Alta was in the same situation as Hammerfest. The inhabitants had returned to rebuild their homes after the Germans' wanton destruction, but the work had still not been completed. Life was far from easy and many commodities were still in short supply. By coincidence, meat rationing was abolished the day Eulalia and Deirdre got there. The roads were in a terrible state and petrol stations few and far between.

'It was a difficult time, but we were welcomed with open arms. The inn in Bossekop was open and the staff were most kind. I have very fond memories of our stay there.'

In Bossekop the two travellers received a pleasant surprise. In the roads lay the *Radiant*, a full rigger chartered by the richest man in England, the Duke of Westminster. Eulalia was a friend of the duke, who was a passionate salmon fisherman and had leased the River Alta for the summer. 'We were invited on board for a magnificent dinner, and the duke gave us an enormous smoked salmon that lasted us all through the summer.'

But the duke's presence did not help Eulalia and Deirdre for long. War had broken out in Korea and the West feared that Stalin would seize the opportunity to cross into Europe. The duke, a major property owner in London and a key figure of the Establishment, could not risk being taken prisoner if Soviet troops were to overrun northern Scandinavia. Accordingly, he upped sticks and set a course for home. Cut short though it was, the season had by no means been a waste of time, as, by the time he left, the duke and his guests had already landed more than two hundred salmon.

'The international situation had taken a dramatic turn,' Deirdre explained, 'but we didn't feel we could leave Finnmark without doing what we had come to do. We had a plan and we intended to follow it.'

Instead of emulating the duke's example and making for home, Eulalia and Deirdre set off eastwards, towards the Soviet frontier. Eulalia wished to see for herself the land over which Hitler and Stalin had fought and spread terror in the greatest bloodbath of modern times. She had heard of the sufferings in the Gulag and knew that hundreds of thousands of innocent people had been arrested and deported to the east. True, Britain and the Soviet Union had been allies in 1943, but the suspicious nature of the KGB (in 1943, the NKGB) was legendary. If Henty and his men had crossed the border without identity papers, there was no telling what might have happened to them.

'Although it was a faint one, we nurtured a hope that he might be in Russia. We were given permission to travel east, but were warned by the police and military authorities under no circumstances to cross into Soviet territory. The situation was tense, and the frontier was tightly sealed.'

While Eulalia was having her work cut out avoiding the puddles and potholes of National Highway 50, the first response to their appeal came in. On Tuesday 4 July Ludvig Rokkan, the captain of a coastal steamer, contacted a Mo i Rana newspaper, the *Helgeland*. 'His ship had been requisitioned by the Germans as a cargo steamer, and when the attack took place it was moored close by the giant German battleship,' the ensuing article said.

According to Rokkan, two midget submarines, each with four men on board, had taken part in the attack. All four had been saved from one of them, but only two from the other. Rokkan says that he saw with his own eyes the British sailors mounting the battleship's gangway. The Germans on board asked the first Englishman over the rail whether the attack was an act of revenge for Scapa Flow, to which he answered yes. However, he also said that in seven minutes the ship would be blown to bits! In the event it wasn't quite that bad, but Rokkan says that the explosion that followed shortly afterwards was the most devastating he had ever heard. He was blown off his feet on to the wharf. Not wanting witnesses, the Germans then chased the men off into the valley.

Rokkan thought that Henty-Creer might have been among the survivors. He had spoken to some of the [Norwegian] soldiers who had been brought to the mainland from Spitsbergen and been in prison with the six Englishmen, and they said that they had been well treated by their captors. The question now is whether the six got back to England. If they didn't, there is a possibility that the missing man was among them.

When the *Vestfinnmark Arbeiderblad* finally traced Eulalia and Deirdre, they were in Vadsø, far to the east. Unfortunately for them Rokkan's testimony contained nothing new: the six survivors – four from *X6* and two from *X7* – had long since returned to Britain and told all they knew. To the journalist who talked to her on the phone, Eulalia seemed to have lost heart, so much so that she had declared her intention of giving up the search. 'Mrs Henty-Creer said that she and her daughter had concluded that her son had lost his life in the attack,' the paper wrote. 'They . . . expect to reach Hammerfest in four days' time. On the way they plan to visit Kvalsund, as she has heard from there that three Englishmen, whose bodies had been recovered from the sea shortly after the *Tirpitz* was attacked, were buried there.'

It is no longer possible to determine what induced Eulalia Henty-Creer to change her opinion and, to all intents and purposes, reconcile herself to the fact that her son was dead. It may have been her disappointment at not having been able to establish contact with the Russians; equally, it could have been nothing more than a reaction to the stresses and strains of her journey. That year, the Arctic summer had been unseasonably cold. The first night-frost was recorded as early as 1 July, with the result that much of the cloudberry harvest was lost. It was enough to discourage any traveller, no matter how resolute. Despite this, Deirdre still thinks the way her mother's attitude changed was strange. 'Mother was an optimist. She wasn't the kind to give up hope – and she continued to hope.'

Meanwhile, another witness had made his way to the Bossekop inn, bringing with him information that was to transform the Henty-Creers' mood entirely. Lars Mathis Aleksandersen Sarilla was seventy years old. A retired sea captain, he lived in Bossekop and from his house had a panoramic view of the whole of the Alta fjord. On all his photographs he comes across as a typical seadog of the old school. Stockily built, legs planted firmly apart, a shiny-peaked cap set square above a rugged, weatherbeaten face, he looks a true veteran of many an Arctic storm. His moustache is white, his gaze steady and authoritative.

'He came to see us at the hotel because he felt he had some important information. Both Mother and I found him highly credible.'

Sarilla had been skipper of a tug in the Kå fjord and was a familiar sight among the German naval personnel stationed there. It was eight o'clock in the morning on Thursday 23 September 1943 when, glancing out of his kitchen window, his attention was caught by something sticking out of the water.

> I took it to be the periscope of a submerged submarine. It was moving quite fast in the direction of Kråknes Point (on the far side of the fjord). The sea was perfectly calm (smooth surface) and I could clearly see a streak of foam on the water in the wake of the periscope. I stood watching the periscope until it was just about in mid-fjord, by which time it was too far away for me to follow any longer. I should imagine that about three or four minutes (five at the most) elapsed from the moment I first saw the periscope . . . until I lost sight of it out in the fjord. There were two other people in the house at the time, though I can't remember who they were, and they saw the same as I did. If I do remember, I shall let you know.

The ageing captain's observation was made the day after the attack by the midget submarines. Eulalia Henty-Creer thought his statement so important that she contacted the local chief of police. Sarilla's testimony was then taken down in the presence of witnesses and duly stamped with the official police stamp. It included the following passage:

When the periscope of the submarine passed the area near my house, some German soldiers, who were working [near] a shore [*sic*] house near my home, became aware of the periscope. They pointed to it and shouted to each other: 'British submarine.' A couple of them ran to the telephone room in the store house probably to report to their superiors. However I could not see that anything was done by the Germans to destroy the submarine.

Sarilla added that, out fishing during the First World War, he had once seen a submerged German U-boat pass his ship. '[A]nd because of this I could with certainty say that what I saw move from Bossekopberget towards Krakenes on the morning of 23rd September was the periscope of a submarine passing in the underwater position.'

Eulalia and Deirdre immediately construed the old captain's story as proof that Henty and his crew had survived the shelling from the *Tirpitz* and the depth charges dropped by *Z29*'s launch. Their despondency gave way to hope and relief: for them, Sarilla's statement gave further justification for their search. Deirdre says:

The periscope Sarilla saw could only have been *X5*'s. Hudspeth's submarine, *X10*, had left the fjord the previous evening. The remaining X-craft had been destroyed, so there were no other possibilities. Henty must have succeeded in stealing out of the Kå fjord *after* having completed his attack. It is probable that he spent the night quietly on the bottom in shallow water off Bossekop making repairs or resting before setting a course for the open sea the next morning. I remember meeting several witnesses who claimed to have seen a submarine further out that same day. That enabled us to piece together what had happened.

When, some weeks later, Eulalia and Deirdre set out on the long drive south, Eulalia thanked the people of Finnmark in an open letter to the *Vestfinnmark Arbeiderblad*:

I cannot leave Alta without thanking the many people who have helped me in my search for my missing son and his three companions. I have spent two months in Finnmark and have travelled a total of nearly 3,000 miles in connection with my investigation. Everywhere, I have met with the utmost friendliness and assistance.

She left for home full of optimism. From her letter it was clear that she was more convinced than ever that her son would one day reappear:

I now have proof that my son in his X5, the day after the attack by the three submarines in the Kå fjord, successfully evaded the German depth charges and made his escape, as next morning the periscope of his submarine was seen close to land off Bossekop. . . . The sight of the periscope occasioned much excitement among people on the dock, Russian prisoners and Germans who were working there. Every effort was made to telephone a report of the sighting to the authorities, but no attack on the submarine resulted.

Eulalia Henty-Creer now felt that she could follow the track of X5 from Bossekop to a lonely bay on an island near the Kå fjord:

Of three clues I have received . . . it is clear that they were having difficulties with the power supply on board and that he was looking for a secluded spot where he could get close inshore, recharge his batteries and give his men some rest. What happened afterwards is a mystery. His mother ship, *Thrasher*, didn't wait long enough for him, and if he got back to the rendezvous too late, there would be only two courses open to him. He would either have to follow the coast to the Kola Peninsula or make his way straight across country and through Finland to Murmansk. There, the Admiralty had made arrangements for him to be assisted to return to England. He wouldn't have tried going through Sweden, as at that time he would have been interned.

Eulalia no longer believed that, if anything had happened to her son in the Soviet Union, the Russian authorities would be willing to help her. But she had still not given up hope that Henty might still be in Norway:

We don't know whether he reached Russia and don't expect to hear anything to that effect either. But I believe he may still be in Norway and that he is ill or has lost his memory. The Norwegians and Lapps helped a lot of people to cross the frontier, and it is conceivable that they have now forgotten most of the young men to whom they rendered assistance six years ago. There is a possibility, though, that someone may recall an incident that would help me in my search, and I ask them to try to remember whether they met or helped a young man, tall, slim, with thick brown eyebrows and very fair, straight hair, about 5'10" in height and 23 years of age. He has bright blue eyes.

It was not only Sarilla's story and what other eye-witnesses had told her that gave Eulalia cause for hope. From her letter it was apparent that she had been in touch with spiritualists and fortune-tellers too.

One thing that encourages me to believe that he may still be somewhere in Norway, either ill or injured, or in shock or suffering from loss of memory, is that twenty-five years ago an [American] Indian prophesied that his name would one day go round the world, and that he would suffer an injury to his head. Many people in London are engaged in psychical research and they are all convinced that he is alive and not far from the place where he was last heard of. One even goes so far as to maintain that his mental and physical health are poor, but that he is being well cared for. He also says that he does not know that the war is over and is waiting for the Navy to come and fetch him. Another says he is living among the Lapps.

There is something very moving and sad about the letter from this grieving mother who, in desperation, had turned to London's mediums and subsequently journeyed thousands of kilometres in search of her missing son. Eulalia died in 1981, but her two daughters, Deirdre and Pamela, are both (2005) still alive. In their conversations with me they continued to speak of their brother with warmth and passion – sixty years after the dramatic events that had taken place in the Kå fjord and Deirdre's and her mother's subsequent odyssey far beyond the Arctic Circle. Listening to them, I could not help but think of the pictures I had seen of the shattered wreck lying at the bottom of the fjord in the shadow of Mount Sakkobadne. If it really was X5, the submarine had been their brother's coffin. It would mean that he *was* close to where he had last been seen, and his name had indeed gone round the world. It was brought home to me what a difficult – and delicate – task lay ahead of us. No matter what the result, someone was bound to be hurt.

CHAPTER FIVE

The Key Theatre in the North

THE BARENTS SEA, 1942/43

While General Eduard Dietl was occupied with the planning of a new offensive to cut the Murmansk railway line once winter released its grip, a bored, unemployed ship's officer was kicking his heels in occupied Copenhagen. The son of a Danish father and Icelandic mother, 27-year-old Ib Arnasson Riis was born and had grown up in the Danish town of Hellerup. He was more strongly attached to his mother and her family than to his father, which is why he adopted Icelandic citizenship.

'I had qualified as a wireless operator and navigator, but after the German occupation the Danish inshore merchant fleet was bottled up in its home ports and many ships were actually laid up. Jobs were hard to come by and there were many applicants for the few that were available. My prospects looked gloomy until, in the autumn of 1940, I was approached by a man who made me an offer I couldn't refuse,' Riis said on the phone when I tracked him down in California in 2003.

Ib Riis had first gone to sea at the age of sixteen, and had four times rounded Cape Horn. Nine years later he sailed through his mate's examination at Svendborg Navigation School and obtained a master's certificate. But this was June 1940. A month earlier, German troops had occupied Denmark and Norway and no one had any use for an Icelandic navigator just out of college.

'The man who came to see me called himself Hansen and spoke Norwegian with a strong German accent. He said that he knew people who could get me a job on a German ship. It seemed that he had looked after a Norwegian delegation at the Summer Olympics in Berlin in 1936. I was suspicious and couldn't help wondering who his contacts were. At the same time, though, I was curious and badly in need of a job.'

At the Clacis café the next day Riis was presented to a rather stout German infantry captain, who introduced himself as Edward Frantz. He was still troubled by malaria after many years spent in the tropics. Frantz asked him whether he would consider taking command of a German ship that was bound for Greenland.

'Without hesitation I said yes. I reasoned that once I got clear of Danish waters it would be easy to slip ashore in Reykjavik. I wanted to get to Iceland,' Riis said.

Riis was wined and dined by Frantz, who seemed to want for nothing. He didn't realise that he was gradually being ensnared in the *Abwehr*'s, that is, the German Military Intelligence Service's, net until, in November 1940, he was told to report to room 248 at the Cosmopolite Hotel in central Copenhagen, headquarters of the occupying forces. At that meeting, all former pleasantries were brushed aside, as the report later compiled by the British following Riis's debriefing confirms: 'At this interview Riis was no longer asked to agree, but rather *told* that he was to go to Iceland by fishing boat in the guise of a refugee, as Greenland was of no further interest. He was told he would have to send back information and that he would be paid a retainer of Kr 200 per month until the trip could be arranged.'

The man who gave the order was a blond giant, over 6 feet tall, with bluish-grey eyes, a bull neck and the battered face of a professional boxer. He called himself Knudsen, but that wasn't his real name. His real name was Otto Kiesel. A key player in the Scandinavian theatre, he held the rank of *Kapitänleutnant* in the *Abwehr* and reported to *Abwehrstelle* Hamburg. His principal task was to recruit Norwegians and Danes to serve as German agents behind enemy lines. When Riis left the hotel that evening, Kiesel could congratulate himself: he had recruited a ship's officer to head a spy ring in Iceland. For administrative purposes Riis was given the cover name Edda, a name with Old Norse connotations.

'By the time I realised what it was all about, it was too late to back out. What is more, I had to think of my parents, who were still living in Hellerup. I might have endangered them if I had refused,' says Riis, who shortly after-wards was sent to Hamburg and spent the next few months undergoing intensive training in secret writing, codes and other shadowy espionage techniques.

'It was tough going. I wasn't allowed contact with other people and most of my evenings were spent alone. What I found most interesting was that Adolf Hitler himself had once stayed in my room, no. 94, at the Phönix Hotel.'

It was not until the winter of 1942, some eighteen months after he had been recruited, that Ib Riis was adjudged ready to set off into the unknown. A somewhat nervous Edward Frantz accompanied him from Hamburg to the island of Heligoland. They travelled on board an armed trawler, the *Kehrwieder*. There was no longer talk of commanding a merchantman. Instead, in all secrecy, Edda was to be set ashore from a U-boat on the northern coast of Iceland. He was provided with an ingenious cover story, being instructed to tell curious relatives that he had been serving on board a German cargo vessel, the *Paul L.M. Russ*, but had jumped ship in Tromsø and paid the captain of a fishing boat, the *Aslaug*, 5,000 kroner to take him across to Iceland. He was twice searched, to ensure that no German or Danish documents of any kind remained in his pockets or wallet. Then he was given false papers, two small-denomination Norwegian banknotes and a falsified diary designed to support his story. One of the notes was marked. If he were forced to flee, he was instructed to make his way to Lisbon, contact the German consul there and produce the banknote, whereupon he would immediately be smuggled to Berlin.

'I spent my last evening, together with Frantz, at a small hotel. We went over the plans for my stay in Iceland. He promised that 500 kroner would be paid into my parents' account every month while I was away, and that I would be given my own ship as soon as the war was over. On the other hand I was enjoined never to forget that my parents' lives depended on my loyalty.'

While out for a walk next morning, seemingly by chance Riis and Frantz encountered three U-boat officers, who invited them for a drink on board their newly commissioned *U-252*, which was moored nearby. *Kapitänleutnant* Kai Lerchner opened a bottle of French cognac in the officers' mess and proposed a toast to the *Führer*. Shortly afterwards, Frantz slipped ashore, unnoticed, and the U-boat cast off and set a course north. Said Riis, 'The voyage was uneventful. We remained submerged during the day and sailed on the surface at night. I got on well with the first officer, a man named Strauss, who had a great sense of humour. In the evenings we used to sit together in the conning tower, the only place where we could smoke. During the day I played poker and lost a lot of money.'

On board, Riis was handed his most important piece of equipment, a suitcase, heavy as lead, covered in black canvas and containing a new Kofferfunkgerät SE 90/40 wireless transmitter, the Penguin edition of Maxim Gorky's *Fragments from My Diary*, on which the sophisticated code he was to use was based, and $US 2,000 in used bills. Agent Edda was ready for action.

'After nine days on board the U-boat, on 6 April I was woken up by the captain at three o'clock in the morning. His navigation had been accurate and we had surfaced at the very spot off Langanes Point where I was to be put ashore. A glance through the periscope showed me that it was snowing and that a strong wind was blowing, which was ideal for my purpose. I told Lerchen to prepare the rubber dinghy.'

After rowing for three-quarters of an hour Ib Riis reached the shore at the mouth of the Finna fjord. But it was still snowing hard and the sea was very rough, with the result that the dinghy capsized in the breakers. Riis – 'Edda' – waded ashore, his clothes soaking wet, his precious case clasped firmly in his hand. When he knocked on the door of the first farmhouse he came to, he was both starving and numb with cold. He had been walking non-stop for sixteen hours. Two days later he phoned the police in Thórshön and said that he had come across from Norway. But Iceland had been occupied by the British since the summer of 1940 and the police were under the jurisdiction of the British military. Riis was instructed to stay where he was until he could be fetched by a representative of the British forces. Fourteen days later he found himself in a warm cell in Reykjavik.

'Almost as soon as I had asked him to sit down and tell me his story he remarked that he had told his Norwegian story to all people, military and civil, he had met before arriving at HQ to preserve secrecy, but that he had a different and correct story to tell now,' wrote Captain T.N. Tawdry of the Royal Artillery, who was the first to question him.

Ib Riis had made a portentous choice. He had landed in Iceland as an agent of the Germans. Thanks to its strategic location in the North Atlantic, the island had become increasingly important as a base for convoys to Russia through the Barents Sea. Merchantmen and their escorts from the USA, Canada and Great Britain converged on the Hval fjord, outside Reykjavik, to form up before setting out on the long and perilous voyage to Murmansk.

'My main task was to report the departure of these convoys by wireless to my masters in the *Abwehr*, but I was no traitor. I had no intention of working for the Germans. I wanted to work for the British,' Riis says.

When Captain Tawdry had recovered from his surprise, Riis was turned over to the British counter-espionage service, MI5, who immediately flew him to London. On arrival in the capital he was taken to a Victorian mansion, Latchmere House, in Surrey, and placed in solitary confinement. Four days later he was taken before a panel of grave-faced officers.

'They told me that after careful consideration of my case, they had come to the conclusion that I could be of great value to them in the struggle against Hitler.'

Latchmere House was the site of MI5's notorious Camp 020, to which were sent all enemy agents who fell into their hands. This was war, and the penalty for espionage was death. The British showed no mercy to captured spies, many of whom were summarily tried and executed. Only those the counter-intelligence service felt they could use, and who declared themselves willing to change sides, were spared. They became double agents, transmitting regular reports to the *Abwehr*, but under strict British supervision. Such messages were compiled by specialists in the art of disinformation and were generally a subtle blend of fact and fiction. Their purpose was to hoodwink and confuse the enemy.

'I agreed to return to Iceland and carry out the German plans. But instead of telling the *Abwehr* what they wanted to know, I would be reporting to them what the British wanted them to know. As long as the Germans believed that I was working for them, my parents would be safe.'

On 29 May Ib Riis was released from Camp 020. One week later he returned to Reykjavik, accompanied by his two controllers from MI5, Ronald Reed and Richmond Stopford. His transmitter was installed in the private residence of the admiral commanding naval forces on the island and contact established with the *Abwehr* in Hamburg. The Germans' response told Reed and Stopford that the first phase of the deception had been successful. In Hamburg and Copenhagen Kiesel, Frantz and the other *Abwehr* officers seemed convinced that 'Edda' had successfully established himself in Iceland. They had no idea that he had been turned and that his reports were actually the work of two British officers. Even Reed, who was trained to be suspicious, began to trust Riis's willingness to cooperate. In his report he wrote:

Cobweb, like most sailors, is somewhat sentimental and very superstitious. I thought it advisable to play on this to a certain extent and having been told by him that his father was extremely pro-British and that his greatest desire was to be taken for 'an English gentleman' (whatever that implies) I stood behind him one day when we were operating from the Admiral's house and said, 'Riis, your father would be the proudest man in the world if he could see you now'. This seemed to produce some emotion and I believe will serve us in good stead in future. I suggested to him that, though he was not probably so anti-Nazi as we were, nevertheless working his transmitter in the way we were at present doing would be of value to us, and I would like him to continue to give us his assistance although I did not know to what extent he was prepared to go in an endeavour to obtain victory for the Allies. He said that he would hardly have given himself up and provided the very copious information which he has done, if he had not wished for the triumph of the British cause.

It was crucial for Reed to feel assured of the Icelander's loyalty. Although Riis was unaware of it, he was at the crux of a top-secret plan, devised by the Admiralty in London, which the British Intelligence Service had aptly named Operation Tarantula. Riis was given a cover name to accord with the object of the plan: Cobweb.

He received the first intimation that something big was afoot when, in mid-June, he was handed an urgent message for immediate transmission to Hamburg. It said that a large fleet of merchant ships was assembling in the Hval fjord and would soon be sailing eastwards with supplies for Murmansk. There was only one problem with the message, which reached the German High Command in the evening of 19 June: it was absolutely true. The ships were gathering to form the war's most famous convoy, PQ17. Three weeks later, they would steam out of the fjord and set a course for the hazardous waters between the coast of Finnmark and Bear Island.

'What a cargo for the Russians; what a prize for the enemy! Seven hundred million dollars' worth of armaments – 297 aircraft, 594 tanks, 2,496 lorries and gun carriers, and over 156,000 tons of general cargo besides – enough to equip an army of fifty thousand men if ever it arrived in Russian ports.'

Why were the British prepared to risk these ships and their immensely valuable cargoes, as well as the lives of those who manned them, by themselves informing the Germans of the convoy's imminent departure? There is only one answer: PQ17 was to be a decoy. The *Tirpitz*, flagship of the German *Kriegsmarine*, was to be lured out into the open sea and ambushed. This was a plan after Churchill's own heart. Britain's prime minister was obsessed with the threat posed by Hitler's gigantic new battleship, which, after a period of intensive training in the Baltic, was now ready for active service. The *Tirpitz* was the *Bismarck's* sister ship, and the *Bismarck* had demonstrated all too clearly what she was capable of. In May 1941, south of Iceland, a single shell from one of her 38cm guns had sufficed to sink the mighty *Hood*, pride of the Home Fleet. Aerial photographs of the *Tirpitz* were enough to send shivers down the spine of even the most battle-hardened sailor. They showed an armoured gun platform more than 242 metres long. Despite the battleship's massive beam, she clove the sea like a destroyer. Experts estimated that, with her boilers working at full pressure, she could attain a speed of at least 30 knots. Her main armament was located in four 1,000-ton turrets, two forward and two aft. The turrets were in themselves highly sophisticated structures balanced on nickel-and-steel ball bearings. The battleship's heavy guns fired shells weighing a good 800 kilograms, the same weight as a Volkswagen, Hitler's 'people's car'. With a muzzle velocity of 820 metres per second, they had an incredible range of more than 34 kilometres. A 15-ton broadside could be fired at one-minute intervals with lethal accuracy, and at a range of 10,000 metres the explosive power of the shells was devastating. They could blast their way through steel plating more than half a metre thick, making the *Tirpitz* one of the deadliest and most efficient warships ever built. In a minute he wrote to General Ismay for the Chiefs of Staff Committee, Churchill made no attempt to conceal his anxiety:

> The destruction or even the crippling of this ship is the greatest event at sea in the present time. No other target is comparable to it. . . . The entire naval situation throughout the world would be altered, and the naval command in the Pacific would be regained. The whole strategy of the war turns at this period on this ship, which is holding four times the number of British ships paralysed, to say nothing of the two new American battleships retained in the Atlantic. I regard the matter as of the highest urgency and importance.

At this time the war was in a critical phase. Hitler's attack on Russia had taken his armies to Leningrad (now St Petersburg) and the suburbs of Moscow. When they were brought to a halt a few kilometres from the centre of the Soviet capital, through their binoculars the forward troops could actually see the onion domes of the Kremlin. In the Pacific, on 7 December 1941 Japan had launched a surprise attack on Pearl Harbor and a number of other naval bases which had resulted in the sinking and disablement of a large part of the American fleet, and Manila, Hong Kong and Singapore were about to fall. And now, early in the new year, Hitler was planning another great offensive eastwards, his object the capture of Stalingrad and the oilfields of the Caucasus. If he could link up with Japan in the Middle East or India, the Axis would have won the war and the world would be ruled from Tokyo and Berlin.

But the dictator was nervous. In the same way that Churchill's mind was preoccupied with the threat represented by the *Tirpitz*, Hitler appeared to be obsessed with Norway. The more he studied the map, the more he feared an Allied counter-attack against the weakest point in the Atlantic Wall – the long, unprotected northern flank between the ports of southern Norway and Dietl's front line on the River Litza. In repeated and increasingly frenetic outbursts, the *Führer* demanded that the *Kriegsmarine*'s heavy battleships be sent to Norway to provide a mobile defence against an Allied landing. The ships he had in mind were not only the Navy's new flagship, the *Tirpitz*, but also the battlecruisers *Scharnhorst*, *Gneisenau* and *Prinz Eugen*, which were bottled up in Brest.

'I am convinced that America and Britain will try to influence the course of the world war through an attack on northern Norway. . . . I want all ships as soon as possible to be concentrated in the north. That is the only thing that will really deter the British,' he told Grand-Admiral Erich Raeder, Commander-in-Chief of the German Navy, in January 1942. In Hitler's mind, Norway was, in a phrase he often used, *eine Schicksalzone*, a zone of destiny, and as such had to be fortified against a surprise attack by the British, no matter what the cost. The Naval High Command did not share Hitler's fear and delayed taking action for as long as it possibly could. True, it had been decided that the *Tirpitz* should be moved to a new anchorage north of Trondheim as soon as her fitting-out was completed that same month, but the admirals were by no means kindly disposed towards a naval build-up in the far north.

The situation was still unresolved when the German admiral in command of naval forces in Norway, Hermann Boehm, intervened. Boehm had been replaced as *Flottenchef* in the autumn of 1939, but he was still widely respected for his professionalism and sound judgement.

'As things stand at present, Norway is becoming an ever greater threat against a belligerent England, just as, if the British had occupied it, it would have been an unacceptable danger to Germany,' Boehm wrote in a personal memorandum to Raeder. Norway was, he said, 'a gun pointed at England's breast'. What is more, it protected the flank of the northern front in the east and kept the German armaments factories supplied with the iron and nickel on which they depended. 'For this reason [he continued] Norway as a whole constitutes a strategic factor of prime importance in the German and European war against England. At the same time it encourages our opponent to mount attacks against this highly important power base for the Reich. . . . At present I consider a major British attack as *more than* probable.'

Boehm's support of Hitler was to have a decisive effect on the discussions that took place in Berlin. Grand-Admiral Raeder was won over. Eighteen months earlier, northern Norway had been a military vacuum; now it had suddenly become the focus of the warring powers' interest. From the end of January onwards, a growing number of units from the *Kriegsmarine* and *Luftwaffe* were transferred to bases in Norway: in January, the *Tirpitz*; in February, the two heavy cruisers *Admiral Scheer* and *Prinz Eugen*; in March and April, the pocket battleship *Lützow* and heavy cruiser *Admiral Hipper* – all backed by twelve destroyers and twenty U-boats. The *Luftwaffe* embarked on a similar build-up, moving elements of the experienced squadrons *KG 26* and *KG 30* to airfields in the region. By the spring of 1942, a formidable force, consisting of more than two hundred Ju 88 bombers, Ju 87 Stuka dive bombers, and Heinkel 111s equipped with torpedoes, had been assembled north of the Arctic Circle.

The build-up occurred at a time when the need for reinforcements was acute. Despite the previous autumn's setbacks, General Dietl had been promoted to command of the entire Lapland army. At his headquarters in Rovaniemi in Finland, he was busy planning a large-scale summer offensive against Kandalaksja on the White Sea coast when alarming reports began to flow in from the Litza front.

Dietl's old Mountain Corps had been taken over by 49-year-old *General-leutnant* Ferdinand Schörner, who had kept the 6th Mountain Division at the front and the 2nd Mountain Division in reserve in Petsamo and Varanger. Like his commanding general, Schörner, a stockily built man with a weatherbeaten face, was a dyed-in-the-wool Nazi and one of Hitler's 'Old Warriors'. The son of a Bavarian policeman, he had begun his military career in the First World War as an NCO on the Western Front, where he was three times wounded. For his gallantry in the hard fighting in the Tyrol he had been awarded Imperial Germany's highest decoration, Pour le Mérite. After serving for a time in the *Freikorps* von Epp, in 1920 he was promoted to lieutenant and served for eleven years, together with Dietl, in the 19th Infantry Regiment. By the outbreak of the Second World War Schörner had risen to command the regiment, and in the spring of 1940 he was made a major-general and given command of the newly formed 6th Mountain Division, which the following year was to play a key role in the Balkans campaign. It was under Schörner's command that, in the course of only twenty-four hours, the division broke through the Metaxas Line to take the mountain passes giving access to Greece, an achievement that won him the Knight's Cross of the Iron Cross. Thus it was one of the *Wehrmacht*'s toughest, most experienced and highly decorated soldiers who, early in 1942, took over where Dietl had had to give up.

What Schörner found on the western bank of the River Litza was far from encouraging. The winter had been a severe trial for the 25,000 men holding a 30-kilometre-long arc on the rocky mountainsides south of the Motovsky fjord. Some summits had been given romantic-sounding names that reminded the soldiers of home: Hertzberg, Eichhorn, Blocksberg. Others were more realistically named: Granatenkopf (Shell Nosecap), Kampenhöhe (Battle Height), Teufelsschlucht (Devil's Gorge). Bunkers had been blasted out of the granite, but they afforded scant protection against the bitter cold and frequent snowstorms.

'The thermometer fell to 42 degrees below zero. Winds of hurricane force raged across the bare slopes. Men crawled about on their hands and knees.

Everyone suffered from frostbite, but there was no point in complaining. Only the most serious cases received treatment,' said a report written early in 1942.

The tundra was almost totally devoid of vegetation, which meant that wood, like everything else, had to be transported through the drifts to the forward positions. This was far from easy, as it was a matter of 310 tons of supplies every single day – a Herculean task not only for the men who had to clear a path through the snow, but also for those who shared the burdens with dogteams and 6,000 horses and mules. 'The Arctic is nothing,' Schörner had said dismissively when, in October, he drove his troops forward along the Arctic Highway in a series of gruelling marches. He was soon forced to revise his opinion. 'To start with Schörner was hated by the men for his hardheartedness. But in time his untiring efforts to prevent a total collapse compelled respect. Only those who were equally tough, adaptable and resourceful won through. In the last resort, it was a toss-up who would survive in that icy waste,' wrote Alex Buchner in his book about the mountain troops.

Only rarely were the men able to snatch a little rest. They had constantly to be on their guard against a Soviet attack, either from regular troops or from partisans operating in their rear. Both Christmas and New Year had been nightmares, as the Soviet infantry had attacked in wave after wave. Nine thousand hand grenades and 250,000 rounds were expended in the course of only a few days, simply to hold the mountain-top known as K4.

After a few uneventful weeks, early in April the Germans again found themselves under a thunderous bombardment and the southern flank was lost after heavy shelling. Before long bitter fighting broke out along the entire front. When, shortly afterwards, a Soviet naval brigade made a surprise landing west of the Litza and advanced on the Arctic Highway, Schörner realised that this was no mere skirmish. A major offensive was under way, supported by thirty-seven fresh infantry battalions numbering close on 40,000 men. The Soviets' intention was obvious: to cut the road from Petsamo, encircle the 6th Mountain Division and annihilate it. Wrote Buchner:

As April gave way to May [1942], the crisis reached its peak. The greatest danger appeared to be in the north, where the enemy's thrust was directed at the Division's supply lines. The situation was perilous in the extreme. The 6th Mountain Division was threatened on both flanks by superior forces. As a last resort Schörner resolved to throw all his reserves into the battle, among them the 2nd Mountain Division then in Kirkenes.

In a wide outflanking movement near the coast, the Soviet 14th Naval Brigade was surrounded. With only a few hundred metres to go, an exceptionally heavy blizzard swept across the battle front, bringing all movement to a halt for three days. When the wind dropped, resistance ceased and the surviving Soviet troops withdrew across the fjord. In the meantime, two battalions of German ski troops, which had skied 150 kilometres south in double-quick time, fell on the advancing Soviet columns from the rear. For a few dramatic hours the battle swung to and fro in no-man's-land. The war diary of the 136th Regiment gives a graphic account of the engagement:

> From well-protected positions on the high ground we are met by a hail of bullets. The mortars are rapidly getting our range. We are under fire from two quarters. The sky darkens. Banks of fog swirl in from the edge of the Arctic Ocean. Above us circle fighters, but they are unable to distinguish friend from foe in the close fighting. Suddenly a thunderous barrage opens up. It is *our* artillery opening fire south of Teufelsschlucht. The Russians pull back. They are pursued by our ski troops.

By 14 May the front had been restabilised after a succession of battles that General Schörner described as the hardest he had ever been engaged in. Both sides had suffered heavy casualties. In a bare five weeks of fighting the Germans lost a total of 3,500 men in killed and wounded, while the Russians left behind on the snowclad banks of the Litza 8,000 frozen corpses and, when they finally withdrew, probably took with them twice as many wounded.

When they came to take stock, the Germans discovered that many of their Soviet antagonists had been re-equipped. They found US weapons, empty corned-beef tins, burned-out GMC trucks and army boots made of real leather. More, the planes harassing them from a low altitude were no longer outmoded Ratas and Yaks but, increasingly, modern Bell-20 Airacobras, Curtiss P-40 Kittyhawks and Douglas Bostons. There was no doubt that aid from the western allies was getting through and doing much to alter the balance of power on the eastern front.

The first convoy, which consisted of only six ships, reached Archangel on 31 August 1941, bringing with it mostly aircraft and urgently needed raw materials – tin, wool and rubber. During the autumn a further fifty-seven merchant ships reached the Kola Peninsula, where they unloaded 1,400 trucks, 800 fighter aircraft, 750 tanks and 100,000 tons of ammunition and other matériel.

The entry of the United States into the war in December meant that the whole of America's enormous production capacity was now at the disposal of the Allies, though it would not have counted for much had the Soviet Union, still reeling from the Nazis' initial hammer blows, collapsed. If Hitler could disengage the forces tied down on the eastern front, the situation would be rendered dramatic in the extreme. At best, the war would be prolonged for many years. For this reason convoys were despatched eastwards with increasing frequency, and they grew bigger and bigger – from PQ8, which consisted of only seven vessels and sailed in January, to PQ16, which comprised no fewer than thirty-five cargo-ships and sailed in May 1942. But now it was June, and for twenty-four hours a day the Barents Sea was bathed in the light of the Midnight Sun. Whereas the first convoys had reached Russia unscathed, German attacks had gained in intensity as spring progressed. Both PQ14 and PQ15 were bombed incessantly, with the loss of four merchantmen. Worse, for the British, was that two cruisers, the *Trinidad* and *Edinburgh*, were sent to the bottom, the latter with a cargo of five tons of gold on board. Not surprisingly, the Admiralty began to have serious misgivings about the wisdom of sending munitions to Russia by the northern route. The First Sea Lord, Admiral Sir Dudley Pound, had long been of the opinion that the convoy service was 'becoming a regular millstone round our necks'. The Commander-in-Chief of the Home Fleet, Admiral John Tovey, wanted to delay sending further convoys until autumn darkness returned to provide a measure of protection against attack from the air.

But for Churchill it was politically impossible to stop the convoys. Stalin was still in a desperate situation and begging for more material aid. 'Not only Premier Stalin but President Roosevelt will object very much to our desisting from running the convoys now. The Russians are in heavy action, and will expect us to run the risk and pay the price entailed by our contribution. The United States ships are queueing up. My own feeling, mingled with much anxiety, is that the convoy [PQ16] ought to sail on the 16th. The operation is justified if a half gets through.'

Churchill's optimism proved well-founded. Despite massive air attacks, only seven ships from convoy PQ16 were lost. Early in June the remaining twenty-eight began unloading 321 tanks, 124 aircraft and more than 2,500 trucks in Murmansk. The British prime minister sent Stalin a jubilant telegram: 'We are resolved to fight our way through to you with the maximum amount of war materials. On account of *Tirpitz* and other enemy surface vessels at Trondheim, the passage of every convoy has become a serious fleet operation. We shall continue to do our utmost.'

In March 1942 the Home Fleet had been reinforced by the addition of America's Task Force 99, which was made up of the battleship USS *Washington*, the aircraft carrier *Wasp* and two cruisers, the *Tuscaloosa* and *Wichita*. Although the British were hard pressed and had suffered heavy losses both in the Mediterranean and in the Pacific, with the help of the Americans Tovey was able to muster a formidable striking force in the north: two battleships, two aircraft carriers, three cruisers and fourteen destroyers. The American presence, coupled with the relative success achieved by PQ16, may have made the admirals over-confident. While the merchantmen that were to sail in the next convoy were forming up in the Hval fjord, Tovey conceived a plan which, in retrospect, seems to have been one of the boldest of the whole war – boldest and most disastrous. Although the *Tirpitz* had made only one sortie since her arrival in Trondheim on 16 January, she remained a great and ever-present threat.

'That ship is an infernal nuisance and the most important business of the war at the present time is to cripple or destroy her. It would just make the whole difference in the way of freeing ships for other theatres. . . . I still think that the most pressing requirement of the war is to dispose of the *Tirpitz*, then things would begin to straighten out a bit,' wrote the commander of the First Cruiser Squadron, Rear-Admiral L.H.K. Hamilton, in a private letter in March. He put into words what both Churchill and most senior officers in the Royal Navy felt: as long as the *Tirpitz* continued to threaten the convoy route from her base in Norway, no one could feel secure. The German battleship had to be destroyed, no matter what the cost. That was undoubtedly Admiral Tovey's intention when, in May 1942 and in the deepest secrecy, he contacted MI5 and asked for their help in putting the *Tirpitz* out of action.

Tovey's request was discussed on 29 May in London between some of the Security Service's most trusted men, among them Commander Ewen Montague, the Royal Navy's liaison with MI5, Major Tar Robertson, head of counter-intelligence against Nazi Germany, and a representative of MI6, Major Frank Foley who, before the outbreak of war, had been MI6's station chief in Berlin and subsequently distinguished himself in the ill-fated Norway campaign. Also present were Reed and Stopford, who were responsible for controlling agents and for disinformation in the field. A draft plan of possible measures to be taken, codenamed Tarantula, was already in being. According to the recently released minutes of the meeting, 'the object of the plan, which has been conceived by C.-in-C. Home Fleet, is primarily to assist the passage of a convoy (P.Q.17) from Iceland to Russia. Secondly, it is hoped that, if this plan is successful, the Home Fleet will be able to bring the German Fleet to battle.'

The means to be adopted were simple: 'The plan is to inform the Germans that a convoy is assembling in Iceland and that another convoy is assembling at Scapa Flow and that it is believed that these two convoys may in all probability be taking troops to effect a landing on the Norwegian coast.'

PQ17 alone was a real convoy. But it was headed for Murmansk, not Norway. The convoy in Scapa Flow was a blind and consisted of a handful of ships that were to sail as though bound for the coast of southern Norway, to mislead German air reconnaissance. But the ships would be in ballast, and would turn round midway between Shetland and Bergen. It was an audacious – and extremely risky – scheme that largely hinged on Hitler's delusions about Norway, as is borne out by an added note reading: 'It is known that the Germans are at the present moment in an extreme state of agitation for fear lest an attack should be made by us on the Norwegian coast.'

MI5 had a whole stable of German spies who had been captured and turned, and their wireless links, which could be utilised to manipulate their controllers in Berlin, were kept open. Two were already earmarked for use in the planned deception. The men chosen to 'inform' the Germans of the assembly and departure of the two convoys were John Moe, a Norwegian double agent whose codename was Mutt, and Ib Riis, Cobweb, who that same day had been released from Camp 020 and was still in ignorance of the role that had been allotted to him. Mutt's task was simple: it was to transmit false information about a non-existent convoy in Scapa Flow. Cobweb had a harder job to do, as he had to transmit genuine information about a real convoy to the very people who were eager to destroy it. It was a deadly game of chance and the stakes were extremely high: 35 ships, most of them American, the lives of more than 2,000 seamen, and cargoes worth some $700 million. None of the minor players could be made privy to the plan, and certainly not Cobweb who, in Reykjavik in June, was merely handed pre-coded messages for transmission to his masters in the *Abwehr*.

'Had I known what those messages contained, I would have refused to send them. The risks to the merchantmen were too great,' Riis says.

The sailors who manned the ships could not be informed of what lay ahead of them either. The nerves of most of them were already badly frayed, so much so that the American crew of the 5,800-ton general cargo carrier *Troubadour*, which sailed under the Panama flag, mutinied when they learned that they were destined for Russia. The Norwegian captain, Georg Salvesen, had to call on an armed guard to put the mutiny down. The ringleaders, herded into the evil-smelling forepeak at gunpoint, gave up after fifty hours' incarceration. Had the news leaked out that PQ17 was being sent to sea as bait for the world's most formidable battleship, the mutiny would undoubtedly have spread and most of the men would have refused to sail. For this reason, only a handful of privileged insiders were aware of what was in the message that Cobweb transmitted to the *Abwehr* in the evening of 17 June, a message that, two days later, was in the hands of the Naval High Command in Berlin: 'V-man Edda of Ast Denmark reports: Friend from Reykjavik says that many merchantmen have recently assembled in Hval fjord. Believes convoy will soon depart.'

The American service chiefs in Iceland were likewise kept in the dark, despite the fact that it was America that had supplied most of the ships and the bulk of their cargoes. On the British side, only two officers were in the know, the admiral and his chief of staff. Neither of them liked the idea. But the grapevine was at work, and many of those involved sensed that something out of the ordinary was in the offing. One was the admiral in command of the cruisers, Rear-Admiral L.H.K. Hamilton, who addressed the officers of HMS *London* as follows: 'The primary object is still to get PQ17 to Russia, but an object only slightly subsidiary is to provide an opportunity for the enemy's heavy ships to be brought to action by our battle fleet and cruiser covering force.'

If the *Tirpitz* put to sea, PQ17 was to turn about off Bear Island and return to Iceland. That would take her into waters where the Home Fleet, led by HMS *King George V* and the USS *Washington*, lay in wait, eager for battle. It would be a perfect ambush and the *Tirpitz* would have little chance of escape.

By this time Tovey knew that the Germans had taken the bait and were preparing a devastating attack on PQ17 with surface ships, aircraft and U-boats. Teleprinter traffic between the Naval High Command in Berlin and the German bases in Trondheim and Narvik passed by landline through Sweden. The landlines were tapped by the Swedish Intelligence Service, which had long since broken the German code. Sweden's defence chiefs were thus fully informed of developments in Norway and on the northern front as a whole. When Colonel Carl Björnstierna, a Swedish intelligence officer, read the detailed instructions sent to the *Tirpitz* and other German units in Norway, he immediately got into touch with the British naval attaché in Stockholm, Henry Denham. In a telegram to the Admiralty, Denham summarised the information he had been given.

Following is German plan of attack on next Arctic convoy. It is hoped to obtain early reconnaissance report when eastbound convoy reaches vicinity of Jan Mayen. Bombing attacks from aircraft based in N. Norway will then commence.

Naval movements may take place from this moment as follows:

1 Pocket-battleships with six destroyers will proceed to Altenfjord anchorage. They may use as *point d'appui* the anchorage in Sörö Sound.

2 *Tirpitz* with *Hipper*, two destroyers and three torpedo boats will proceed to Narvik area, probably Bogenfjord.

Naval forces may be expected to operate from these anchorages once the convoy has reached the meridian of 5 degrees East. The intention for the two groups of surface forces is to make a rendezvous on the Bear Island meridian and to make a simultaneous attack on convoy supported by U-boats and air units.

This was a remarkably correct summing-up of the German plan, which was codenamed Operation *Rösselsprung* (Knight's Move). The Germans had learned from Edda/Cobweb that PQ17 was preparing to depart. It was intended that as soon as the convoy had been located by long-range reconnaissance aircraft, the *Tirpitz*, *Lützow*, *Admiral Scheer*, *Hipper* and eleven destroyers should deploy by stages to the Kå fjord. The plan was to fall upon the convoy when it reached Bear Island and despatch both the merchantmen and their escorts in a lightning attack.

Tovey had achieved his purpose: the Germans knew of PQ17 and were preparing to intercept it. But there was one small item in the message he had received from Stockholm that worried him. The Naval High Command in Berlin was intending to attack the convoy *east* of Bear Island, in a stretch of water well within the range of German aircraft based in northern Norway. Tovey had planned to ambush the German fleet in a different part of the ocean altogether, an area *west* of Bear Island.

Early in the afternoon of Saturday 27 June, the thirty-three ships of PQ17 sailed out of the Hval fjord. From the bridge of the USS *Wichita* film star Douglas Fairbanks Jr, who was serving as the American admiral's flag lieutenant, watched the ships leave. 'No honors or salutes were paid to them as they passed, such as there are for naval vessels. But every one who was watching paid them a silent tribute and offered them some half-thought prayer.'

Four days later, at half-past three in the afternoon of Wednesday 1 July, the convoy was sighted off Jan Mayen by a Focke-Wulf *Kondor* from the airfield at Bardufoss. About two hours later the smoke from the ships' funnels was observed by two U-boat captains, Max-Martin Teichert, commander of *U-456*, and Reinhard Reche, who commanded *U-255*. That same evening, under the watchful eye of Ronald Reed, Cobweb again went on the air from Reykjavik to transmit the following message, which was dated two days earlier, that is, Monday 29 June: 'Important. Good friend in Reykjavik says large convoy left Saturday evening.'

For the benefit of the Germans, MI5 wished to reaffirm that PQ17 really was on its way and at the same time enhance Cobweb's credibility.

I think it may reasonably [be] assumed that the enemy now repose considerable confidence in Cobweb, as, far from blowing him, operation E.S. has supported his bona fides. I made the decision together with the Chief of Staff on Friday, 26th June, that we would not go off the air in order to avoid reporting the departure of PQ.17 but would stay off on Sunday as if he had gone into Reykjavik to visit some friends and would come up on Monday, pretending that he was unable to get through due to bad conditions. We thought that the convoy would probably be reported on Tuesday and that he could therefore send over a message about its departure on Tuesday evening. A.C.I.C. did not hear that the convoy had been sighted by reconnaissance aircraft until Wednesday 1st July at 13.30 GMT and consider that this was sufficient justification for our reporting to them on the evening transmission, that the convoy had left the previous Saturday evening. This we did in a message dated Monday 29th June as if he had heard about the convoy's departure on Sunday while in Reykjavik. We also had another message saying that he had had great difficulty in obtaining contact during the last few days in spite of the fact that he wished to get a most important message to them, and complained that they could not have been listening very carefully. Doubtless, Franz's [sic] reaction to this was to tear his hair with rage for had the control station picked up Cobweb's signals on the Monday, his report would have beaten all the reconnaissance aircraft by two days instead of the aircraft beating Cobweb by a few hours.

Two days later, on Friday 3 July, as the convoy neared the edge of the ice barrier north of Bear Island, the *Tirpitz*, together with the rest of the German fleet, weighed anchor. Operation *Rösselsprung* had begun.

At five o'clock next morning the convoy suffered its first loss, a 7,000-ton Liberty ship, the *Christopher Newton*, which was sunk north of Bear Island by a torpedo dropped by a Heinkel operating from the float-plane base in the Bille fjord. Fifteen hours later the first torpedo-bombers from Bardufoss-based *KG 26* struck. The attack lasted for ten minutes, and when it was over it left three ships, the *William Hooper*, *Navarino* and *Azerbaijan*, a tanker laden with linseed oil, helpless, blazing wrecks. It was good flying weather, there was virtually no wind and it was broad daylight. The wretched seamen fighting for their lives in the icy water knew nothing of the machinations that had taken place in London and Berlin prior to the convoy's departure, but it was becoming increasingly apparent that a bloodbath was pending and that many men would die.

For Admiral John Tovey, who with his battle fleet was still some 200 nautical miles west of the convoy, the situation was desperate. Operation Tarantula was in danger of ending in total failure. The Germans had not been deceived into thinking that the ships steaming towards Norway further south heralded a landing on the coast; the diversionary convoy that set out from Scapa Flow had not even been discovered. On the contrary, the German Naval High Command had drawn the correct conclusion, thanks in part to the information they had received from Cobweb. They were aware that PQ17 was a genuine convoy en route to Murmansk with invaluable supplies and munitions for Russia. From that point onwards it would be subjected to systematic and increasingly intensive attacks from the air and by U-boats. Worst of all, the prize that was to have justified the bloody sacrifice had failed to show up. The *Tirpitz* seemed to have completely disappeared. The fjords of Finnmark were blanketed in fog and reconnaissance aircraft sent out from Scotland had been forced to return with their mission unaccomplished. Nor had the submarines patrolling off the North Cape seen anything, and there had been no wireless traffic to indicate the battleship's whereabouts. The risks that had been taken and all the meticulous planning had been in vain. For all Tovey knew, the *Tirpitz* was closing on the convoy at that very moment. If it was, he had no chance of reaching the scene in time.

At the Admiralty, gloom prevailed. The First Sea Lord, the ageing Admiral Sir Dudley Pound, had been opposed to despatching PQ17 to Russia from the outset, and as the evening of Saturday 4 July wore on without news of the *Tirpitz*, his anxiety increased. When, at long last, he learned that the battleship had reported her arrival in the Kå fjord at nine o'clock that same morning, he knew exactly how matters stood. If the German squadron had left its base immediately, it would by then be only a few hours' sailing from PQ17. For Pound, this was the moment of truth. He had to assume that the *Tirpitz* had sortied, although he had no sound information to tell him that it had. But if it had, the Navy's rash and cynical plan was destined to end in tragedy. The Admiralty was inextricably entangled in a web of duplicity and disinformation that was entirely of its own making. The Home Fleet was too far away from the scene to intervene, which meant that unless something drastic were done, the merchant ships would be blown out of the water by the German battleship's heavy guns. The responsibility was Pound's: it was he who had to decide the course of action.

[T]he First Sea Lord leaned back in his leather-backed chair and closed his eyes — an invariable attitude of deep meditation when making difficult decisions; his hands gripped the arms of his chair, and his features, which had seemed almost ill and strained, became peaceful and composed. . . . After thirty long seconds, Admiral Pound reached for a Naval Message pad and announced, 'The convoy is to be dispersed.'

The signal conveying the admiral's fateful decision reached the convoy and its escorts two hours later, at half-past nine on Saturday evening. The commander of the escorting squadron, Captain J.R. Broome, could hardly believe his eyes when he read the decoded message. But an order was an order and he assumed that the Admiralty knew something he didn't. He radioed the commodore in charge of the convoy, Rear-Admiral J.C. Dowding, 'Sorry to leave you like this. Good luck. Looks like a bloody business.' 'Many thanks. Good-bye and good hunting,' Dowding replied.

On board the cargo-ships, the news was received with a mixture of disappointment, bewilderment and fury. In his diary, Nathaniel Platt, first officer of the 7,000-ton *John Witherspoon*, wrote: 'Received orders to disband convoy. It is unbelievable that we are being put on our own without protection – some ships with no guns at all. Everyone going every way on horizon. Some ships sticking two or three together. We are going off alone . . .'

The tragic part about it all was that the source of the panic was lying securely at anchor inside her anti-torpedo nets in the Kå fjord, only a few cable-lengths from the *Black Watch*, General Eduard Dietl's one-time floating headquarters.

On board the *Tirpitz*, the convoy's progress was being carefully followed from hour to hour; but in Berlin, the naval chiefs continued to hold back. Not until the morning of Sunday 5 July was the squadron, which was under the command of *Vize-Admiral* Otto Schniewind, given permission to put to sea. Some time later, off the North Cape, the *Tirpitz* was sighted, first by Captain Nicolai Lunin, commander of the Soviet submarine *K-21*, then by Lieutenant Westmacott in command of the British submarine *Unshaken*. The signals they transmitted to Murmansk and London respectively were picked up by a German monitoring station in Kirkenes and immediately relayed to Berlin. That was all Grand-Admiral Raeder needed. He knew that PQ17 was unprotected and would be subjected to continuous attack by aircraft and U-boats. That being so, he no longer saw any reason to hazard his capital ships, with the consequence that at ten o'clock on Sunday evening the *Tirpitz* and the ships that accompanied her were ordered to reverse course and return to the Kå fjord.

For the next few days German U-boats and aircraft maintained a relentless assault on PQ17, whose ships tried desperately to make their way to Murmansk individually and unescorted. The convoy's losses were horrendous, no fewer than twenty-two merchantmen, one rescue-ship and one tanker being sunk. One hundred and fifty-three seamen lost their lives and 3,350 trucks, 430 tanks, 210 bombers and 99,316 tons of ammunition, armour-steel, radar equipment, motor vehicles, field rations and other matériel were sent to the bottom. It was without doubt one of the greatest disasters to befall any Allied convoy throughout the war – and it had been precipitated by one thing and one thing only: the British admirals' fear of the *Tirpitz*, which, for the first time, had dropped anchor at the German naval base in the Kå fjord.

CHAPTER SIX

The Search

THE KÅ FJORD, 1973–76

In an open letter to readers of the *Vestfinnmark Arbeiderblad* in the autumn of 1950, Eulalia Henty-Creer had promised to return and resume the search for her missing son. But nearly twenty-three years were to elapse before a member of the family finally managed to get back to Alta. This was Eulalia's youngest daughter, Pamela, who, in June 1973, journeyed to the Kå fjord to carry on where Deirdre and their mother had temporarily abandoned their task.

> Quite by chance I happened to see an item in the *Daily Telegraph* about the recovery of a midget submarine [she wrote]. The journalist responsible for the article put me in touch with Peter Cornish, then a prominent member of the British Sub-Aqua Club, who specialised in finding and salvaging wrecked vessels. Not only was Peter intrigued by the story of *X5*, he was also planning to go to Norway to help recover a Halifax bomber that had been found at the bottom of a lake in [the county of] Trøndelag. He declared his willingness to meet my husband Gerard and myself in the Kå fjord and look around, with the possible intention of putting together a team to explore the seabed.

Thirty years old at the time, Peter Cornish was a pharmaceutical chemist and one of Britain's foremost amateur divers. In 1972 he had helped to find and recover the wreck of the midget submarine *XE8*, which had sunk in 30 metres of water off Portland Bill shortly after the war. The article that had caught Pamela Mellor's eye and prompted her to contact Cornish dealt with this incident. 'We tried to interest a few politicians and the Royal Navy, but without success. Besides, Peter wished to keep our reconnaissance trip a secret, as he didn't want a lot of amateurs diving in waters that until then had remained unexplored.'

Some twenty-three years or so earlier Eulalia and Deirdre Henty-Creer, encouraged by the testimonies of Mathis Sarilla and a number of others, had left Finnmark with high hopes. But in London no one seemed willing to take the matter seriously. 'Mother got into touch with an admiral, a one-time classmate of my father, who she hoped would help. He sent his chief-of-staff home to us. The chap listened politely to what we had to say, but the letter he wrote to us a few days later held out no hope of assistance. There was nothing he could do, he said, the matter was closed. No one would help us.'

The family's bitterness was manifest in the notice Eulalia later placed in the In Memoriam column of *The Times*.

HENTY-CREER, LIEUT., R.N.V.R., commanding midget submarine X5, only son of Mrs. Henty-Creer, Cornwall Gardens, S.W.7, reported missing with his gallant crew since his attack with X6 and X7 on German battleship *Tirpitz* in Kaa Fjord, North Finnmark, on Sept. 22, 1943, and last seen the following day (Sept. 23) leaving Altan [*sic*] Fjord. A naval expendable.

It was a concise summation of the case, the way Eulalia saw it, a terse and stinging indictment in a newspaper that was read by the whole of the British Establishment. The day it appeared, many an admiral must have choked over his morning coffee. If the Admiralty had been disinclined to change its stance before, it would hardly be more willing to do so after such an unveiled criticism of its averred policy. 'Mother was terribly disappointed and indignant. I understand her. It still angers me to think of the way we were treated.'

The relatives of the other members of X5's crew were equally despondent and frustrated. They included Mervyn Malcolm, brother of the submarine's second-in-command, Sub-Lieutenant Alastair Malcolm, and Ruby Simpson, sister of the diver, Sub-Lieutenant Tom Nelson. Not long after the war Tom's family had advertised in Norwegian newspapers for help in determining the fate of the missing men, but the letters they received did nothing to solve the mystery.

'The Germans kept the prisoners on board for a few days. They held a party for them, as they thought that what the Englishmen had done was a great achievement. Afterwards, when they were driven off, heading for Narvik, two of them in each car, they were smoking fat cigars. They looked quite cheerful,' wrote a man from Oslo, who claimed to have been an eye-witness to the attack.

When Ruby Simpson heard of the expedition Peter Cornish was planning to mount, she had only one brief comment to make: 'I just want the record put straight for Tom's sake. We just want to know what happened.'

In the summer of 1973 Cornish was a member of the team that raised the wreck of a Halifax shot down near Trondheim on 29 April 1942 when it took part in an unsuccessful attack on the *Tirpitz*. His task completed, he immediately made his way to Alta, where Pamela and her husband, Lieutenant-Colonel Gerard Mellor, were waiting for him. There they hired a boat, from which Cornish slipped into the cold, dark water.

The fjord's water was clear, the bottom level at some 140 feet and littered with war debris, untouched since the Germans had left some thirty years before. Amongst the litter were discarded crockery and beer bottles as well as a largish number of canisters which looked as if they might have been unexploded depth charges, but which, more probably, were discarded smoke canisters. . . . Peter's enthusiasm was kindled and he became determined to organise a full-scale expedition as soon as possible to fully explore the whole bottom of the fjord.

Peter himself was equally optimistic: 'I dived six times around the fjord – twice at the spot where X5 supposedly sank but I did not locate her. I found, however, so much wreckage and other material that I resolved to get together a good team and suitable equipment for a thorough search for the missing submarine.'

A year later, on Midsummer's Eve 1974, in a light drizzle, a DC-9 landed at Alta airport. On board was Peter Cornish. By some miracle, despite a marked lack of enthusiasm in high places for the Henty-Creers' persistence, he had succeeded in gathering together sixteen of Britain's most adventurous amateur divers, two tons of sophisticated equipment for underwater exploration and a good £3,000 pounds in cash, then quite a considerable sum. The newspaper for which I had been working as a journalist since 1968, the *Finnmark Dagblad*, was the successor of the *Vestfinnmark Arbeiderblad*, the paper which in 1950 had printed Eulalia Henty-Creer's plea for help. Two weeks later one of the paper's reporters wrote the first on-the-spot report of the search. It was headlined 'British frogmen hunt submarine in the Kå fjord. Searching for the midget submarine that disabled the *Tirpitz*.'

The summer of 1974 was a truly arctic one, cold and wet, very similar to that of 1950, when Eulalia and Deirdre had struggled to keep warm in their tent beside National Highway 50. Said one despatch from the Kå fjord: "'In weather like this you never know where you are, on the surface or below," laughed one of the high-spirited young divers we spoke to.' I personally remember playing football on days when my fingers were numb with cold, and evenings when the rain beat endlessly against the window-panes. The dripping, low clouds were like molten lead, and day after day passed without a glimpse of the sun.

I had a desk job in those days and am pretty sure that it was I who fleshed out the X5 article and brought it to life in the pages of the newspaper. It made a vivid impression on me when I read it, and I set out to bring out the drama and convey to our readers something of the excitement surrounding the unsolved mystery.

'We're having to do a lot of diving because there's a great deal of metal on the bottom,' say the divers to the *Finnmark Dagblad*. The seabed is strewn with pieces of the old anti-torpedo nets, as well as with wires and cables and other wartime relics. A few days ago the frogmen found a wreck dating from the war, and in the inner recesses of the fjord they have come across many objects on the sea floor where the battleship was moored. They are now working their way towards the mouth of the fjord in an endeavour to find the wreck of X5. . . . If they find the submarine and it proves that the charges had been released from the hull, steps will probably be taken to ensure that the four members of the crew who lost their lives when the submarine disappeared are given the credit they deserve.

Written on 7 July, the report reflected the expedition's continuing optimism, which was maintained in spite of the difficulties surrounding the search. The divers' high hopes were largely ascribable to the equipment Cornish had brought with him: a state-of-the-art side-scan sonar, a Sea-Fix Decca Navigation Chain and a proton magnetometer. Not even the North Sea oil rigs were better equipped. With sixteen divers available to carry out underwater inspection of all irregularities that showed up on the seabed, it is not surprising that, a few days later, the *Finnmark Dagblad* could jubilantly announce: 'Midget submarine X5 found.'

In the mud at the bottom of the fjord the divers had discovered some pieces of steel that were so mangled as to be practically unidentifiable. However, closer inspection revealed that they came from the bow of a submarine. Their optimism increased. 'When it became clear that X5 had been found, the news was immediately despatched to England. Prince Charles sent the frogmen working in the Kå fjord a congratulatory telegram,' we reported on Friday 12 July.

At a depth of 40 metres visibility was poor, however, and water from the rivers flowing into the fjord had left objects on the bottom covered with greyish-brown ooze. When he returned to England in August, Peter Cornish was personally far from confident that they had found the wreck of the submarine. 'I can't be really certain, but under the circumstances I'd say there's a good chance the wreckage was that of the X5. But it's not my position to voice an opinion of what we found, that's for the naval historians,' he said.

CHAPTER SEVEN

In Love and War

FINNMARK, 1943

Many paths crossed in the northern theatre of war in autumn 1942 and winter 1943. Far to the south, Hitler had launched a new offensive against the Soviet forces, an offensive that was not brought to a halt until it reached Stalingrad. The endless steppe took a heavy toll of both men and machines, with the consequence that neither the Germans nor the Russians had reserves to fling into battle between the White Sea and the Motovsky fjord in the far north. True, there were some violent clashes east of Salla, where fire from mortars and howitzers set the Finnish forests alight. But on Schörner's front beside the Litza, things were quiet: both sides had expended most of their strength in the bloody battles fought in May.

In the Barents Sea, too, the sound of gunfire had died away. The near-annihilation of PQ17 had impelled the Allies to discontinue the convoys until September, thus allowing the *Luftwaffe* to concentrate on other targets. Says the history of the *Eismeer* fighter squadron:

August is a grim month for the Soviet Union. *KG 30* launches a massive attack. When vast fleets of warplanes appear over Petsamo, all hell breaks loose. This late summer of 1942, the north-eastern area of Murmansk is burning day and night. It has been a dry summer. The old two-storey timber houses fall easy victim to the flames. The smokeclouds form enormous mountains of cumulus that are visible from as far away as the Norwegian border.

At this time *Leutnant* Heinrich Ehrler was almost daily in the air above the Kola Peninsula in his Messerchmitt Bf109. The fighters' task was to provide cover for the Ju 88 bombers stationed at Banak, which were systematically destroying Russian towns and villages. On 21 August, while returning from a major attack on the airfield at Murmaschi, they were set upon by thirty-five Soviet fighters. A large-scale air battle ensued in which fourteen Russian planes were shot down. Ehrler was credited with two kills. However, the Germans also suffered losses. One pilot who failed to return was *Premierleutnant* Hartwein, leader of No. 6 flight. That same day Ehrler was promoted and ordered to take Hartwein's place. For the one-time butcher's apprentice, this was indeed a big step up. *JG 5* was fast becoming one of the *Luftwaffe's* most renowned fighter squadrons and Ehrler one of its most distinguished pilots. He was well on his way to the top.

Many Germans viewed service in the north as a hard and thankless task. For those with no fondness for fishing or the outdoor life, apart from visits to the local brothels and gambling dens there was little to do in one's spare time. On both sides of the front, fear was a constant companion. No one who fell into the hands of the enemy could expect to be shown mercy. The Germans treated Soviet prisoners like cattle, starving, maltreating and working them to death. According to the Nazis' demented ideology, Russians were *Untermenschen*, subhumans with no rights whatsoever. In what was known as the Commissar Order, and other criminal decrees, Hitler had authorised the *Wehrmacht* to summarily execute Jews and Bolsheviks. His orders found an echo in the second-class guard battalions stationed on the Finnmark coast. 'The Russians have in this war renounced all right to humane treatment,' said a circular that went the rounds of the 230th Division in the winter of 1942.

Conditions in Soviet prison camps were little better, and at the front no holds were barred. Both Soviet special forces and Finnish frontier detachments made full use of fear and terror. One day the commander of an Austrian battalion, *Major* Holzinger, found that he had lost touch with a rifle company positioned on the shore of Støvelsjøen [Lake Boot] on the Litza front. The patrol sent out to investigate was met with a gruesome sight.

Undetected, a Soviet reconnaissance patrol had sneaked up on the men and bayoneted all twenty-two of them to death. But not content with killing them, they then proceeded to flay them. The faces of the corpses were terribly mutilated and the lifeless bodies had been repeatedly slashed and stabbed. They found it hard to understand that the Russians had stripped the bloody corpses of their uniforms and taken them with them. Holzinger mined the surrounding area, then withdrew. When, some time later, the Soviet infantry advanced, many of them suffered grievous wounds in the minefield. 'Hour after hour they cried for help.

Some called for their mothers. Not one of my men lifted a finger. Admittedly, those infantrymen bore no responsibity for the atrocities we had witnessed, but the memory of our flayed comrades precluded all thought of mercy.'

It was a brutal, bitterly fought war that many had begun to hate, though few dared say so. For anyone who protested, the way to a firing squad was short indeed. Some men broke down altogether, and suicides and desertions increased. The vast majority of the Germans suffered intense homesickness. There was little to brighten their cold, grey lives. One thing that did so was the wireless, which, through the medium of request and entertainment programmes, gave expression to the soldiers' yearnings. In the north, the Norwegian Broadcasting Corporation's station in Vadsø had been taken over by the occupiers and renamed *Soldatensender Finnmark*. Because of its location and powerful 10kW transmitter it became the Germans' principal radio station in Norway, along with the main transmitter located on the eastern outskirts of Oslo. The station's star was a young Norwegian singer from Vadsø, Gudrun Niska. The programmes were intended to indoctrinate their listeners in the spirit of National Socialism, but it was the music that the thousands of soldiers, sailors and airmen in northern Norway wanted to hear, and especially the Sunday afternoon concert with its greetings from families and friends back home. 'Best of all,' says the history of Reconnaissance Group 124, which was stationed at Høybuktmoen airfield, 'we liked the voices of Gudrun Niska and Will Höhne, who often visited the squadron.'

Request programmes and romantic ballads formed the background of our evenings off and long nights on duty. Often heard on both sides of the line was the French song *J'attendrai*, sung by Gudrun Niska, which put into words the longing we felt for our loved ones so far away, along with *Sing, Nachtigall sing* and, last but by no means least, Hans Liep's haunting melody that became popular all over the world, *Vor der Lanterne, vor dem grossen Tor* [*Lili Marlen*], sung by sultry voiced Lale Andersen. The Vadsø transmitter closed down at midnight, rounding off the evening's programme with *Die kleine Stadt muss schlafen gehen*. That set many listeners thinking of their loved ones at home.

Gudrun Niska's pure, sweet voice brought a little cheer to the dark autumn days and also to those who, as agents, were risking their lives behind enemy lines. One night in October 1942 a darkened Soviet submarine nosed its way into the Kongs fjord in eastern Finnmark, far behind the German lines, and hove to some 500 metres offshore. On board were three of the men who had fled from Kiberg to the Soviet Union in the autumn of 1940 and there been trained as partisans under Naval Group 4090: Trygve Eriksen, Harald Utne and Utne's nephew, nineteen-year-old Leif Utne.

After his capture by the Germans some months later, Harald Utne gave the following account of the landing:

> The diesel engine was switched off, but the electric motors were left running to keep the propellers going. With the motors barely ticking over, the submarine maintained its position bow-on to the shore. . . . Our gear was hauled up into the conning tower and then transferred to three rubber dinghies. In the first were Trygve and Leif, together with the transmitter and other equipment, in the second Åge Halvari, who had come along to give us a helping hand. I was in the third dinghy with the rest of the equipment. The landing took an hour from start to finish. The sea was calm and all went smoothly.

The submarine restarted its main engine and was soon out of sight in the autumn darkness, while the three partisans busied themselves setting up their transmitter in a mountain cave looking out across an expanse of the Arctic Ocean. From its mouth they could keep watch on all the ships bringing supplies to Schörner's Mountain Corps entrenched on the banks of the Litza. Before long the first reports began to reach the KGB's receiving station in Murmansk.

In the late summer of 1941 all civilian wireless sets in Norway were seized by the Germans, leaving people without access to underground newspapers or clandestine receivers ignorant of the progress of the war. The population had largely to make do with such newspapers as were still published, but censorship was very strict and their Nazification became ever more pronounced. Reliable news and comment were gradually replaced by propaganda, public announcements and advertisements. The Labour newspaper *Finmarken*, which had been published in the small border town of Vardø since 1899, soon became the unwilling mouthpiece of the *Nasjonal Samling* [Vidkun Quisling's National Union Party] in eastern Finnmark, ending up with an *Abwehr* agent, Christopher Dahl, as editor. One man who was especially put out by the way this time-honoured Labour newspaper had been made into an instrument of the occupying power was a patriotic printer named Ragnvald Wærnes. Wærnes was a firm believer in the eventual victory of democracy, but there was little he could do to bring it about. He continued to make up the paper's few pages right up until the time that Vardø was bombed in 1944 and the *Finmarken* temporarily ceased publication.

Whereas detachments of the *Wehrmacht* and *Luftwaffe* were in the majority in the Soviet border areas, it was the *Kriegsmarine* that dominated the scene further to the west. Because of Hitler's fear of an Allied landing, the whole of the western part of the county had been transformed into a gigantic naval base. The Kå and Lang fjords afforded safe anchorages for the German Navy's flagship, the *Tirpitz*, and the other ships of the 1st Battle Group, the Reppar fjord was the assembly point for convoys bringing in supplies, and Hammerfest was a U-boat base. The two approaches to the main base in the Kå fjord were protected by minefields and hydrophones. Carefully sited on strategic headlands round about were no fewer than fourteen coastal batteries, many of them equipped with 15.5cm cannon. The contract for building and improving some of the wharves had been entrusted to a small but respected company from Schleswig-Holstein, Tiefbaufirma Robert Looft. One of the company's secretaries was a slim, twenty-year-old woman with chestnut hair and laughing eyes named Regina Looft, who came from the small town of Wilster. Her father owned a shop called Mode Looft [Looft Fashions]. Although the building contractor and shopkeeper shared the same surname, they were not related. Says Regina:

> One day I was drawn aside by my boss and asked if I would consider taking on a special assignment. It appeared that the company was having problems in the Administration Department in Alta and needed a secretary who could straighten things out. The question was whether I was willing to go. I was twenty years old and legally still a minor, but the job was well paid and when my father gave his permission, I agreed to go and set off north right away.

Regina travelled by train through Sweden to Narvik, where she was allotted a berth on board a troopship that took her to Bossekop, where Bauamt Alta, the authority responsible for the building project, had its offices in a barrack hut. Tiefbaufirma Robert Looft's chartered cutter *Lieselotte* took her the last few kilometres to the Kå fjord, where she was found lodgings in a private house. The contractor was engaged in building and upgrading wharves and mooring facilities for the *Tirpitz*, the *Scharnhorst* and the U-boats, but was having a lot of trouble with the planning and finding it difficult to obtain the requisite materials.

> The Kå fjord was cold and wintry and completely different from everything to which I had been accustomed. But I had more than enough to do and was

often invited on board the ships anchored there. The *Tirpitz* was especially important, as it was the only ship with a direct teleprinter link to Naval Headquarters in Kiel. In my free time I went skiing. There was a fine slope nearby called Dietlschanze after General Eduard Dietl, who was the first to take command in the Kå fjord area.

Whenever she had to go to the nearby town of Hammerfest, Regina used to spend the night in a bed-sitter belonging to the Lohmann fish-filleting plant. Under the plans for the future Thousand Year Reich, northern Norway had been allocated a special role as principal supplier of protein-rich fish to the Continent. Among those who grasped the opportunities offered for industrial expansion was an enterprising manufacturer of fishmeal from Cuxhaven, Heinz Lohmann. The German occupation had barely begun when he set about building a new state-of-the-art filleting and freezing plant. It was designed to supply the *Wehrmacht* and other purchasers of field rations with tinned and frozen fish. Lohmann brought in labour from the Ukraine, where, one night in the spring of 1942, German troops swooped on a suburb of the industrial city of Dnepropetrovsk. Physically fit young girls were taken away and made an offer it was impossible for them to refuse. They were 'invited' to take paid employment under the Germans. All they were permitted to take with them were a few clothes and personal belongings.

'It was useless to protest,' Anny Evensen remembers. 'There were a hundred and fifty women from my home town. I was only seventeen at the time and had never been far from home. Now we found ourselves bundled on to a train and sent north.' She was one of the girls who, that fateful night, had been forcibly recruited as an *Ostarbeider* and sent off into the unknown. After a journey lasting several days the train came to a halt in Stettin (now Szczecin) in Poland, where the girls were transferred to the troopship *Levant*. On board were several hundred young women. In the days and nights that followed, the ship slowly made its way northwards, along a coast none of the girls had seen before.

'After three weeks at sea, on 22 June 1942 we finally reached our destination and were allowed to go ashore. The small town in which we found ourselves was the world's northernmost, Hammerfest, but I'd have been hard put to it to place it on a map of the world. I had never seen a saltwater fish before, but we were there to work in a fish factory.' From the *Levant* the girls, all one hundred and fifty of them, were taken to a camp on Fuglenes Point, where they were housed in barrack huts, ten to a room. They were issued with working clothes – simple dresses and headscarves. They were paid a few hundred kroner a month.

'Compared with ordinary prisoners of war, we were well treated,' Anny says. 'But we weren't free – we were forced labour.'

For a brief period, Regina and Anny worked in close proximity to each other, though they were unaware of each other's existence and never conversed. Their circumstances were totally different. Regina was a secretary in a position of trust, Anny had been abducted and was a forced worker. The one thing they had in common was that both were young and attractive.

The new installations on the shores of the Alta fjord required men to guard them. The soldiers charged with the task of defending the 100-kilometre-long expanse of coastline were members of Pioneer Regiment 349, which came under the command of the recently formed 230th Division under *General der Infanterie* Conrad Menke. Some of the men had landed in Oslo with the invasion force on 9 April 1940 and made their way north in the wake of the retreating British and Norwegians. One of them was Karl Lausch, a well-built, straight-backed corporal from Salzgitter. He had dark hair, brushed back, a strong nose and wore horn-rimmed spectacles. In 1941 he was stationed with his battalion at Talvik, only a few kilometres from the German naval base in the Kå fjord. 'Our job was to protect the naval bases round about from attack by land. The battalion set up its headquarters in the old school, where I was in the Staff Office,' he says.

The young corporal's days passed quietly, filled as they were with routine duties and devoid of dramatic incidents. Talvik was a small, isolated rural community of a bare hundred inhabitants, who mostly made a living from small-scale farming and fishing. With some six hundred young soldiers quartered in barrack huts and elsewhere, contact with the locals was necessarily close. Like many of his comrades, Karl Lausch was happy in this quiet backwater on the shore of the Alta fjord – not least because of a dark-haired young girl with an engaging smile who used to pass his office every day carrying milk pails. 'I thought she was terribly pretty. We used to pass each other every single day, but it was many months before I ventured to say hello. The first time we fell into conversation was during an alert. I discovered that her name was Solveig and that she was eighteen. From that moment I was lost.'

In September 1942 the Allied convoys had been discontinued for a period of two months. Although the days were drawing in when the thirty-nine vessels of the eastbound convoy PQ18 set sail in the middle of the month, for two weeks they found themselves under constant attack from German aircraft and U-boats. Thirteen heavily laden ships were lost, proving that it was still too great a risk to send merchant ships through the Barents Sea while it was light. Much against his will, Churchill was forced to postpone further sailings for another three months. In the meantime, American and British troops had landed in Algeria and Morocco, bringing Rommel's *Afrika Korps* under attack on two fronts. In an attempt to avert disaster in the desert war, the Germans rushed reinforcements to the Mediterranean, with the result that the Arctic theatre lost most of the crack squadrons which, for the last six months, had enjoyed undisputed command of the skies above the Barents Sea. The convoys were resumed in December, and in the darkest winter months the Allies succeeded in getting three convoys through to Murmansk. The *Luftwaffe* had been manifestly weakened and the *Kriegsmarine* had squandered a golden opportunity to inflict serious damage on a convoy when, in what has become known as the Battle of the Barents Sea, the *Hipper* and *Lützow* endeavoured to attack it on New Year's Eve. Only six out of a total of seventy-four merchantmen were lost.

The fourth convoy, JW54, was on the point of departure when, in March 1943, sailings were again suspended indefinitely. Intelligence officers in London had learned that a strong new German battle fleet had assembled in the north.

What Churchill once called, among other choice epithets, 'that damned ship,' the *Tirpitz*, was back in the Kå fjord.

CHAPTER EIGHT

The Divers Return

THE KÅ FJORD, SUMMER 1976

It took two years for Peter Cornish finally to determine which midget submarine he had found on the bottom of the Kå fjord. Expectations had risen to new heights when news of the find was released in August 1974. The discovery was reported in many British newspapers and fuelled the hope that one of the great mysteries of the war had finally been solved. David Mudd, a Member of Parliament, even went so far as to demand a full investigation of the affair. 'The fact that the hull is recognisable would suggest that the submarine was not subjected to an explosive charge of a size consistent with the amatol charges the X5 carried into the fjord,' he said in an interview published in the *Daily Telegraph*. For all who could read between the lines, the implication was clear: if it really was X5 that had been found, Lieutenant Henty Henty-Creer had been cheated of a well-deserved Victoria Cross, in which case there would inevitably be a public outcry.

Cornish himself was more reserved in his comments. He knew better than anyone the difficulties confronting the expedition to the Kå fjord. It had rained non-stop for eleven days and for much of the time the temperature had been barely above freezing point. The water had been ice-cold and visibility often near zero. Constantly descending to depths of 45 metres imposed considerable strain on the divers. His official report described the actual finding of the wreck:

Our three week stay at Kaafjord was coming to an end and still nothing resembling an X-craft had been found in the fjord. We were beginning to wonder if our searching was in vain. With very little time remaining our Geophysicist, Nigel Kelland, undertook reappraisal of our search technique results and listed eight anomalies already checked but in need of further inspection.

On Tuesday 9th July, 1974, at 11.25 a.m. a pair of divers comprising Tony Rodgers and our Australian diver, Lindsey Coles, dived on anomaly No. 23 again. On surfacing they reported that this wreckage appeared to be part of a submarine. After closer study of the craft photographs, further dives confirmed that this was the entire bow section of an X-craft, upside down in thirty centimetres of mud at a depth of forty-two metres.

Much closer scrutiny was now given to the other anomalies in the vicinity of No. 23 and it was quickly found that No. 31 was the shattered remains of the pressure hull of an X-craft. It is relevant that the area where these anomalies were located is more or less equidistant between where the gunnery target was sited and where X5 was shelled.

I sympathised with Peter Cornish and his team. I knew all too well from my own attempts to locate the wrecks of the trawler *Gaul* and the German battlecruiser *Scharnhorst*, not to mention, off the island of Senja, the main engine of the fishing boat *Utvik Senior*, what they had been up against. The sea seems limitless, and it is very, very easy to make mistakes. What looks simple on the surface often proves incredibly difficult and complicated underwater. I made one mistake after another, and it took me four years to locate the missing engine, which was itself about the size of a midget submarine. Cornish and his fellow divers had experienced many of the same frustrations as I had. The side scanner had registered the presence of the bow section quite early on, and the divers had repeatedly passed over it without realising what lay beneath them on the bottom. It was only when they reassessed the echo readings and again investigated the objects on the sea floor that it was brought home to them that the tortured pieces of metal embedded in the mud were actually parts of a midget submarine. By then they had only two days left before their plane was due to depart, and were thus unable to complete their investigations at their leisure.

With permission from the British Ministry of Defence, on 11 June the bow section was raised with the aid of a lifting bag to a position 10 metres below the surface. It was a great moment when the object, which weighed two tons, finally wrenched itself free from the mud and came into view for the first time in thirty years.

We then started to fill with the twin set and after a while she slowly lifted out of the mud and rapidly shot to the surface in a cloud of silt. Great care was taken in case it came hurtling back down again.

Decompressed for five minutes at seven metres and five minutes at three metres and then inspected our efforts.

Unmistakably an X-craft nose cone.

The mud covered surface of the nose cone was cleaned to ensure that it could be clearly photographed.

In the mud inside the bow were found bits of an old rubber diving suit and an electric cell. These objects were reverently crated and taken back to England for closer inspection, before the bow was lowered back into place on the seabed.

Closer study revealed that the pieces of rubber came from a Sladen diving suit of the type used by the British during the war. Chloride Industrial Batteries confirmed that the cell was from a battery of the type installed in wartime midget submarines. But was it the wreck of X5 that Cornish and his salvage team had found or was it that of X7, which had been depth-charged not far from the target raft?

After poring over the results, Peter Cornish came to the following disappointing conclusion: 'It seems increasingly certain that the wreckage located at Anomaly Nos. 23 and 31 is from X7 and not X5. This is supported by the fact that H.M.S. X7 was located on the 27th September, 1943, at 0930 hrs. by 'ARNGAST' at a position 350 metres, 40° from 'TIRPITZ'. Subsequently, this was recovered on 1st October, 1943, and found to have an estimated 5.5 metre length of bow missing.'

He did not give up, however. In July 1976 he returned to Alta at the head of a new and bigger expedition. More money had been raised, and a side-scan sonar, a Hi-Fix Decca station and an underwater television camera borrowed for a second time. With him he brought twenty-four amateur divers, drawn from all over Great Britain, volunteers from other parts of the world, and ten Royal Engineers, who had with them a transportable decompression chamber. In the course of four weeks more than five hundred dives were carried out in the Kå fjord – from the head of the fjord and right out to the 50-metre line. The bow section and the part of the pressure hull that had been found in 1974 were recovered and shipped off to the Imperial War Museum in London.

Cornish was again interviewed by a reporter from my newspaper, the *Finnmark Dagblad*. 'We hoped it was X5 we had found a part of, but I think it is actually a bit of X7. . . . There's enormous interest in the project at home in

England,' he said. 'We've already made a film that we've sent to a British television company, and we are in constant communication with English newspapers that are interested in what we are doing.'

'Is it known for certain that X5 was inside the Kå fjord?'

'Yes, that we do know. It was observed in the fjord during the attack on the *Tirpitz*. It was outside the anti-torpedo net at the time but close by the giant it had come to destroy.'

'What will happen if you find it?'

'There's talk in the Navy of recovering it. It depends on whether it's intact or in bits and pieces. It had a crew of four, and if we find them they will have to be identified. The same applies to the submarine, or what's left of it. If we do find it and it turns out to be X5, I'm sure awards will be made to the men who manned it and lost their lives in it.'

'But isn't it established practice to leave such wrecks where they are as war graves for those who died in them?'

'Yes, that's the way in Britain. But I think we may say that this is a very special case. If we find X5, in all probability it will cast new light on one of the war's most dramatic incidents. I think everyone is interested in doing that. The relatives of the crew have all requested that they be brought ashore and given a proper burial in their own country.'

From then on, up to 18 August 1976, a massive search operation was carried out. The bottom of the fjord was combed yet again. The divers found parts of an aircraft that had crashed in a bombing raid on the *Tirpitz*, sunken lighters and tugs, depth charges, shells and pieces of anti-submarine and -torpedo nets. But of the craft the team had come to find, X5, there was not a trace. In a letter he wrote to Pamela Mellor on his return home Peter Cornish made no attempt to hide his disappointment: 'We never found X5. I think I can now quite definitely say that she does not exist in Kaafjord at the 58-yard depth limit. Where she is, is now pure conjecture. She could be anywhere and it ceases to be a diving task. We tried very hard to find her but she is not there.'

The more I read, the more doubtful I became about our own project. Cornish and his team had twice made a thorough search of the fjord with the aid of a side-scan sonar. Although, in the course of forty-five days, they had made more than eight hundred and fifty dives, a truly fantastic accomplishment, they had found no trace of Henty-Creer's missing midget submarine. But the films made by Jon Røkenes and other members of the Alta Diving Club showed what looked very much like the wreck of a small underwater craft on the spot where X5 had gone down – and, some hundreds of metres away, an unexploded side-charge. Visibility was notoriously poor in the depths of the fjord. Had the British quite simply overlooked the mangled remains and the mine? Or had they found them and for some reason concluded that they were not those of a submarine and its side-charge? It was all very mystifying. Supported as it was by the Imperial War Museum and the Winston Churchill Memorial Trust, the expedition had been a prestigious undertaking carried out in a blaze of publicity.

In 1978 Cornish, along with a few other members of the expedition, was summoned to Buckingham Palace to receive the Duke of Edinburgh's Gold Medal for their endeavours. The Prince himself made the presentation. The more I read, too, the more I realised that not only did we risk hurting people, we also risked incurring the displeasure – and even the antagonism – of the many who were convinced that X5 was not in the Kå fjord at all.

There was only one thing to do, and that was to try to return to the original sources and determine exactly what the eye-witnesses had seen. The events that took place in the fjord on that fateful morning of Wednesday 22 September 1943 would have to be reconstructed as accurately as possible. But time was fast running out. The attack had taken place sixty years earlier and it was by no means certain that any of those who had witnessed it were still alive.

PART II

CHAPTER NINE

Waiting

THE SHETLANDS AND ARCTIC, JULY 1943

The Minches (Little Minch and North Minch) is the collective name of the stretch of water that divides the Hebrides from the west coast of the Scottish mainland. But the Minches are more than a sound: together they make up an inland sea. In the south lie the islands of Skye, Rum and Eigg, with their precipitous cliffs and green littoral strip; in the north, Atlantic storms lash the beetling, windswept bulk of Cape Wrath. Between these outer limits the coast is cleft by numerous lochs and inlets. First among them is Loch Ewe, where convoys assembled before setting out on the long and hazardous voyage to Murmansk. Then, a short distance further north, comes Eddrachillis Bay, from the head of which a narrow inlet leads to a secluded lagoon edged by sheltered coves and dotted with wooded islets. This is Loch Cairnbawn, which then branches in the east into two further inlets, Loch Glendu and Loch Glencoul. When, in 1943, the admiral in charge of submarines, Rear-Admiral Claud Barry, chose this desolate arm of the sea as a forward base for the new hush-hush Twelfth Submarine Flotilla, he did so not only because it was sparsely populated and outside the range of German reconnaissance aircraft, but primarily because Loch Cairnbawn was very like a certain expanse of country further to the north, that surrounding the Alta fjord, together with its two branches, the Lang and Kå fjords, where the German High Seas Fleet had found a snug retreat.

Said Sub-Lieutenant Ivor Jarvis: 'The location really was very remote. Some of us loved it. Others plainly didn't. . . . A day off, a run ashore from Kylesku, was across Scotland, driven at high speed by a Marine driver, sometimes in fog, on the switchback single-track road, to Invergordon. A distance of some 70 miles each way. . . . I remember that there was very little to do in Invergordon when we got there. Especially on a Sunday. Oh, those Scottish Sabbaths.'

On Sunday 4 July 1943, the people living on the sheep farms bordering the loch realised that there was something out of the ordinary going on. In from the west steamed a grey-hulled 10,000-tonner with an upright funnel and a 100-ton derrick athwart the forward hold. This vessel, HMS *Bonaventure*, was a depot ship. She was escorted by an assortment of smaller craft, among them a one-time drifter pressed into service as a rescue ship and the oddly (and aptly) named HMS *Present Help*. 'She [HMS *Bonaventure*] was a Clan Line vessel, which had been taken over by the Navy as mothership for X-craft while she was still building. A Clan boat was chosen because this line specialises in transporting heavy equipment and so has much more powerful lifting gear than is usual. This was essential in our case, of course, since the craft were frequently lifted out of or into the water . . .'

The depot ship was transformed into a hive of industry the moment she dropped anchor just offshore. The hatch-covers were removed and from the depths of the holds six black-painted steel cylinders were hoisted up, swung out over the side, lowered into the water and carefully unshackled. They floated low in the water, only their flat decks being visible. From a distance they looked like so many whales basking in the sunshine beneath the twin peaks of Quinag. Nothing could have been further from the truth. The 16-metre-long cylinders were the Royal Navy's deadly new weapons, underwater minelayers. Each of them could carry four tons of high explosive over long distances. Operated by a four-man crew, they were, in fact, midget submarines – which is what they were called. Their mothership, HMS *Bonaventure*, had brought them, the first six operational units, to Loch Cairnbawn for proving trials and the crews' arduous final training. In northern Norway the moon would be on the wane at the end of September, which would make it the ideal time for an attack on the German naval bases there. A bare ten weeks were thus left before one of Churchill's many bold and original ideas was to be put to the test.

'Please report what is being done to emulate the exploits of the Italians in Alexandria harbour and similar methods of this kind,' the Prime Minister had written, eighteen months earlier, in a sharply worded minute to General Ismay for the Chiefs of Staff Committee. Just before Christmas 1941 Italian frogmen mounted on 'two-man torpedoes' had penetrated the heavily guarded British naval base at Alexandria and placed 300-kilogram explosive charges on the seabed beneath two battleships, the *Valiant* and *Queen Elizabeth*. When the charges went off, both ships were severely damaged. The *Valiant* was out of action for six months and the *Queen Elizabeth* for a year and a half. This daring attack left the British Mediterranean Fleet without heavy warships for several critical months. Moreover, it proved that a great deal could be achieved by small units and that the Italians had developed a totally new weapon which could be used to decisive effect in the heart of an enemy fortress. Mussolini's navy had won an underwater race. With every report from Alexandria, where divers were attempting to recover what was left of the Italian craft, Churchill's dissatisfaction increased, prompting him to write:

> At the beginning of the war Colonel Jefferis had a number of bright ideas on this subject, which received very little encouragement. Is there any reason why we should be incapable of the same kind of scientific aggressive action that the Italians have shown? One would have thought we should have been in the lead.
>
> Please state the exact position.

Churchill's many minutes and directives, which all too often bore the injunction 'Action this Day', were feared by all who received them – and with good reason. On this occasion, however, General Ismay had no cause to hang his head before the ageing warrior at No. 10. The Royal Navy already had the matter in hand, although progress had been slow. For some years past a handful of enthusiasts had busied themselves developing a midget submarine with the requisite properties, and a prototype, codenamed *X3*, was already under construction at Varley-Marine Works at Burlesdon, near Southampton. Launch was scheduled for March 1942, but as the technology involved was completely new, not a few teething troubles were foreseen. This meant that it would be many months before such a submarine could play an active role in operations. In the meantime steps would have to be taken to assemble a band of courageous young men who would be willing to take these new and untried craft into a strongly defended enemy naval base. Finding them was bound to take time, and Churchill was not exactly noted for his patience.

In an endeavour to speed things up, two parallel programmes were embarked upon. While *X3* was undergoing her preliminary trials in Portsmouth, the first 'human torpedo' was built in the same port. It was based on photographs and drawings of the *Maiale* (Pig) that had so successfully been deployed by the Italian navy in Alexandria and Gibraltar. The British version, named the Chariot, was in reality a 7.5-metre-long torpedo armed with a 300-kilogram warhead. It was designed to be guided to its target by two 'Charioteers' in frogmen's suits. The first of these, who sat astride the torpedo forward, was the driver, the helmsman. In front of him was an instrument panel complete with compass and controls for the hydroplanes and vertical rudder. His companion sat behind him, rather in the manner of a pillion rider on a motorcycle. He was responsible for the tools employed to cut through anti-torpedo and -submarine nets and to remove various obstacles. The torpedo riders' job was a cold one and called for steady nerves. Should they be discovered and come under fire, there was nothing to protect them. What is more, their breathing apparatus was primitive in the extreme. In those days little was known of the effects of oxygen on the human organism. Diving suits were all rubber and were known to the men who wore them as 'Clammy Death' suits. Most of the Charioteers preferred to work without gloves. The Chariots could do 4 knots and, at that speed, had a theoretical range of 16 nautical miles. Needless to say, long before the target was reached, the hands and feet of the men manning these human torpedoes were frozen stiff.

With nose tightly clipped for hours, swollen and raw from the previous day's dive, with gums cut and puffed from constant gripping of the mouthpiece, and with hands cold to the point of numbness, cut and torn from each day's diving . . . and when one surfaced and hands thawed out while one undressed, there was the feeling that all hell had broken loose with the remaining circulation.

Two of Britain's leading submarine officers were put in charge of the arduous and highly secret training programme, Captains William Fell and Geoffrey Sladen. Both knew Norway well. Fell had taken part in the Commando raids against Vågsøy and Floro and Sladen had commanded the submarine HMS *Trident*, which, in the autumn of 1941, sank two German troopships, the *Bahia Laura* and *Donau*, in the Arctic Ocean, an action that did much to prevent vital reinforcements reaching Dietl's Mountain Corps on the banks of the Litza.

Although X3 had been built to a different concept and had room for a crew of four *inside* its pressure hull, there was nothing luxurious about it. The batteries that powered the electric motor were located forward, which meant that if water were to penetrate them the chlorine gas thus generated would soon make it impossible to breathe. The control room amidships was crammed with technical gear – a periscope, navigational aids, a sonar and handles and wheels to control the rudder and pumps. Headroom was a bare metre and a half, which meant that none of the crew could stand upright to stretch their cramped limbs; they had to remain seated or shuffle about on hands and knees. Between the control room and diesel engine aft lay what was known as the W&D (Wet and Dry) compartment, a pressure tank that could be sealed off and filled with water. When the internal and external pressures were equalised, a hatch in the compartment could be opened. A diver wearing a Clammy Death suit and equipped with bottles of oxygen could then make his way out of the submarine and, with the aid of hydraulically powered cutters, cut an opening in whatever net happened to be blocking the submarine's passage, to enable it to slip through. The pressure hulls were welded from high-quality steel, permitting the submarines to dive to depths of more than 100 metres. Driven by an electric motor, submerged they could maintain a speed of 5 knots, while on the surface their pounding diesel engine gave them a speed of some 6 to 7 knots. They were ingenious little craft, but sensitive weapons of war that demanded a lot in terms of seamanship and mental and physical endurance. Service on board was limited to ten days; not even the strongest of men could endure more.

With special training they might be able to last 14 days, wrote Walker, but the last few days would be little short of hell. Even the first few days were arduous. On the surface only one man could go on deck at a time, and even that was a mixed blessing. He had to be lashed to a stanchion or be washed overboard. He got fresh air but he also got a cold bath. One thing he did not ever get was warm. The only wash the crew had was the involuntary one when they were lashed to the stanchion on deck. The air inside the submarine was always foul, even when running on the surface, and always dank and humid. The bulkheads were always dripping with condensation, which played merry hell with the sensitive electrical gear. Food was not exactly cordon bleu. The only cooking device was a little electric pot and that could be used only when the boat was on the surface, otherwise the steam would add to the unbearable moisture in the boat. Built to meticulous standards though they were, the X-craft remained constantly troubled by leaks. As historian Paul Kemp wrote:

> The crews, augmented by volunteers arriving from Fort Blockhouse, soon discovered some serious snags; water dripped everywhere, and there was great humidity below. There were two periscopes, one fixed, specially for night use. The motor for raising the attack periscope often failed. Sometimes water got into the the optical system, so that it was impossible to see anything at all. The crew tried hard to find ways of remedying this, but throughout the war this main defect of the X-craft was never overcome.

One of those who joined the new submarine arm in 1942 was a 22-year-old from Sydney. Known on account of his coppery hair as 'Tiger', Henty Henty-Creer was the son of an Australian father and an English mother. When his parents divorced in the 1920s, he accompanied his mother, Eulalia, and two younger sisters on travels that took them all over Asia and Europe. Something of a tearaway, Henty found school irksome. A born adventurer, he dreamed of becoming a film actor, and at the tender age of fourteen actually found himself a job as assistant to the Grand Old Man of Britain's budding film industry, the producer and director Alexander Korda, then head of London Film Productions. Henty never made the silver screen, but he did work in the film industry and contribute to a number of the studio's productions, among them the great propaganda epic *49th Parallel*, in which a German U-boat was hunted down and destroyed in Canada's icy waters. As soon as filming finished in the autumn of 1940, he volunteered for the Royal Navy. Talented as he was, and a hard worker to boot, he was selected for officer training and, despite his lack of formal education, passed out third of an intake numbering a hundred cadets.

'Because he had done so well, Henty was allowed to choose which branch of the service he wished to enter. As he very much wanted to be his own master, he was keen on MTBs, but he had read about Japan's midget subs, so he opted for midget submarines,' says his youngest sister, Pamela Mellor. When, in the summer of 1942, he reported to the ship that was to take the first batch of volunteers to Scotland, he was full of excitement. In the diary he left behind, and which he was destined never to complete, Henty wrote:

Two months had gone by since our initial duckings in the DSEA [Davis Submarine Escape Apparatus] tank at Fort Blockhouse and here at last was our big moment, around the last bend of the loch. We were all rather tense and just a bit keyed up, so many stories had filtered down. Some said you just couldn't see her – she was supposed to be so low in the water.

We waited and waited. The little drifter, her parent ship, so aptly named *Present Help*, was the only thing in sight. A thin plume of smoke from her galley wound up into the cold still air and it was just after 0800. As we circled her the first class were on deck and shouting about mail and laundry. One had the impression that here indeed was utter desolation!

Lying alongside was a low flat object that looked like a long black drain-pipe floating just above the water. That was all we saw before we were pulled ashore to the little concrete causeway.

Shortly afterwards they were taken on board the *Present Help* and introduced to 26-year-old Lieutenant Donald Cameron, who had been in charge of the early trials conducted by *X3*. Cameron, a Scot, was a sailor and submariner to the core. Quietly spoken, he possessed an underlying strength of will that soon won the respect of all about him.

His air of quiet authority was refreshing and his eyes were full of humour as he smoked his enormous rough wood pipe. His cap looked altogether far too big for his small face with that pugnacious chin. We crowded round on the little deck and looked down on the rusty casing of the *Tiddler*, she was an impressive little thing and the very 'first of the few'. Only about 18 inches of her bows showed above the water and with the inner feeling of hope and success we listened to explanations. The idea really was immense and one couldn't help feeling proud.

My first impression was of the inside of a Wellington bomber – that maze of instruments, levers and electrical gadgets, the dim lighting and lack of standing room. The many cocks, valves, switches and pipe lines, pump motors, gyro, all so compact.

A year had now passed since Henty-Creer and his fellow volunteers had first been introduced to the prototype craft. An intensive training programme was nearing its end and most of those involved felt relieved and happy that their long wait would soon be over.

The worst enemies of these long training periods were boredom and frustration. Doing the same old thing over and over again, carrying out the same tests of equipment, watching the same old scenery slip by your periscope, seeing the same old faces in the wardroom month after month after month, and in the back of one's mind all the time the nagging knowledge that at some time enemy waters had to be penetrated and an enemy battleship attacked. The combination of extreme monotony over a very long period, and almost complete ignorance of what was in store – nobody had ever before attacked a battleship in precisely this manner – had at times a devastating effect psychologically, and we went through stages of intense gloom, which, however, would lift as suddenly as they had descended.

The keels of the first six midget submarines had been laid down in September 1942 at the Vickers yard at Barrow-in-Furness. They were numbered consecutively from X5 to X10. Lieutenant Henty-Creer was given command of the first of them, X5. He was enabled to follow the building process from the outset, which, besides being an eye-opening experience, afforded him a welcome break from his long period of training.

I had an extraordinary sense of freedom as the train took the final turns up on that rain-soaked corner of the north-west English coast. It was late autumn and the last bright leaves were falling from the nearly naked trees. . . . The immensity of it all was staggering. Warships and submarines nearing completion filled the waterways and great billows of black smoke poured out of the tall chimneys, to drift lazily past the incredibly large cranes. . . . Lorries and locomotives with their squeaking wheels appeared from nowhere and, as soon, disappeared into this monstrous hive that was in itself a complete city. . . . Walking over the cobbled roads that led to our boat, we passed shed after shed whose large open doors gave us an insight into another side of war. Great sheets of flame and white hot metal blazed in the inner darkness, where men became silhouettes as they tended their weird charges. The music of metal in all its stages, forged and struck with mighty living slabs of iron, echoed out to us as we passed on down the yards. . . . It was hard to make oneself believe that what appeared now just a collection of old iron, would in a month or so be a unit of the Royal Navy – spotless in its first coat of paint. . . . As the days went on and the boat gradually filled with more and more pipes and valves, and the maze of electric cables began to mean something, my confidence in myself fell hour by hour. Would I ever know the boat? Each day produced new gadgets and things seemed to get more obscure and I would go to the drawing office to get an interpretation of it all.

X5 was launched on New Year's Eve 1942, the other craft following early in January 1943.

Such small craft would never rate official names from the Admiralty, yet it seemed all wrong to let them cross the sea, dive and fight merely as X5, X6, X7 etc. They must have names of their own, at least for private use. Yes, but what names? Those of towns, flowers, plants, birds, fishes, national heroes, admirals, had all been taken apparently by earlier vessels.

After prolonged discussions and visits to the library it was agreed that all the names should begin with a 'P' and have underwater connections.

'Well, I'm going Down Under to find a name for mine,' said Henty-Creer. 'I shall name her "Platypus".' He went on to explain to his bewildered companions that the platypus is an Australian mammal that lives in water and lays its eggs there, adding, 'My "Platypus" will carry its huge eggs and lay them under enemy ships. They'll hatch out there quite suddenly and go off with a bang.'

Lieutenant Donald Cameron called his submarine, X6, 'Piker', while Godfrey Place chose for his X7 'Pdinichthys', which, he explained, was a fierce prehistoric fish.

By this time it was July 1943. Cameron, Place and Henty-Creer had now been in command of their own craft for six months. Their doubts about what had once looked to them like 'a heap of scrap iron' had long been dispelled. Using the battleship *Malaya* and their mothership *Bonaventure* as targets, time and again they had successfully forced anti-torpedo nets, guard posts and hydrophones to lay their side-charges on the bottom. They worked smoothly together and had complete confidence in their craft, which they could handle virtually blindfold. Six months of intensive preparation were nearing their end. Now they were chafing at the bit, their one desire to set off on their first operation.

*

On board the *Tirpitz*, which still lay snugly at anchor behind her anti-torpedo nets in the Kå fjord, Admiral Oskar Kummetz was in a grim mood. So far, the summer had been a washout, and Sunday 4 July was no exception. The sky was heavily overcast and the temperature was a mere 7°C. A light breeze, blowing from the north, set the men gathered on the open deck for the weekly service of worship shivering with cold. The ship's complement of 2,300 men comprised both Protestants and Roman Catholics, for which reason the *Tirpitz* carried two padres, one Evagelical-Lutheran, the other Catholic. Fifty-one-year-old Kummetz, who was not particularly religious in the first place, was hardly rendered more so by the teleprinter message that came ticking in that same morning from Naval Headquarters in Kiel.

'Despite all attempts to reconcile [our] differing points of view, the *Luftwaffe* is now showing itself it its true colours. In addition to the tone of the communication and the reproaches levelled at *Admiral Nordmeer* [Admiral Northern Seas], there is a clear lack of understanding in regard to the demands imposed by the war at sea,' reads an angry entry in the ship's war diary.

Kummetz was born in 1891 in a small country town in East Prussia, close to the border with White Russia. Entering the Imperial Navy in 1910 as a cadet, he had sailed as an officer on liners and destroyers throughout the whole of the First World War. Hard work and dedication in a succession of command and staff posts had taken him into the highest echelons of the *Kriegsmarine* by the time, in the winter of 1940, he was promoted to *Konter-Admiral* and entrusted with command of the squadron selected to take Norway's capital city, Oslo. Lean, and of short stature, Kummetz was a proud, ambitious man with piercing eyes, a weatherbeaten face and full lips that gave him an arrogant and rather acerbic appearance. Of all Hitler's admirals, it was he who had longest exercised operational command of Germany's capital ships since the outbreak of war, that is, for close on two years. He had done well to do so, for the Fates had been anything but kind to him. On the night of 8/9 April his flagship, the *Blücher*, was sunk in the narrow confines of Drøbak Sound, not far from Oslo, its goal. Kummetz and the rest of his staff had survived by the skin of their teeth after swimming ashore, a distance of some 200 metres, in the icy water. Kummetz was widely criticised for the loss of this brand-new cruiser, on account of his having insisted on negotiating the sound, which was overlooked by Oscarsborg Fort, at reduced speed. It was the fort's heavy guns and torpedo batteries that sent the *Blücher* to the bottom.

But Hitler and Germany's Naval High Command saw things differently. Kummetz was promoted to Inspector of Torpedoes and awarded the Knight's Cross to the Iron Cross. In spring 1942 he received a further boost when he was promoted to *Vizeadmiral* and given command of the *Kriegsmarine*'s remaining cruisers, with the *Admiral Hipper* as his flagship. But when, on New Year's Eve 1942, he attacked a British convoy south of Bear Island, Kummetz again met with disaster. An inferior British force routed the attackers and the convoy it was escorting reached Archangel without loss, causing Hitler to lose all confidence in the Battle Fleet and, in his fury, order the Navy's big ships to be decommissioned. Only the stubbornness and powers of persuasion of the new naval chief, *Gross-Admiral* Karl Dönitz, saved what was left of the 1st Battle Group – the *Tirpitz*, the battlecruiser *Scharnhorst* and the 'pocket battleship' *Lützow*. Dönitz made a deal with Hitler, promising to deploy his ships for 'an annihilating blow' against the convoys passing through the Barents Sea, and to this end, in March 1943 he despatched the whole squadron to the Kå fjord. To many people's surprise, the man responsible for the New Year's Eve débâcle, Oskar Kummetz, was made a full admiral and placed in command of the group, where he flew his flag in the *Tirpitz*. In all probability this was a power-political ploy on

Dönitz' part. He no doubt assumed that Kummetz would be burning for revenge and, more so than any of the other ranking officers available, be prepared to 'fight and, if need be, die' to redeem his honour and that of the Battle Group.

In the mahogany-panelled Admiral's Cabin on board the *Tirpitz*, Kummetz had been working hard all through the spring to prepare for what he referred to as his 'principal task', which was to prevent supplies reaching Murmansk. Many conferences had been held in the cabin and many had been the distinguished visitors to the flagship. They included *Fliegerführer Lofoten, Generalmajor* Ernst-August Roth, who, from his headquarters at Bardufoss, was in command of the bombers and reconnaissance aircraft stationed in Troms and western Finnmark, and *Fregattenkapitän* Prützmann, the *Kriegsmarine*'s liaison with *Luftflotte 5*, the Air Fleet of which Roth was a part. The convoys had been temporarily suspended, but Kummetz wished to be ready for action the day the British and Americans again ventured to send merchant ships into the Barents Sea. However, he was nothing if not a realist: he realised that, by themselves, his surface ships could never destroy a whole convoy, and most certainly not if it was protected by battleships and aircraft carriers. He needed the help of the *Luftwaffe*, both for reconnaissance and for defence against heavily armed escort vessels.

'It is Prützmann's duty to impress upon Luftflotte 5, over and over again, that our common goal of destroying a convoy can be achieved only if all prestige is put aside and replaced by sensible operational and tactical cooperation,' Kummetz wrote in the war diary.

All the Admiral's efforts to bring this about had so far been in vain, hence his grim mood. The rivalry between the *Kriegsmarine* and the *Luftwaffe* was legendary. There was more than a little truth in the hoary old joke that the top brass expended more of their energy on fighting each other than on fighting the enemy. To the Navy's chagrin, the *Luftwaffe* insisted that it was the torpedo carriers and bombers of *KG 26* and *KG 30* that had ensured victory in the great battles fought against the convoys in the summer of 1942. Göring and his fellow officers insisted that the *Luftwaffe* was to play a new – and leading – role once convoy sailings were resumed. It was the *Luftwaffe* that would sink the merchantmen, leaving the 1st Battle Group to deal with their escort. Kummetz wanted the roles reversed: 'I am of the opinion that attacking merchantmen should not be the task of the Luftwaffe,' he wrote, 'as a convoy can be destroyed more quickly and completely by naval forces.'

It was a bitter and destructive conflict that was destined never to be resolved. Göring's generals refused to concentrate on the escorts in future attacks and were determined not to employ fighter aircraft for reconnaissance purposes.

'This means that I shall be unable to count on any support worth mentioning from the *Luftwaffe* for operations in the Barents Sea. Although I have earlier declared such support a vital prerequisite, I believe that we can achieve results even so. To do so we need luck and the addition of a sufficient number of light forces. Every vessel will be of the utmost importance,' Kummetz wrote in the war diary.

It was probably with some relief that, at eight o'clock in the evening of the following day, for the first time since his arrival in the Kå fjord three months earlier, he weighed anchor and took the entire battle fleet to sea. The wind had veered to the south-east, bringing with it a welcome rise in temperature. The orb of the sun was faintly discernible through the light overcast when the *Tirpitz, Scharnhorst, Lützow* and twelve destroyers set a course for Bear Island on the night of 5/6 July. They were to take part in a war game in which the *Tirpitz, Scharnhorst* and seven of the destroyers would attack a British escort force represented by the *Lützow* and the remaining destroyers. Although the exercise had to be broken off after only four hours owing to a critical shortage of fuel, Kummetz was feeling reasonably satisfied with the result when the *Tirpitz* slipped back into her berth in the Kå fjord on the morning of 7 July.

> This exercise in the open sea gave the Group a boost of sorts, but it also made clear how essential training of this nature is. It cannot be expected that a group penned up in a narrow fjord, and only able to carry out brief training exercises involving one or two ships at a time, should act as a coordinated whole and perform tactically correctly in whatever situations may arise. . . . Such exercises must therefore be regularly carried out.

Considering the way the war was going for Germany, Kummetz most probably knew that this was wishful thinking. Oil was strictly rationed, forcing the big ships to lie idle at their moorings, engines shut down, for long periods at a time. Power and heating had to be provided by auxiliary vessels equipped with electric generators and coal-fired steam engines. But even they were not without their problems. In July, for example, the generators on board the *Karl Junge* and *Wilhelm Bremen* broke down and no spare parts to repair them were available. Not until another auxiliary vessel, the *Watt*, was summoned from Narvik did the big ships get their power back. On board the twelve-year-old, diesel-driven *Lützow*, the situation was especially critical. The year before, the *Admiral Scheer* had sailed deep into the Kara Sea to wreak havoc among the convoys hugging Russia's arctic coast, and Berlin was eager to repeat her success, only this time with the *Lützow* as the intruder. *Kapitän-zur-See* Rudolf Stange and his men had been training for weeks with this object in view, and were now only waiting to hear that the ice had receded sufficiently to provide a free passage. But the *Lützow* was badly run down after a hard winter in the north and was living on borrowed time. The list of repairs that needed to be done grew longer with every passing day. Stange had managed to keep up with the squadron on the Bear Island foray, but two weeks later, while testing the ship's radar in the Alta fjord against the armoured vessel *Thetis*, four of the battleship's generators broke down at the same time. That was the end. 'That is fifty per cent of the total, including the most efficient of the engines. . . . With the engines in their present state, it must be expected that similar breakdowns will continue to occur, especially if they are in operation for any length of time at sea. I can therefore no longer regard the ship as fully battleworthy,' Stange wrote in the war diary.

One of the men who toiled day and night to make the *Lützow* seaworthy again was a 34-year-old specialist from the Carl Zeiss works in Jena, Robert Ehrhardt. Renowned world-wide for the quality of its cameras and binoculars, Zeiss was a major supplier to the German Navy. Radar was still in its infancy, which meant that all the *Kriegsmarine*'s vessels were equipped with large numbers of optical rangefinders. The biggest of these was 10.5 metres across and could detect an aircraft at a range little short of 100 kilometres. A ship's ability to bring its big guns to bear depended on its rangefinders' supplying the gun crews with accurate data, and for that the powerful lenses and prisms had to be kept finely adjusted at all times. Because the *Kriegsmarine* continued to despatch an increasing number of its heavy battleships to Norway, Zeiss found it expedient to open an office in Horten, on the western shore of the Oslo fjord. Robert Ehrhardt was one of the company's leading experts on marine optics and for this reason was appointed technical manager. There was a pressing need to maintain these sophisticated instruments, and from 1943 onwards Ehrhardt found himself on board the ships of the 1st Battle Group at anchor in the Kå and Lang fjords.

'My father was a specialist and he was sent for whenever anything went wrong. He was very proud of his expertise. I was an only child. I remember him as a kind man and a good father. I loved him dearly and missed him terribly when he was away in Norway. His letters kept our spirits up and gave us hope that one day peace would come,' says Ehrhardt's daughter, Inge, who still lives in Jena.

On his photographs Robert Ehrhardt always seems to have a playful smile about his lips. He has a straight nose and looks calm and assured. It is the face of a sensitive man. In one of the letters he wrote to his daughter from the Kå fjord he said:

It's not that we're bored on board, but these last few days the weather has taken a turn for the worse, making it impossible to do any work. Without warning, winter returned and thus put paid to all hope that summer would soon be here. The day before yesterday the temperature dropped to two degrees below zero and it snowed all day long. Things are looking better today and the snow is all wet and slushy. Most of it will be gone by Whitsuntide, especially as here on board the holiday has been put back by a week. The job I came to do is actually finished, I am just waiting for a spare part from Jena, so I should be through for good within the next eight days . . . which means that I should be home some time in July. If you can get away, I can take my holiday then. The garden may need a lot doing to it. It must be wonderful to see apple and cherry trees in blossom. I haven't seen that for three years. Here, it's all very different. . . . The birches usually burst into leaf in the course of only a few days, then Nature's reawakening is over. We've not reached that point yet, though. Only the waterfalls tell us that a change won't be long in coming. . . . Well, one day the war will come to an end and everything will be back to normal. . . . I wish you and Mother a happy Whitsun.

Lots of love to you both

Your father

The dilapidated state of the Navy's ships was a general cause for concern. In Kiel, the High Command had more than once proposed transferring the Battle Group from Alta to the Bogen fjord near Narvik, where maintenance facilities were better. But Kummetz was averse to such a move:

In the past I considered Alta most suitable as a secondary anchorage, with the Bogen fjord as a permanent base. I have now changed my opinion. Now that the Lang and Kå fjords are established bases, complete with provisioning facilities, anti-aircraft batteries, anti-submarine nets and the like, I believe that Alta is the best place for the fleet to be. There is no difference between Alta and the Bogen fjord in regard to the threat from the air, but from an operational point of view the former is much to be preferred, as there are several good exits from the base.

The naval chiefs were also eager to see the big ships dispersed among the various fjords, to make attacking them more difficult. Kummetz was opposed to this, too. 'The suggestion that anchorages should be changed to guard against sabotage is not new. The matter was raised as early as February 1942, but nothing came of it because of the fuel situation. It would be the same now, as fuel would be consumed not only in moving the big ships, but also for water and power supplies and for the guardships.'

One reason Kummetz felt secure where he was in the Kå fjord was, not least, that he had received some comforting news from General Conrad Menke, commander of the 230th Infantry Division, which was responsible for safeguarding the area. Menke's headquarters were at Skoganvarre, while the 349th Pioneer Regiment, which was stationed at Talvik, covered the Alta fjord. 'It emerged from the discussion that, since redeployment of his forces to well-established bases, the Commander-in-Chief of the Army now feels capable of repulsing any action on the part of the enemy. It is gratifying to learn that arms and ammunition are up to strength, also where new weapons are concerned.'

What was foremost in the minds of the two officers responsible for guarding the Kå fjord area was the possibility of a landing by British forces on a broad front. They had no idea that the real danger would come from a totally different quarter.

*

Fear of sabotage stemmed from news received in spring 1943 from the neighbouring division in eastern Finnmark, the 210th Infantry Division under *Generalleutnant* Karl Wintergerst. In April, a Russian prisoner had revealed the presence of more than sixty Norwegian refugees in the Murmansk region and said that many of them had been trained as partisans for operations behind the German lines. 'There are indications that we must now expect regular acts of sabotage and espionage on the part of the enemy also in northern Norway,' warned General Eduard Dietl's headquarters in Rovaniemi.

Early in 1942 the Soviet Northern Fleet began to deploy an increasing number of submarines along the coast of Finnmark in an attempt to sever the Mountain Corps' supply lines. The targets were both many and tempting. In 1943, 6.3 million tons of war materials were shipped along the coastal route. Every week, anything up to fifty merchantmen plied the exposed waters between Tromsø and Kirkenes. Eastbound vessels were laden with ammunition, petrol, food, fresh troops and weaponry. On the return voyage some of them carried invaluable cargoes of nickel from the Petsamo mines.

Throughout the whole of 1942 and 1943 the duel between Soviet aircraft and submarines and the German Navy grew ever harder and bloodier. Many cargo ships were sunk, most notably between Nordkyn and Vardø, an expanse of sea that was completely unprotected. What were little short of full-scale battles ensued between the planes and submarines and the German escorts, which largely consisted of commandeered Norwegian whaling vessels. The Germans lost twelve submarine chasers, and eight Soviet submarines were sent to the bottom.

Strange as it may seem, the Germans did not realise that the Russians were receiving help from the shore until late in the spring of 1943. By then, Norwegian partisans recruited from the Kiberg refugees had been keeping coastal shipping under surveillance from caves in the mountains for more than eighteen months, and had been in almost daily wireless communication with their base in Murmansk. 'Our suspicions relating to Norwegian/Russian agents operating in the Varanger area were confirmed by information obtained from a prisoner,' wrote *Premierleutnant* Fritz Pardon in a report he compiled at a later date.

Thirty-eight-year-old Pardon had been a member of Hitler's 'Brownshirts' [*Sturmabteilung*] since 1933. A judge by profession, before being called up he had been a district stipendiary magistrate in Burgsteinfürt. He was married and had two children. He had been in Norway since the spring of 1940 as adjutant of the 2nd Mountain Division and had taken part in the first two years' bitter fighting on the Litza front. In the spring of 1943 he was assigned a task more in keeping with his former profession, being appointed intelligence officer of the 210th Division, which was responsible for security in eastern Finnmark. One of his first tasks was to interrogate a twenty-year-old Red Guardsman, Georgy Wertyanski, who had been captured six months earlier on the Fisherman's Peninsula. The ambitious lieutenant was startled by what the prisoner had to tell.

When, in September 1941, he reached . . . Polyarnoe . . . he got to know some fifty Norwegians who were being trained as spies. . . . They had made their way to Russia in 1940 on board various fishing boats, along with a number of women and children. . . . One month later, three Norwegians and a Russian wireless operator reported to a reconnaissance unit there [i.e. in Polyarnoe], where they planned to spend the night. Next morning Wertyanski had to help load two rubber dinghies on board a submarine, together with provisions for several months: tinned food, tobacco, chocolate, pistols and hand grenades. In April 1942, together with another party of four men, he came *back* from Norway in a submarine. . . . The wireless operator, Tschishewski, was a friend of Wertyanski, who learned from him that they had spent several months in the Kirkenes area, where Tschishewski had even managed to visit the local cinema. Among other things, he had brought back with him a Norwegian *sparkstøtting* [chair-sledge]. . . . The dinghies were employed to put the men ashore from submarines in lonely fjords. The men's duties included gathering intelligence on shipping and troop movements, establishing contact with Norwegians and spreading propaganda among the local population.

Pardon came to the following conclusion: 'The fact that some sixty Communist-minded Norwegians from Kiberg emigrated to Russia early in the war makes it reasonable to suppose that the enemy has landed, and is maintaining in the Varanger area, groups of agents who are in contact with the locals in out-of-the-way places.'

The lieutenant was responsible for counter-espionage in the 210th Division's field of operations, which extended from Kirkenes in the east to Laksefjord in the west. He approached his task with zeal. Only two days after questioning the Russian prisoner, he contacted the officer commanding naval forces in Kirkenes, the *Abwehr* and the *Gestapo*, and exhorted them to mount a concerted campaign to hunt down the partisans.

Early in May 1943 a wireless-detection unit from the Navy's Direction Finding and Monitoring Station (MPHS Kirkenes) was despatched to Vardø to track down enemy wireless transmissions. It drew a blank. Although many transmissions were picked up, they were found to be in Finnish. This prompted the experts at the Monitoring Service's headquarters in Berlin to put a damper on the proceedings. 'The monitoring proved unsuccessful. Berlin refused to believe that the transmissions came from Russian agents. They would not agree with the unit's findings,' Pardon wrote.

However, bearings had been taken on strong signals emanating from the sparsely populated area surrounding the Sylte fjord. Although Berlin remained unresponsive, Pardon was convinced that he was on to something big. 'The Division urged the *Abwehr* to step up surveillance in the area, which was not occupied by the *Wehrmacht* and was thus a good place for agents to avoid detection.'

When the *Abwehr*'s efforts proved equally unsuccessful, Pardon determined to take the matter into his own hands. On 2 July, several hundred men from the 210th Division, naval headquarters in Kirkenes and coastal batteries in the region were set ashore at various places on the Varanger Peninsula. In the course of one week an exhaustive house-to-house search, Operation *Mitternachtssonne* [Midnight Sun], was carried out in every fishing village and isolated community. Papers were carefully scrutinised and substantial rewards in the shape of money and food were offered to anyone coming forward with information on strangers in the locality.

Yet again, eager-beaver Pardon was doomed to disappointment, as nothing came of the search. When, on Friday 9 July, the time came to sum up the results of the operation, he had to acknowledge that the operation had been a failure. True, four people had been arrested for unlawful possession of arms, and in the Sylte fjord district an anti-Nazi leaflet headed '*Ti bud for en ekte nordmann*' [Ten precepts for a true Norwegian] had been found. But of the agents and saboteurs he had set out to uncover, there was not a trace.

*

While Pardon was in Kirkenes planning a new offensive and Kummetz, in Alta, was engaged in puzzling out how to manage without the *Luftwaffe*, a dramatic development occurred on Spitsbergen, 500 kilometres to the north. In mid-June 1943 a Norwegian patrol of ten men, led by Captain Ernst Ullring, had set out on a reconnaissance patrol in a 30-foot open motorboat, bound for the Kross fjord, north of New Ålesund. In Signehamna the patrol made some surprising discoveries, among them an automatic weather station, two rowing boats and a varied store of equipment. Leaving five men to keep watch on their find, Ullring then hastened back to Barentsburg to bring in reinforcements.

Although he did not know it, he had stumbled on the German Navy's most important weather station on Spitsbergen; manned by six men, it had been there since the autumn of 1941. When the war spread to the Arctic, the meteorologists had followed in its wake. The region was one of the world's most important sources of weather. What happened there, at the interface of warm air from the south and cold air from the north, did much to determine weather conditions in the whole of the northern hemisphere – making the Arctic of vital importance to the planning of military operations on land, at sea and in the air. German meteorologists, who were among the best in their field, quickly set up a chain of observation posts extending from Labrador and Greenland in the west to Franz Josef's Land and Novaya Zemlya in the east. With its specially equipped Heinkel 111s, Meteorological Squadron 5, stationed at Banak on the

Norwegian mainland, made daily flights far out across the Barents Sea. Wrote the German historian Franz Selinger:

> With the outbreak of war, international exchanges of meteorological reports ceased. This meant that Germany found herself in need of information from territories in the Arctic that were under Allied control. What occurs in the atmosphere in the northern polar regions largely determines the weather in Europe and the Atlantic. For this reason, continuous reports on conditions in the Arctic were essential for accurate weather forecasting in these theatres.

The station at Signehamna was one of the most important of these German weather stations. Equipped with radiosondes and other sophisticated equipment, it transmitted daily reports to the Norwegian mainland. In 1943 it was called *Nussbaum* [Walnut Tree], after the distinguished meteorologist in charge, Dr Franz Nusser. His deputy, Dr Heinz Köhler, was a gifted painter. On Sunday 20 June Köhler was engaged in photographing birdlife beside a mountain lake when he was seen by two of the Norwegian soldiers who had been left behind. When they attempted to apprehend him, he panicked. 'Warning shots were fired, and in the chase that followed Köhler tripped and fell. Seated on the ground, at a range of 15 to 20 metres he fired several shots at his two pursuers, but missed. He then put the pistol to his head and shot himself.'

The five remaining German weathermen thought they were under attack from a large force of infantry and radioed for help. A German U-boat commander, 26-year-old *Kapitänleutnant* Hans Benker, an Arctic veteran, happened to be in Hammerfest with his boat, *U-625*, when the call for assistance was received. Benker knew the waters off Spitsbergen well. In November of the previous year he had sunk two British merchant ships, the *Chumleigh* and *Empire Sky*, off South Cape. He immediately put to sea, reaching the Kross fjord on Wednesday 23 June. As soon as the five survivors from the *Nussbaum* station were safely on board, the 4.7-inch gun on the foredeck was loaded and the U-boat headed for Signehamna, where a force of sixteen Norwegians was busy dismantling the German weather station. Benker's first shot blew the patrol's motorboat out of the water.

'The two men on board jumped into the sea and swam for the shore, still under German fire. They clambered up on to the ice and made their way inland, intent on seeking refuge in a crack in the rock. But Harald Andersen lost his footing, fell into the sea and was unable to get out by his own efforts.' Only when, half an hour later, Benker withdrew, was Andersen pulled out of the water; but by then it was too late – he had frozen to death in the ice-cold water.

The patrol buried the two dead men, collected the most important pieces of equipment and set fire to the station. Among the papers they retrieved was one that made a vivid impression on the Norwegians, the diary the thirty-year-old Berliner Heinz Köhler had so assiduously kept all winter. 'His last entry was a wish that his wife was all right. He had dreamed one night that she had died in his arms.'

When Dr Nusser and his four surviving companions were set ashore in the Bogen fjord near Narvik on 28 June, there was consternation among the German military staffs. Accurate weather reports would be of vital importance in the forthcoming operations in the north. The Norwegian company stationed at Barentsburg had long been a thorn in the Germans' side, and now one of the *Kriegsmarine*'s key weather stations was no more. The admirals in Berlin, Narvik and Alta were unanimous in agreeing that the time had come to teach the Norwegians a lesson.

CHAPTER TEN

The Passage

SCOTLAND AND FINNMARK, AUGUST/SEPTEMBER 1943

It was nearing four o'clock in the afternoon of Saturday 11 September when Lieutenant Robert Alexander gave the order to start HMS *Truculent*'s diesels. Slowly, the submarine began to gain headway and the towrope, which was nearly 300 metres long, took up the strain. A sudden jerk told the passage crew on board 'Piker' that both submarines were on their way to the mouth of Eddrachillis Bay. Eighteen months after Churchill had fired off his impatient minute to the Chiefs-of-Staff about the *Tirpitz*, Operation Source had begun. In the course of the next twenty-four hours, all six midget submarines of the Twelfth Submarine Flotilla were on their way to the island of Sørøy in western Finnmark.

On board the *Bonaventure* the Chief Electrical Artificer, James Williams, witnessed the departure of the X-craft with a mixture of pride and sadness. 'I'm not ashamed to say we had pride in our hearts and a tear in our eye, tough as we were. Then when they had all left we were somehow lost, our "babies" had gone. It was hard going . . . but I wouldn't have missed it then for any other project.'

The previous day, Sir Claud Barry, Rear-Admiral Submarines, had flown in to Loch Cairnbawn, bringing with him the latest updates on the plans. That same evening he invited the twelve midget-submarine commanders to a farewell dinner on board HMS *Titania*. Six of them would sail their craft to the release point west of Sørøy; the other six would take them through Stjern Sound into the Kå fjord. The Admiral later wrote:

They were like boys on the last day of term, their spirits ran so high. This confidence was not in any way the outcome of youthful dare-devilry, but was based on the firm conviction, formed during many months of arduous training, that their submarines were capable of doing all that their crews demanded of them, and the crews were quite capable of surmounting any difficulties or hazards which it was possible for human beings to conquer.

With his twenty-six years, and seagoing experience in the Merchant Navy, Lieutenant Donald Cameron was the leading figure of the intrepid little band. A few days earlier he had said goodbye to his wife, Eve, and Iain, his four-month-old son. Late that night, after the party, he retired to his cabin and sat down to write in his private notebook:

Darling, I am writing this for your enjoyment, I hope, and also for Iain's when he is old enough to take an interest in such matters. . . . Excellent dinner sitting on Claud's left. . . . Usual shop. Very optimistic, perhaps a trifle too much so. . . . My condition a trifle hazy on return to *Bonaventure*! Lovely clear night, moon almost full, good weather ahead, thank God. Turn in for my last night in a comfortable bed. Goodnight.

Tubs

Cameron had followed the progress of the midget submarines ever since the time when the prototype, *X3*, was launched in mid-March 1942. Better than any of his fellow commanders, he knew that Operation Source was going to be a hazardous undertaking, no matter by what standards it was judged. Ever since the flotilla's arrival in Loch Cairnbawn on Sunday 4 July training had been intensified. It was originally intended that the submarines should carry a crew of no more than three: a commander, who doubled as navigator, a second-in-command, who would be responsible for the electrical equipment, and an Engine Room Artificer (ERA) to deal with mechanical problems. That meant that one or more of the men needed to be trained as a diver, ready to leave the submarine if it were trapped in an anti-torpedo net. But when two men were drowned in training, Admiral Barry and his staff realised that this would be asking too much of the men, and it was hastily decided to add a qualified diver to each crew.

'It was a wartime emergency. Both the planners and the men in charge of the operation were under tremendous pressure. By rights the attack should have been mounted in March, but the submarines weren't ready. We had to set out in September, otherwise it would have been too late. Summer had already come when the decision to increase the crew from three to four was made. We had only had some four to six weeks together with the others, and spent most of our time on net exercises,' says Robert Aitken, an Ipswich man who had volunteered as a navy diver and in July was welcomed aboard X7, 'Pdinichtys'.

The crews' intensive training continued all through August. Much time and effort went into determining what kind of explosive would be most effective. The 8-metre-long charges, which resembled large metal troughs, were shaped to fit snugly on each side of the submarine's hull, but they proved far from ideal. Wrote Frank Walker:

Large masses of explosive are difficult to detonate evenly and in the case of the mines carried by the X-craft there was an additional problem – their shape was determined by the shape of the boat, not by detonation effectiveness. The usual criterion of optimum shape for maximum detonation did not apply. The experts resigned themselves to the fact that detonation efficiency probably lay within the range of 25 to 65 per cent. One hundred per cent was highly unlikely, in view of the shape of the mines.

Peter Smail, a Shipwright Artificer on the *Bonaventure*, was one of those whose job it was to handle the charges. 'The amatol explosive that went into the side cargoes took the form of grey granules, rather like instant gravy. After fitting and securing "fit for release", I often had the task of being hoisted up and out with the craft and then when she was waterborne, lying along the top of the charge half in and half out of the water, readjusting the tension of the charge bottle screws to get them "spot on" for release.'

Although the charges caused the men who had to manhandle them into position considerable trouble, their explosive power was formidable indeed. The surface of the sea heaved and boiled when they were exploded during trials, and it was clear that if they were correctly laid, even the strongest armour-steel would be hard put to it to withstand the shock. Complete with ballast tank, each charge weighed 2.75 tons, two tons of which was explosive. The timers could be set from inside the submarine. The addition of 5.5 tons extra weight, coupled with the danger of leaking casings, made trimming the small craft a difficult task.

More than 1,000 nautical miles separated Scotland from northern Norway, and the skies above most of the intervening ocean were regularly patrolled by German aircraft. The midget submarines could not carry sufficient fuel to make the trip under their own power, and in consequence had to be towed. After numerous trials, and no little discussion, it was resolved to employ standard diesel-driven submarines to do the towing. But to avoid detection, as much as possible of the eight-day crossing would have to be carried out submerged, which gave rise to new and complicated problems. In the first place, extra crews had to be trained for the passage, and in the second place, never before had an attempt been made to tow one submarine behind another over such a great distance. The strain on the two craft, the men who manned them and, not least, the towline, would be extremely great. The Royal Air Force used nylon towlines to tow gliders, but this was still a secret; moreover, nylon was in short supply and strictly rationed. The Air Ministry refused to release more than 600 precious pounds, which was too little to provide nylon towlines for all six X-craft. The consequence was that most of them had to make do with manila ropes woven round a telephone line. Hemp is a strong and well-tested material, but trials had shown that manila ropes had a tendency to part after some sixty to eighty hours' use. If that were to happen, it would find the unfortunate submarine on tow far from its designated release point. Accordingly, the crews had to keep on their toes. If a towline were to break while the submarine was submerged, the weight of the waterlogged line would soon drag the hapless little craft remorselessly into the depths.

While the crews struggled to overcome their difficulties, the planners had problems of their own. In 1942 the *Tirpitz* had moved successively from Trondheim to Narvik to Alta, and it was not until late in the winter of 1943 that it became reasonably certain that Alta had become the 1st Battle Group's permanent base. This meant that a lot of work had to be done to find out what defence measures the midget submarines would have to contend with.

'Preliminary photographic reconnaissance of the anchorages, with specific reference to net defences, was considered most necessary for the success of the operation, and last minute reconnaissances, to give the disposition of targets, essential,' wrote Rear-Admiral Barry in his report.

Alta presented special problems. The bases in the Kå and Lang fjords were beyond the range of British reconnaissance aircraft. Strange though it may seem, neither the Norwegian Resistance nor the British had infiltrated agents into Finnmark, despite the county's having for two years been the most important theatre of war in the north. The nearest Soviet agents equipped with wireless facilities were in hiding on the island of Arnøy; the nearest British were in Tromsø, more than 200 kilometres distant.

The solution was to employ long-range Spitfires specially equipped for aerial photography and capable of operating from bases in north-western Russia. Several such aircraft had been supplied to the Russians the previous year, but the Soviet pilots lacked the experience required for such work. In any case, it was a long flight from the airfield at Vaenga to the Kå fjord, and much of the intervening airspace was dominated by the German squadrons in Petsamo and Kirkenes. Accordingly, early that spring Rear-Admiral Barry had requested that a new British Photographic Reconnaissance Unit should be allowed to operate from Soviet territory. The problem was that the Russians were clearly far from happy with the idea. It took them several weeks to give their consent, which meant that it was not until 27 August that two destroyers, the *Musketeer* and *Mahratta*, were able to set sail for Murmansk carrying three suitably equipped Spitfires, together with their pilots and ground staff. Flight Lieutenant Mike Hodsman, a photographic interpreter, found the atmosphere at Vaenga anything but friendly. 'Although willy-nilly "we" the British and "them" the Russians were allies, the atmosphere between us was distinctly odd, with doubt and mistrust on both sides,' he wrote.

In the meantime MI6 and the Norwegian Intelligence Centre in London had alerted their veteran agent in Tromsø, Egil Lindberg who, from his hideout in the loft of the local hospital, operated a wireless transmitter codenamed Upsilon. Early in August Lindberg received a signal urging him to send someone north without delay to chart the German naval base's defences. The choice fell on a 23-year-old student, Torbjørn Johansen, who, a few days later, took the steamer from Tromsø to Alteidet and from there bicycled the more than 100 kilometres from Langfjordbotn to Alta. On the way he drew accurate maps showing the berths occupied by the *Tirpitz*, *Scharnhorst* and *Lützow*, along with their net defences, surrounding gun emplacements and auxiliary vessels. He stayed for a week at a fox farm that gave him an uninterrupted view of the *Tirpitz* and also secured a number of water samples from the fjord. When Johansen returned to Tromsø on 16 August, Lindberg immediately radioed his report, which was highly detailed and contained accurate map coordinates, to London. It read in part: 'Kaafjord. A double net from Auskarnes towards Hjemmeluftnes where the gate is always open. Type of net as given above. A net of the same type as that in Sopnesbukt has been laid in the bay SW of Auskarnes. In the centre of the fjord off Auskarnes in a southerly direction, there is a square net about 200 metres long each side.'

While the report and original maps were on their way by courier to Stockholm, Lindberg had received further enquiries about the net defences in the Kå fjord. On 21 August he sent the following signal:

The gate is in the corner on the eastern side. The net is a single net with equipment as given in one of my previous reports, but is not secured ashore. The net which closes Indre Kvaenvik has a gate near both shore[s]. It is not secured ashore.

The nets are anchored at corners and at the ends. All shore anchorages are of ½" wire. Heavy seas or ice do not reduce the efficacy of the nets. Aukarneset is strongly defended with many types of defence. Smoke apparatus round the whole of the fjord. Distance between buoys approximately three metres.

Thanks to the information received from Lindberg and Johansen, preparations in Scotland went ahead with increasing speed. On 30 August HMS *Titania* was despatched to Loch Cairnbawn to act as mothership to the six standard, diesel-driven submarines that were to tow the X-craft north. Two days later, on Wednesday 1 September, all leave was cancelled and the region surrounding Loch Cairnbawn cordoned off. Eulalia Henty-Creer and her two daughters, Deirdre and Pamela, were staying at an inn some 15 kilometres from the base. Just a few days earlier they had managed to bid their son and brother farewell. Says Pamela Mellor:

Henty was very optimistic and was looking forward to setting off. He knew what was at stake, although he couldn't reveal the details to us. He said it was a job that could qualify for a Victoria Cross, and that was something he dreamed of winning. He was convinced that he would return safely. The last thing we did was to agree on where he could find us. We were going back to London, but we didn't have a permanent address there, so we agreed that he should contact us through our bank.

The next five days were devoted to more arduous training in the arts of towing and changing crews at sea. On Sunday 5 September the midget submarines were hauled aboard the *Bonaventure* for a final check, the loading of fuel and provisions, and to fit the side-charges. Near-panic ensued when a wayward flame from a blowlamp caused a small outbreak of fire on the *Bonaventure*'s deck, close to six of the charges. 'There was quite a to-do before the fire was put out. Only afterwards did we discover that there had never been any danger. The amatol would simply have melted from the heat; only a detonation could have made it explode,' says John Lorimer, who was Cameron's second-in-command.

That same evening the crews were summoned to the first detailed briefing by Commander G.D.S. Davies, who had been provided with maps and topographical descriptions by geographers attached to the Norwegian Intelligence Centre in London. Only then did Cameron, Place and Henty-Creer, along with the others directly concerned, learn that what they had long suspected was true: their targets were indeed the *Tirpitz*, *Scharnhorst* and *Lützow*, which were to be destroyed in one devastating blow. In terms of boldness and initiative the plan was almost without parallel in the annals of the Royal Navy. When the men realised the scope of the operation they were about to embark upon, and the risk attaching to it, most fell silent, wrapped in their own thoughts. As John Lorimer wrote some years later: 'This was it, the climax of 18 months of intensive training. Operation "Source" was beginning. The midget submarines were going to war for the first time. Over 1,000 miles away across the North Sea lay their targets, three German battleships.

'A tremendous responsibility too, for the crews of the X-craft. If they succeeded in destroying or crippling the *Tirpitz*, the British Home Fleet could give its protection to the U-boat-haunted Atlantic convoys and the lives of thousands of Merchant Seamen might be saved.'

The next few days were spent in readying the midget submarines for what lay ahead. 'Feverish activity during afternoon, final check-up and trial dive with full operational equipment and crew. "Piker" behaving very well. Will trust in Cameron luck to pull us through,' Cameron noted in his log.

In the meantime the Vaenga-based Spitfires had at last made a reconnaissance flight over the Kå and Lang fjords. Disappointment was great when the results reached London on the morning of Wednesday 8 September. The *Tirpitz*, *Scharnhorst* and their attendant destroyers had vanished. Only the ageing *Lützow* and a few auxiliary vessels were left in the anchorage. And only three days remained before the twelve submarines were scheduled to set off on their momentous mission. Eighteen months of intensive training were at an end – and now it looked as though all might have been in vain.

*

When that Spitfire flew over the Kå fjord, the *Tirpitz*, the *Scharnhorst* and the twelve destroyers of the 4th, 5th and 6th Flotillas were midway between Bear Island and Spitsbergen. The plane was seen by observers on the ground. Two hours later the Battle Group was alerted by a signal from *Admiral Nordmeer*, Otto Klüber, in Narvik reading: '16.45 ALTA ANCHORAGE OVERFLOWN BY SPITFIRE.'

On board the *Tirpitz*, both Squadron Commander Kummetz and the ship's captain, Hans Meyer, greeted the news with equanimity. Their relentless badgering of the *Luftwaffe* had finally achieved the desired result. From Trondheim in the south to Banak in the north some ten or more reconnaissance aircraft had combed the vast expanse of ocean between Jan Mayen and the Norwegian coast. On board both the *Tirpitz* and the *Scharnhorst* wireless operators sat glued to their sets, monitoring the airwaves. The wind was from the south-east and the fine autumn weather ensured both good visibility and a minimum of static. There appeared to be no enemy warships in the area and enemy wireless traffic was non-existent. All evidence suggested that surprise would be complete: the British Home Fleet had no inkling that the 1st Battle Group was at sea for the third time in six months.

On the bridge of destroyer *Z29*, 43-year-old *Kapitän-zur-See* Rolf Johannesson, commander of the 4th Destroyer Flotilla, expressed his feelings when, at eight o'clock in the evening, he wrote in the war diary: 'So far, no information has been forthcoming to suggest that our departure from Alta has been reported. It is now highly improbable that any such information will be received.'

For Kummetz, the lack of such information represented a small, but important, personal victory. When news of Berlin's angry response to the attack on the German meteorological station on Spitsbergen reached him, he had immediately seen it as a new opportunity to get the Battle Group out of its defensive nets and into action. A surprise attack on the Norwegian garrison at Barentsburg would assure the world that the *Kriegsmarine* was still a force to be reckoned with and, in addition, ensure for the German meteorologists stationed in the Arctic the peace of mind and secure working conditions they needed. In August the three services had agreed to collaborate. The *Wehrmacht* would release 600 men from the 349th Pioneer Regiment at Talvik, the *Luftwaffe* would provide for the essential reconnaissance, and the 1st Battle Group would contribute transport and concentrated covering fire. The plan was a simple one: to destroy all military, industrial and civil installations in Barentsburg and Longyearbyen. But it had to be done quickly. No more than eleven hours could be spared to shell the buildings and coalmines and put the troops ashore. That was all the Germans could allow themselves if an Allied counter-attack was to be avoided. Success presupposed absolute secrecy, for which reason no reference to the operation, which was codenamed *Sizilien*, was made in wireless communications. Only a handful of the naval commanders were informed, and that was by word of mouth a mere two weeks before the operation was due to commence. The remainder only learned of where they were going six hours before weighing anchor.

Shortly after midnight on Wednesday 8 September the coast of Spitsbergen came into view. Three hours later the Battle Group approached Cape Linné and the entrance to the Is fjord. With a blend of reverence and awe, through his binoculars Flotilla Commander Johannesson watched the mountains ahead of him grow ever larger: 'Dawn is breaking. In the north-east, the horizon is slowly turning red and the clouds are beginning to disperse. Ahead of us tower the primaeval mountains, jagged, bistre. In the valleys, glaciers shimmer with a bluish-white light that occasionally takes on a pinkish shade in the morning sun. The plains are a uniform reddish-brown. There is no greenery, no trees or grass, as far as the eye can see.'

Five weeks had passed since Johannesson had steamed into the Alta fjord after a trouble-free journey from Germany of more than 1,600 nautical miles; the only untoward incident had been an unfortunate fire in a boiler on board *Z29*. Highly principled and deeply religious, and a man who never attempted to disguise his feelings, Johannesson was one of the German Navy's most experienced destroyer commanders. Prior to his arrival in Alta in late July, as captain of the commandeered Greek destroyer *Hermes* he had spent more than a year fighting a losing battle in the Mediterranean, winning in the process a Knight's Cross. He was thus well fitted to analyse the Battle Group's true position and put it into words: 'Apart from such exercises as have been carried out,' he wrote in the war diary in mid-August, 'the military situation in the north has for more than half a year been characterised by inactivity.' He continued:

Lying at anchor in the impenetrable reaches of the Kå fjord and the Lang fjord, not far from Hammerfest, is Germany's last means of forcing a decision in the war at sea. Numerically, if not qualitatively, it constitutes a bare one-third of the tonnage the Treaty of Versailles allowed us to maintain: two battleships, twelve destroyers and the venerable *Lützow*. Lacking as it does aircraft carriers and cruisers, it is not a squadron in the modern sense of the word. Those who are really in command on the few exercises that have been conducted are the engine-room staffs, who in their turn are subject to the dictatorship of the fuel gauges.

The situation on both the big ships and their escorts left much to be desired. They had sailed northwards to fight, but as long as the Allies continued to hold their convoys back, there were no suitable targets to be had in the Barents Sea.

The heavily censored news from the continent was gloomy in the extreme. The great German offensive at Kursk had ground to a halt; and a Russian counter-attack in August had driven the German forces back to the Dnepr. In the Mediterranean, the Allies had landed in Sicily, precipitating Mussolini's fall. And in Germany itself, the Allied air offensive was gaining in intensity with every passing week. In the course of the five months' long campaign embarked upon by Bomber Command in 1943, nearly 50,000 tons of bombs had been dropped on the industrial cities of the Ruhr. The destruction was indescribable. Moreover, heavy raids on Hamburg at the end of July had left large areas of the city in ruins and nearly 100,000 people dead. Men returning from home leave to the Kå fjord brought with them heart-rending accounts of the sufferings of the civilian population. Early in August, on her way north to the naval base in Hammerfest, a brand-new U-boat, *U-716*, had put into Hamburg. Her commander, *Oberleutnant-zur-See* Hans Dunkelberg, and his youthful crew were horrified by what they saw. 'The destruction made an indelible impression on all on board. I remember Dunkelberg shaking his head and saying, "We can no longer win. The war is lost."'

Johannesson noted that the majority of the young men under his command still retained their optimism, despite the rumours that were rife; some of the older petty officers were less sanguine, however: 'In a situation in which there is nothing to occupy us, it is important to maintain morale. There is very little to do here, apart from visits to the cinema, fishing and going for walks. . . . For this reason officers have to show understanding and tolerance in their dealings with the men. Il Duce's unforeseen deposition has done a great deal of damage, though so far I have not noticed any decline in the men's will to fight or in their confidence in their officers.'

As an example, the Flotilla Commander quoted an incident involving a party of cadets who had reached the ship at two o'clock in the morning. Nothing had been done to find them a place to sleep, and they were left standing shivering on the afterdeck, whereupon some of the older hands voluntarily turned over their hammocks to the new arrivals and took their places on deck. 'Nothing of the kind would ever have happened when I was a cadet in the First World War,' Johannesson wrote.

On board the battlecruiser *Scharnhorst*, which continued to alternate between its anchorages in the Lang fjord and Kå fjord, *Kapitän-zur-See* Friedrich Hüffmaier's captaincy was coming to an end. He was scheduled to take command over the *Wehrgeistiger Fürungsstab* in Berlin, which would make him the Navy's new ideological 'caretaker' and, towards the end of the war, the last commander of the Channel Islands. He was concerned about the effect the long months of idleness would have on the men's faith in a Nazi victory. In an endeavour to boost morale, he had introduced a variety of measures designed to strengthen the sense of comradeship on board his own ship and between the other ships in the Group. He started courses in raffia weaving, organised shore expeditions to gather mushrooms and berries, and held an athletics meeting grandly entitled the Polar Championships. 'In August we set up a stage on the afterdeck and put on eleven variety shows for the men of the big ships, the destroyers, torpedo boats, supply ships, tugs and Army detachments in the neighbourhood. They were greeted with considerable enthusiasm and produced encouraging results.'

The athletics meetings on the gravelled sports field in the Kå fjord and the revue 'From St Pauli to Shanghai' were indeed morale boosters, but Hüffmaier was nothing if not a realist, writing: 'These events could not dispel the uncomfortable feeling we have that up here in the north we are much safer than are our loved ones, exposed as they are to constant bombing attacks, especially in the Ruhr, where many of the men are from. The desire to avenge these attacks on families and friends with the aid of the ships, or in some other way, is very widespread.'

The sudden order issued on Monday 6 September to weigh anchor had been greeted with great enthusiasm by nearly all concerned. Now, two days later, shadowy grey shapes were approaching the entrance to the Is fjord. The guns were manned and below deck, on board the destroyers, the men of *IR 349* were clutching their machine-guns and light hand weapons. To preserve the element of surprise for as long as possible, Kummetz had ordered all his ships to fly British flags. On board *Z29* Johannesson recorded: 'We are about 14 nautical miles from the coast. The glimmer of the bluish-white glaciers is clearly visible.' The time was two o'clock in the morning.

Three-quarters of an hour later, at 02.43, Norwegian lookouts on Cape Heer spotted a number of silhouettes on the horizon and raised the alarm. Shortly afterwards the wireless station in Barentsburg transmitted the following signal: 'SEVEN DESTROYERS, THREE CRUISERS.' On board the *Tirpitz* an unsuccessful attempt was made to jam the transmission, but the signal was picked up by a British station in Reykjavik, which at 04.00 passed it on to the Home Fleet's main base at Scapa Flow. The German operators monitoring the Allied frequencies also picked it up, and only a few minutes later the text was on the Admiral's desk, together with the following comment: 'The signal has been received by the British. Accordingly intervention must be expected from forces in Iceland and Scapa Flow.'

Once again, Kummetz remained calm. The *Tirpitz* had launched two of its Arados, which were equipped for both reconnaissance and bombing missions, and immediately brought its massive 38cm guns to bear on the shore. Shortly before 04.30, the first shells were hurtling towards their target. The range was only 13,000 metres.

'The effect was devastating. It was like an express train when the heavy death-dealing shells from the *Tirpitz* came screaming through the air towards us,' says Thoralv Lund in his book *Kalde krigsår* ('Cold Years of War'). As a soldier serving in the garrison, which at that time was manned by 148 Norwegians and a handful of British service personnel under the command of Captain Peter Bredsdorff, he experienced the bombardment at first hand. Some 100 men were stationed in and around Barentsburg, while the rest were dispersed between the Advent fjord and Longyearbyen. They were armed with three 10.5cm naval guns, eight 40mm Bofors and 28mm Oerlikon anti-aircraft guns, and a number of machine-guns.

Flotilla Commander Rolf Johannesson and *Fregattenkapitän* Theodor von Mutius on board *Z29* had been allotted a leading role in the operation. The destroyer was ordered to make a frontal attack on Barentsburg by sailing straight up to the little jetty and landing troops right in the centre of the abandoned settlement.

Shortly before four o'clock in the morning, *Z29* swept into the Grøn fjord at a speed of 27 knots, with *Z33* a few cable-lengths astern. On the bridge, Johannesson watched as the old Russian mining town came into sight off the port bow. 'The place looked deserted. Black smoke was rising from a heap of coal. One large building had been burned to the ground.'

Johannesson had no idea that the coal had been alight since the autumn of 1941, when the British had set fire to the abandoned stocks. He beckoned to a signaller: 'They must have been warned we were coming. Signal *Tirpitz* – she's a thousand metres astern – that Barentsburg is burning.'

On the shore, the Norwegian defenders watched with growing anxiety as the German ships came racing towards them. They were ensconced in makeshift bunkers between slagheaps and ruined buildings. Most of them were sailors, sealers and whalers who had received weapons training with the Norwegian brigade stationed in Scotland. Few of them had seen action. Captain Bredsdorff himself was with the main battery on the mountainside behind the town, which gave him an overall view of the harbour. He had at his disposal a 10.5cm naval gun, a Bofors and an Oerlikon.

'The men stationed on Cape Heer had been instructed not to open fire until ordered to do so. . . . The Norwegians knew they were in a sticky situation, but were determined to put up a strong resistance.' At 04.12, *Z29* was only 500 metres from the jetty. Through his binoculars, Johannesson could see that as a landing place it left much to be desired. 'The jetty had just one bollard, rather tall, which meant that only one hawser could be made fast. For that reason the destroyer had to maintain station alongside the jetty with the aid of its propellers.'

As Johannesson and Mutius stood discussing the situation, there was a loud report from among the slagheaps and two 10.5cm shells blew holes in the destroyer's hull. Then the decks were swept by machine-gun fire.

'The infantrymen were lined up on the destroyers' decks, ready to go ashore. Taking matters into his own hands, Second Lieutenant Gustav Bowitz ordered his men to open fire on the destroyer making for Cape Heer. The waiting soldiers were raked by a stream of bullets from the battery's Oerlikon, but the return fire was deadly. Guns opened up from Barentsburg, too, but the defenders found it difficult to get the range, as they were under heavy fire from the destroyers' guns,' said a Norwegian report.

On board *Z29*, three men were killed and many more wounded. The destroyer's 15cm guns, backed by those of her secondary armament, fired round after round. When *Z29* closed the jetty and the first troops leaped ashore, Johannesson signalled the *Tirpitz*: 'Strong resistance.' Lying as it was alongside the jetty, the destroyer was no longer visible to the Norwegians manning the gun tucked away among the slagheaps, so they turned their attention to *Z33*, which had followed in *Z29's* wake. 'Second Lieutenant Rasmus Breidablikk, in command of the 40mm gun, brought the destroyer under withering fire. The range was about 500 metres and the deck was packed with soldiers waiting to embark in the boats that would ferry them ashore. Shells from the battery struck the turret and deck.'

On board *Z29*, Johannesson watched anxiously as his fellow destroyer suffered repeated hits. '*Z33* was under such heavy fire that I was very worried about the state she was in. She seemed to be drifting aimlessly and steam was billowing from the engine-room. There was no response to my signals, which were sent by lamp over a distance of no more than a thousand metres. I witnessed many hits, and countless near-misses.'

In the meantime, with the aid of machine-guns and hand grenades, the German infantrymen had worked their way up close to the Norwegian defenders. Shells from the destroyers' heavy guns crept ever closer, while the two Arados flew backwards and forwards over the Norwegian positions, bombing and strafing. Captain Bredsdorff was wounded in his foot and the

Norwegians were forced to give ground. By this time their fire was more sporadic, while out in the fjord *Fregattenkapitän* Holtorp had regained control of *Z33*.

'So far, we have two men killed and several severely wounded. We shall have to reckon with further casualties. We have taken many hits from 20mm guns and guns of smaller calibre on the foreship and near the bridge,' said the destroyer's situation report. The engines were still functioning, however, and a work party was busy welding the holes in the hull.

To the German soldiers, Barentsburg was a raging inferno. The thunder of heavy artillery and the staccato chatter of machine-guns were deafening. Exploding shells filled the air with dust and flying fragments of coal. In some places the infantrymen advancing towards the towering heaps of coal and slag found themselves sinking to their knees in ash from earlier fires. When, after about an hour, the *Tirpitz* again opened up with her heavy guns, the devastation was complete. Fresh fires were started and the whole area was soon shrouded in choking black smoke. The main defences were overrun at about 05.00. Four men were killed and four, among them Bredsdorff, taken prisoner. One German detachment worked its way along the aerial cableway used to convey coal from the mines to the sea. Said the report of the action:

It was hard to make headway. Forcing the many obstacles was a tough job and all around us stacks of coal were on fire. The moment we reached the cableway, we came under machine-gun fire from a nearby emplacement. When we turned all our machine-guns on it and attacked with hand grenades, the defenders withdrew towards the slagheaps and ravines higher up the mountainside. . . . Our other detachment came under fire from the entrance to a mine. The position was stormed with hand grenades, machine pistols and rifles, and completely wiped out. One man was killed and three prisoners were taken.

A stream of wounded and prisoners made their way back to *Z29*. 'Round about five o'clock resistance in Barentsburg ceased. The infantry's operations are now proceeding according to plan. The place has been reduced to a desolate, burning scrapheap,' wrote Johannesson.

The German troops pursued the fleeing Norwegians inland for a few kilometres, but at eight o'clock they were recalled. On their way back they blew up all the buildings that were still standing and set fire to them. 'The place is a sea of flame. Smoke and tongues of fire rise from the oil tanks, wooden buildings and stacks of timber. The *Tirpitz* has also fired a few salvoes into the centre of the town. The fires are spreading rapidly thanks to a strong wind from the south. . . . It is clear that the mission has been successfully accomplished, though things looked critical at the start.'

Later that morning the squadron was ordered to rejoin the *Tirpitz*, which then fired a few final rounds from its heavy guns to destroy such buildings as were still intact. A little later the *Scharnhorst* and the rest of the destroyers came in from the Advent fjord, where Longyearbyen had been similarly razed. Between them the destroyers had lost ten men killed, while sixteen Germans and eleven Norwegians had been taken to the sickbay on board the *Tirpitz*, suffering from wounds. Five Norwegians and one Briton had been killed in the fighting and forty-one men had been taken prisoner. Three prisoners died on the return voyage and were buried at sea, bringing the total number of Norwegians and British killed to nine.

Kummetz didn't waste words when he congratulated the 4th Destroyer Flotilla on their achievement: 'I wish to express my admiration for the excellent and successful execution of the landing operation,' was all he said.

Shortly before noon the admiral gave the order to head for home and the twelve ships sped southwards. From start to finish the attack had taken less than eight hours. The mood on board was one of exultation mingled with relief. When the Battle Group rounded the entrance to the Kå fjord in the afternoon of Thursday 9 September, Johannesson summed up the situation as follows: 'The 4th Destroyer Flotilla has now undergone its baptism of fire. Successful completion of this unusual operation has welded the crew together in a common experience of war. With renewed self-confidence, they are now ready for new tasks.'

In London, and among those in the know at Loch Cairnbawn, there was widespread gloom when the initial reconnaissance flight disclosed that neither the *Tirpitz* nor the *Scharnhorst* remained in the Kå fjord. However, all doubts were soon dispelled when, on the morning of Wednesday 8 September, an urgent report about the ships approaching Barentsburg reached the Admiralty. Later that same morning the British succeeded in deciphering additional wireless messages which suggested that two of these vessels were the missing *Tirpitz* and *Scharnhorst*. When, later in the day, the Ministry of Propaganda in Berlin jubilantly announced that German naval forces had destroyed 'extensive military installations' on Spitsbergen, the last pieces of the jigsaw puzzle fell into place.

There was no time for the Home Fleet to intercept the *Tirpitz* on her way home, but in Loch Cairnbawn the midget submarines were poised ready for action. In the morning of Friday 10 September the British learned from more wireless signals that the *Tirpitz* and the rest of the Battle Group were again safely at anchor in the Kå fjord. A Spitfire flew over the base later that same day and confirmed that the three capital ships were indeed back in their berths.

For Rear-Admiral Claud Barry, who had flown up from London to Loch Cairnbawn that same Friday, the choice was simple. It was now or never. The operation was on.

CHAPTER ELEVEN

Approaching the Target

THE KÅ FJORD, 11–22 SEPTEMBER 1943

It was getting on for 21.00 when Donald Cameron first sighted the Norwegian coast. 'Piker' was still deep in the minefields guarding the entrance to the Germans' main base in the Arctic. Trimmed low, the little submarine was barely visible in the long rollers coming in from the Atlantic. Cameron was standing in the W&D compartment, the upper part of his body halfway out of the open hatch. A light south-westerly wind was blowing, but the temperature was only a degree or two above freezing point. Cameron's clothes were soaking wet from the spray, but he was oblivious both to that and to the cold. He was less than a day's sailing from his target, the *Tirpitz*, which lay at anchor somewhere in the darkness ahead. From his observation post a bare metre above the surface of the sea he had an unimpeded view in every direction. To port, rising seemingly sheer from the water, he could see the precipitous cliffs of Stjern Island. Further away, and to starboard, gleamed the 1,200-metre-high Øksfjord glacier, magical in the fading light.

'Night wonderfully still, and moon by now well on its way above the horizon. We were treated to a wonderful display of Northern Lights. High land to eastward now in sight, with moon glistening on snow-drifts; also entrance to Stjernsund,' he noted in his private log.

The passage had been as dramatic as the planners had long feared. HMS *Truculent*, with 'Piker' (X6) trailing 300 metres astern, had set off first, in the afternoon of Saturday 11 September. In the course of the next eighteen hours all six tows were on their way, on courses that would take them midway between the Faeroes and Shetlands, due north past the Lofotens and out into the open expanse of sea west of Sørøy Island. For the *Truculent* and little 'Piker', which had been allotted the westernmost route, the distance was not far short of 1,500 nautical miles. On trials, towing had been successfully carried out at speeds of up to 10 knots, but it was out of the question to maintain the same speed all the way. The midget submarines had to surface every six hours to air the boat and recharge their batteries, and there was always the threat of bad weather and breakdowns. Nerve-racking throughout, the crossing might well take a week, perhaps even longer.

Cameron had remained in the *Truculent*'s conning tower until the Scottish coast disappeared into the blackness astern and he could no longer see the outline of the superstructure, such as it was, of *X6*, which in passage was under the command of Lieutenant Willy Wilson. He felt vaguely uneasy, as he had forgotten to bring with him the little red cap he always used to wear on such occasions. As if that were not enough, Wilson had had to dismantle and pitch overboard a loose cover from the periscope on which was inscribed the boat's pet name, 'Piker'. Cameron tightened his grip on Bungay, a small wooden dog given him by his wife, which he always kept in his pocket. 'Is it my Highland blood taking this as an omen?' he wrote. 'However, I have still got Bungay, so all's well. Why should I, a product of modern civilisation, be affected by such things? No logic in it, but there it is. I look at the familiar hills and islands and wonder when I shall see them again. Said a little prayer for all of us, darling . . .'

Whereas the attacking crews were able to relax in relative comfort on board the towing submarines, the passage crews were having a hard time.

[A]fter a few hours they began to feel a weight on the neck and a stiffness in the limbs; the crouching position had never seemed so painful to them. Damp was oozing everywhere. Two people out of three had to be on watch for most of the twenty-four hours, someone had to be watching the depth-gauge and the inclinometer bubble all the time; there was endless maintenance to be done, a thousand and one odd jobs to be seen to, plus the cooking and cleaning; and they had to be continually prepared for emergency signals from the parent submarine.

Twelve hours after setting out, Peter Philip, passage commander on board *X7*, 'Pdinichthys', was the first to run into trouble. When he began to dive after having ventilated the boat, the hatch wasn't closed in time and water poured in. But he and his crew kept their heads. They allowed the boat to sink until the pressure of water forced the hatch firmly down on to its seating. 'The minutes passed very slowly. At last Philip could surface again – the manoeuvre had succeeded. After this excitement, they cheerfully baled out the water that had come in, while ventilating the craft and recharging the batteries; then they cleaned the soaked bulkheads.'

On Tuesday 14 September a Spitfire had flown over western Finnmark and taken more photographs. They showed that the *Tirpitz* and *Scharnhorst* were back behind their defensive nets in the Kå fjord, while the *Lützow* had shifted her berth to the Lang fjord. The photographs had been transported to London by a Catalina flying-boat. After close study, Rear-Admiral Barry decided to put Plan 4 into operation. That meant that *X5*, *X6* and *X7* would attack the *Tirpitz*, *X9* and *X10* the *Scharnhorst*, and *X8* would take on the *Lützow*.

The order was radioed to the parent submarines the following day, but they already had their hands full. Some 300 nautical miles west of the Norwegian coast they had run into gale-force winds and were being tossed about like corks. Peter Philip in *X7* said the conditions were worse than he had ever known. 'We are rolling as well as pitching, and every few minutes our bows are hauled over to port with a corkscrew motion. We heel over, and rise, then go down in a power dive. Perfectly bloody. I expect the tow to part at any moment. Also I have a vague suspicion that one, if not both of our side-charges have [*sic*] gone, or are at least flooded. Heigh ho. P.S. The telephone appears to have packed up, too.'

The strain proved too much for the manila towrope and it snapped. The little submarine sank like a stone at an angle of 45° and could not be stabilised until the ballast tanks had been brought up to full pressure. When Philip reached the surface and opened the conning-tower hatch, he found that the wind had dropped a little, though the sea was still running high.

[W]aves were sweeping over the casing, their force enough to grab anyone who tried to come out and hurl him into the sea. Without hesitation, holding on with both hands, Philip levered himself on to the casing. Soaked and buffeted, he groped along for the induction trunk, found it, clung to it. Between two waves he at last saw *Stubborn*; then a larger wave broke. He would have to go below and wait. It was *Stubborn*'s business to manoeuvre, not his.

It was the diver, Robert Aitken, who finally made his way to *X7* in a rubber dinghy, bringing with him a new tow. But also the grassline from the *Stubborn* to the dinghy parted, leaving him stranded. Fortunately he managed to get hold of the tow, which was almost submerged, and slowly, hand over hand and leaning on the sea, he succeeded in dragging himself back to the parent submarine. 'It was tough going,' he said, 'but I made it.'

Early that same morning Lieutenant Jack Oakley, commanding another of the parent submarines, the *Seanymph*, had had an equally unpleasant experience. When he tried to contact *X8* by telephone he found that the line was dead. The tow had parted during the night without anyone realising it, and their charge had disappeared. The *Seanymph* immediately reversed course, while the lookouts scanned the surface of the sea through their binoculars. Hour after hour passed without a sign of *X8*. Late in the evening of Wednesday 15 September, as Oakley and his crew were slowly beginning to reconcile themselves to the thought that the little submarine they had been towing was lost, a signal was received from London to say that, by chance, *X8* had been found by the *Stubborn*. Late in the afternoon of the following day the towline was again securely in place.

X8 had been missing for thirty-seven hours. It was still afloat, but the transit crew were worn out and the submarine was taking in water. It was still 200 nautical miles to the release point. Lieutenant McFarlane, who was to be in command during the attack, insisted on taking over straight away, to enable the crew to get some much-needed rest. The weather wasn't at all bad and, in two operations, the crews exchanged places without mishap.

By this time the force had reached a critical point in the crossing. The six tows had passed the Lofoten Islands and were now on a north-easterly course. They were approaching the danger zone and their problems had only just begun. The *Syrtis*, which was towing *X9*, had so far had a smooth voyage. But when, in the morning of Thursday 16 September, three hand grenades were tossed overboard to warn *X9*'s crew that it was time to ventilate their boat, nothing happened. Another towline had snapped.

'From the log readings and the fuel consumption this [the parting of the tow] was estimated to have been between 01.45 and 03.00. But the morning passed and part of the afternoon without any sign of *X9*. At 15.45 Jupp saw a long narrow oil track running in a direction 088, which happened to be the direct course for the point of attack 200 miles away.' Theoretically, *X9* could have set a new course for the Norwegian mainland and the crew might have been saved. The more likely possibility, however, was that the submarine was lost.

In the meantime, on board *X8*, McFarlane was having trouble trimming his craft. Air was streaming from one of the side-charges and the little submarine was listing more and more to starboard. After having struggled unavailingly for some hours to correct the list, McFarlane came to a dramatic conclusion: both side-charges would have to be jettisoned. The explosion of the second one generated a violent shock wave. Two hours had passed since it had been released, but even so the explosion was so violent that men were thrown off their feet.

Water flooded into the W&D compartment and pipes were distorted and fractured. On Saturday 18 September it was decided that there was no alternative but to call the operation off. There was no point in going on. *X8* was scuttled in deep water some 100 nautical miles west of the Norwegian mainland. Six midget submarines had set out from Scotland; now only four were left – and it would still take three long days to reach the German anchorages for which they were bound. Those days would be the most hazardous of the entire voyage.

*

In the Kå fjord, autumn was by this time well advanced. The birchwoods in the Mathis valley were aflame with red, russet and gold, and the sun was sinking lower with every day that passed. Early in the evenings the anchorages found themselves enveloped in a deep-blue, melancholy darkness. The nights were cold and clear. The men manning the anti-aircraft guns on the nearby headlands watched fascinated as the silken streamers of the Northern Lights weaved their way from horizon to horizon. On lower decks and in barrack rooms wireless sets were switched on and tuned to *Soldatensender Finnmark*. Even the most hard-boiled of men found it hard to hold back a tear when Gudrun Niska signed off with her goodnight song, *Die kleine Stadt muss schlafen gehen*. 'Gudrun was dearly loved by all. She had a voice that went right to the heart.'

Hein Hellendoorn, who came from Bad Bentheim, a small town near the Dutch border, found life in the Kå fjord very much to his liking, primarily because being a naval officer meant so much to him. His father, a printer who also published the local newspaper, *Grafschafter Nachrichten*, had been very proud when, in 1939, after rigorous testing, his son was accepted for officer training at the Naval College in Mürwik. Says Hellendoorn:

The entrance exams were very difficult and there was strong competition. One thing I remember is being shown drawings of sixteen musical instruments, which we had to name. Then we were handed a colour chart with the same number of colours and had to identify them – and after that say which instrument matched which colour! I wasn't very good at that kind of thing, but I was athletic, and I think that's why I passed.

After having trained as a gunner, in February 1941, at the age of twenty-one Hellendoorn was posted to the *Bismarck*, where he was one of the battleship's youngest officers of his rank. But a few weeks before this mighty ship set out on what was to be its first and only sortie, Fate took a hand. Hellendoorn was taken off the ship to attend a two-month course at Swinemünde, where he was to receive further training as an anti-aircraft gunner. The course had barely begun when the devastating news was received that the *Bismarck* had been sunk in the Atlantic with the loss of more than 2,000 men; only 115 of those on board were rescued.

'I lost many of my friends. You could say that I was lucky, but it didn't seem like that to me. I had some agonising moments.'

On completing the course, Hellendoorn was posted to the *Bismarck*'s sister ship, the *Tirpitz*, which was fitting out in the Baltic. Now, in September 1943, he was a full lieutenant and third in command of the battleship's anti-aircraft defences. In the course of the two years he had spent on board he had found himself edging further and further north – from Trondheim to Narvik and, finally, to Alta. In all that time he had never been granted leave. But he was not unduly concerned: his duties were exacting and kept him very much on his toes. The battleship's anti-aircraft gunners had more to do than most of the men on board. The ship's secondary armament consisted of more than sixty guns of varying calibres, ranging from 20mm to 15.5cm, and had successfully defended her against several attacks by enemy aircraft.

'We maintained a very high degree of preparedness. We kept a twenty-four-hour watch, both at the guns and in the Fire-Control Room. We never knew when we might be attacked from the air. It was attack from other quarters that we were not sufficiently on our guard against.'

Tall and in fine physical trim, before the war Hein Hellendoorn had entertained hopes of becoming one of Germany's leading athletes. Now, however, he was only able to compete in local events. 'I remember I did well in the Polar Championships. I was the ship's champion in both the long jump and putting the shot.'

Although, by the time the ships got back from Spitsbergen, the mountain peaks were already capped with white and winter was fast approaching, the mood of the German sailors was one of satisfaction and relief. They had accomplished what they had set out to do and had done so without unduly heavy losses – despite the fact that the landing had taken place under direct enemy fire. On Saturday 11 September – by coincidence, the same day the midget submarines left Loch Cairnbawn – the dead from the destroyers and *IR 349* were buried with full honours in the military cemetery in Alta. Inspection of the three destroyers that had come off worst in the frontal attack, *Z29*, *Z31* and *Z33*, showed that it would take only ten days to repair the damage and that their state of readiness would not be greatly impaired. All three were reberthed alongside the repair ship *Neumark*, which was anchored in mid-fjord and carried a full complement of highly qualified mechanics and welders. 'At the behest of the Battle Group, all the anti-aircraft guns that had been damaged were replaced by new ones from the supply ships,' Johannesson recorded with satisfaction.

Goebbels' propaganda machine in Berlin had trumpeted *Operation Sizilien* as a major victory, and for a few days the 10,000 young soldiers and sailors pent up in the narrow confines of the Kå and Lang fjords were able to reap their reward. After hurried consideration, between five hundred and a thousand Iron Crosses were awarded to the 1st Battle Group. Presentation of the more prestigious Iron Cross First Class took place on Friday 17 September. On *Z29*, which had landed its troops straight on to the jetty in Barentsburg, five men received First Class crosses. The Second Class crosses were presented before a large crowd on the assault course on the shore of the Kå fjord shortly afterwards. Four hundred went to the *Tirpitz*, one hundred and sixty-two to the *Scharnhorst*, forty-six to *Z29* and a goodly number to the remaining destroyers. Before the stores lining the Grøn fjord and Advent fjord were burned to the ground, they had been systematically searched and plundered and large quantities of butter, chocolate, canned goods and Russian cigarettes seized. It was a lively weekend! Schnapps and beer flowed freely and at the poker tables stakes were high. 'There was a prodigious amount of gambling on board. Vast sums were won and lost,' says a postwar report.

The jubilation was not universal, however. *Kapitän-zur-See* Stange, captain of the *Lützow*, had been both disappointed and angered when, on 6 September, he was ordered to shift berth to the Kå fjord and take the place of the *Tirpitz*. For two months he had been poised ready to make a dashing raid on Soviet shipping in the Kara Sea. Instead, the *Lützow* had been allocated the humble role of stand-in for the flagship.

'It is a bitter pill for the men to swallow that the Battle Group should put to sea without the *Lützow*,' he wrote in the ship's war diary. To mollify them he made a fiery speech on the afterdeck before taking those not on watch for a mountain ramble. 'It didn't help much,' was his ironic comment. 'Among the men, the following joke went the rounds. Question: "What's the difference between the *Tirpitz* and the *Lützow*?" Answer: *"Tirpitz kämpft um Spitsbergen, Lützow kämpft um Bergspitzen"* [*Tirpitz* fights over Spitsbergen, *Lützow* fights over mountain-tops].'

On board the *Scharnhorst*, which was anchored all by itself at the head of the Lang fjord, four hours' sailing from the flagship, disaffection was also widespread. There had always been a great deal of rivalry among the big ships of the *Kriegsmarine*. The *Draft Interrogation Report on Prisoners of War from the Scharnhorst* compiled by the Director of Naval Intelligence in London (23 February 1944) stated: 'That the ship's company was proud of *Scharnhorst* and had immense faith in the ship's capabilities and fighting qualities has been only too apparent. Even *Gneisenau,* the sister-ship[,] was looked upon as a poor relation and relations with the crew of the *Tirpitz* were far from cordial, probably as the result of a feeling of rivalry.'

The men had disliked seeing the *Scharnhorst* ordered into the Advent fjord 'as though she were an ordinary minesweeper' while the *Tirpitz* lay to off the entrance to the Grøn fjord. Resistance had been much weaker in Longyearbyen than in Barentsburg and there had been little call for the *Scharnhorst*'s heavy guns. When, just after half-past nine in the morning, *Admiral* Kummetz had ordered the squadron to close the flagship, *Kapitän-zur-See* Hüffmaier was still engaged in shelling an unmanned weather station perched on a mountain. As the wind rose, the waters of the fjord were whipped up and the ship's Arado had difficulty in making a landing. On its third attempt the plane was damaged, thus further delaying the ship's departure. It hadn't helped matters that Hüffmaier had neglected to inform the *Tirpitz* of what had happened. By the time the *Scharnhorst* reached the assembly point, it was half-past eleven and the *Tirpitz* and the rest of the squadron had been waiting for an hour and a half. Kummetz was furious.

'This resulted in a most unsatisfactory situation. . . . The Squadron Commander had no idea of what the ship was doing between half-past nine and half-past eleven . . . a delay which in an operational context might have had most regrettable consequences' was the stinging comment in the war diary.

The ill-feeling aroused by this incident was still in evidence four months later when *Scharnhorst* survivors were interrogated by British intelligence officers:

Discipline in *Tirpitz* was said to be much stricter than in *Scharnhorst* and the ship's company very much younger and more inexperienced. The Commanding Officer, Captain Meyer, was always referred to in derogatory terms and many of the *Scharnhorst* survivors said that nothing would induce them to transfer to *Tirpitz*. They described her men as having a hang-dog look about them.

Some leading stokers who had been transferred to *Tirpitz* from *Scharnhorst* used to meet their former shipmates and bewail their fate, complaining that their new ship was run like a detention barracks.

Some of the scathing comments made by the *Scharnhorst* survivors concerning *Tirpitz* and her men may well be due to the fact that they considered the crew of the flagship received better treatment than they did.

In the matter of counting 'points' for the award of the Iron Cross Second Class, *Tirpitz* was considered especially favoured. . . . After the Spitzbergen raid, more than 400 of *Tirpitz*'s men qualified for the Iron Cross, while *Scharnhorst*, which had done all the hard work and had been in service considerably longer, only received 160 Iron Crosses. *Tirpitz* was strongly suspected of cheating in the necessary calculations.

In his lofty and tastefully furnished cabin *Admiral* Kummetz was far removed from the talk and banter of the lower deck. A Ju 88 had flown over Barentsburg a few days after the raid and been surprised by fire from an anti-aircraft gun. Commenting on the operation, the *Luftwaffe* had hinted that the job hadn't been properly done. The insinuation left the Squadron Commander fuming. 'Either the men of the garrison who sought refuge in the mountains have repaired one of the guns that were damaged or the submarine that was observed later provided them with a gun. . . . The fact that fires are still burning on the island is sufficient proof of how thorough the destruction was.' But he was well aware that the 1st Battle Group was in urgent need of further training.

I cannot emphasise too strongly how important it is to mount frequent operations of this kind that last for several days. They are essential to maintenance of the Battle Group's effectiveness and striking power. In the war diaries of all units under my command the need to be at sea is stressed time and time again. Many report, for example, that a lot of men became seasick when the height of the waves was no more than two to three metres. . . . A Battle Group that never leaves its base loses its edge. It will never be capable of meeting major challenges.

Kummetz knew that time was running short. The *Lützow*, old as it was, was badly run down and there were plans to transfer it, early in the new year, to the Baltic, to serve as a training ship for officer cadets. It had, in fact, already been determined that it should sail for Kiel at the first opportunity. Moreover, the *Tirpitz* had not been drydocked since leaving Germany early in 1942. True, it had undergone certain repairs while in the Trondheim fjord, but that had been almost a year ago. Very soon a decision would have to be taken: if the battleship were to retain its fighting capability, it would have to be put in for repair. A memo to the Naval High Command made the situation clear:

> The Battle Group will be weakened if the *Tirpitz* is sent home. However, as the days are drawing in, operational conditions for the battleship will be so unfavourable that her return home will be acceptable. There will be a new moon on 29 October, so she could sail in the latter half of the month. . . . Eight destroyers will be needed as escort. The return [to Germany] of the *Tirpitz* is such an important operation that the destroyers must be made available regardless of the fuel situation . . . and without regard to the fact that the northern theatre will for a time be totally without destroyers.

In the light of the foregoing, Kummetz had applied for compassionate leave and was preparing to go home as soon as his replacement arrived.

The men were, of course, ignorant of the deliberations of the admirals in Alta, Narvik and Kiel. One such was Karl Heinz Lohse from Ottenbüttel in Schleswig-Holstein. He had attended school in the neighbouring town of Wilster before being apprenticed to a carpenter. 'My father had served in the Imperial Navy, but he didn't want me to go to sea. I had a hard job persuading him. He didn't give in until I told him that I intended to volunteer as a paratrooper.'

A strongly built man who could turn his hand to almost anything, Lohse was twenty when he joined the *Tirpitz* in Gotenhafen. 'I well remember the first time we entered Narvik harbour in 1942. I thought the landscape looked incredibly bare and inhospitable. It occurred to me that home was a long way off if anything were to go wrong. I said to myself: "Dear God, I don't want to be buried here."'

In Alta, work on the defences was still in progress when the *Tirpitz*, along with the rest of the 1st Battle Group, arrived at the end of March 1943. For a carpenter there was more than enough to do, both on board and ashore. 'I was kept busy and never had a dull moment. I had lots of friends and we were a happy crowd.'

One day Karl Heinz Lohse was returning from the Carpenters' Shop when, to his surprise, he ran into a familiar figure. 'It was a cheery young girl I'd been at school with in Wilster, Regina Looft – we just used to call her Gina. There weren't many German girls in the Kå fjord, so the few there were stood out. Besides, Gina was pretty and good company. I asked her what she was doing there and she said she was working for a construction company and was running the local office.'

Regina's job necessitated regular contact with the company's head office in Germany, and her sole means of communication was the teleprinter on board the *Tirpitz*. 'I often had to go on board the ship and I got to know Karl Heinz and some of the other men. They were smart-looking chaps and I was never short of male company.'

One of the ratings was a dark and distinguished-looking Chief Engine Room Artificer from Niedersheim on the Dutch border, Werner Brand. Thirty years of age, he was rather older than the rest of the men. His father was a stationmaster and Werner had originally foreseen a career on the railways for himself. But when Hitler announced his plan for a rapid build-up of Germany's armed forces, he allowed himself to be tempted by visions of adventures in foreign lands. He joined the *Kriegsmarine* and in 1935 mustered as a pump man.

Werner was already acquainted with Kummetz, having been in the engine-room when the *Blücher* was torpedoed in the Oslo fjord on 9 April 1940. Like the admiral, after a long swim in the icy water he had made it safely to the shore. Enterprising and resourceful, he had constructed a small smokehouse on the shore in which he smoked herring and salmon bought from local fishermen. One day *Kapitän-zur-See* Meyer approached him with a fine salmon he had caught in the River Alta. 'He wanted it smoked, but I misjudged the setting and it was burned to a cinder. There was hell to pay, but there was nothing I could do about it. It was an accident, that's all.'

Among those who enjoyed listening to Werner's stories was the young secretary from Tiefbaufirma Robert Looft, and it wasn't long before it became obvious to all and sundry that there was something going on between her and Werner. 'I fell for him. The first time I set eyes on him, I knew he was the one for me. It happened in a flash, just like that. Werner was the man I'd been waiting for.'

Werner felt the same about Regina, who was ten years younger than he was, and began to court her in earnest. He gave her some of the chocolate that had been seized on Spitsbergen and also found her a bicycle. 'He was very protective and repeatedly warned me against the other sailors. He claimed that most of them were married or had girlfriends in Germany. He, on the other hand, was single and could be trusted. I couldn't help but laugh.'

Werner made no attempt to hide his love in the letters he sent to Regina by the local steamer in the weeks when her work took her to Hammerfest.

My dear Gina, it is now eight hours since you left, but it seems like eight weeks. My chest seems as if it's bursting, but now, at least, I know what I feel for you. I pine for you all day long. My eyes are permanently glazed with tears. Dear Gina, come back soon! I must close now, as my heart is growing ever heavier.

Love and kisses
Your Werner

Werner and Regina weren't the only young lovers strolling hand-in-hand along the gravelled roads of Alta in the autumn darkness. Only a few kilometres distant, in Talvik, on the other side of the mountains, Karl Lausch, serving on the staff of *IR 349*, had helped to equip the 600 men who had taken part in the raid on Spitsbergen. It had made an interesting break in what was otherwise very much an unvarying routine. Now it was over – and Karl had at last found out the name of the Norwegian girl with the milk pails who passed his office every day.

'Solveig was the daughter of a local smallholder. When we first began to say hello, the rest followed as a matter of course. We started seeing each other regularly. I was German and she was Norwegian, but love knows no bounds. We were soon very much in love.'

In the evening of Monday 20 September *Kapitän-zur-See* Rolf Johannesson invited his captains, first officers and chief engineers to dine on board *Z29*. They had a lot to talk about. At the presentation on the assault course earlier that afternoon, the 4th Destroyer Flotilla had been highly praised for its accomplishments in Barentsburg. It was rare for nearly fifty Iron Crosses to be awarded to the same ship and the occasion called for a celebration. Outside, the fjord was shrouded in velvety darkness and the sky was ablaze with the rippling rays of the Northern Lights. The men on watch on the lonely guardships and manning the hydrophone defences peered out across the blackness of the ocean and thought of their homes, far to the south. The steel buoys supporting the defence nets gleamed in the moonlight. There was nothing to be seen, but they knew that, out there, beyond the horizon, lurked the enemy, along with his planes and deadly submarines. Here, however, tucked away behind anti-submarine and anti-torpedo nets, deep in the recesses of the fjord, they were in no danger. In their snug little base they felt safe.

*

At his provisional headquarters in Vardø in eastern Finnmark, the intelligence officer of the 210th Division, *Premierleutnant* Fritz Pardon, was also feeling pleased with himself. Despite Berlin's resistance, he had not hesitated in placing complete confidence in the intercepted signals the head of *MPHS Kirkenes*, *Kapitänleutnant* Bankstahl, had shown him. They were conclusive proof that one or more wireless transmitters were operating in the neighbourhood, in all probability in the inaccessible country surrounding the Kongs fjord. *Luftwaffe* reports pointed to the same conclusion. Oil slicks had been observed from the air and Soviet planes had many times been seen over the area. *Operation Mitternachtssonne* had been a failure, but the very next day, Saturday 10 July, Pardon had been given permission to mount another search. Codenamed *Wildente* [Wild Duck], it was to be concentrated further to the west, to encompass the steep slopes and deep inlets between the Kongs fjord and Berlevåg. As the crow flies, this was a distance of a bare 25 kilometres. But for thousands of years the landscape had been battered by raging storms from the Arctic Ocean and the sandstone was badly eroded and deeply fissured. There were countless ravines and caves where agents could hide.

Pardon had an agonising wait while the first patrols began to work their way eastwards from Berlevåg shortly after midnight on Monday 12 July. Valleys and mountainsides were combed, houses ransacked, identification papers checked, barns and byres thoroughly searched. The first day's search yielded nothing, but on Tuesday 13 July the situation changed dramatically. A few hundred metres from the small community of Løkvik a party of soldiers came upon a cleft in the rock covered over with branches, leaves and heather. Beneath the camouflage they found parts of a wireless transmitter of Russian make, complete with batteries. Stacked in a corner were crates of tinned food and sacks of flour and sugar. They also found winter clothing, rucksacks and a number of Russian hand grenades. The find convinced Pardon that his assumption was correct; it was clearly the hideout of Soviet agents. But where were they? They appeared to have left in a hurry – they had even left behind two personal diaries that had been kept from 22 January to 29 May.

While the soldiers were carefully removing and noting down all they had found, the three agents were only a few hundred metres away. Three weeks earlier, their leader, Franz Mathisen, and his two companions, Harald and Leif Utne, had decided to move to a mountain cave some 20 kilometres further east, on the other side of the fjord. It was rumoured that the Germans were intending to build a road along the coast. Moreover, people in Berlevåg were beginning to talk about the men from Løkvik who were so well supplied with money, spirits and cigarettes and were prepared to pay handsomely for information. Mathisen was keen to find somewhere safer, and on Midsummer Eve he had got Kristian

Olsen, a thirty-year-old fisherman who lived on a small farm nearby, and who was one of the group's regular contacts, to ferry all three of them, together with two wireless transmitters and provisions, to the new hiding place. 'We had a better view of the sea from this cave than from the crevice in Løkvik. We were planning to collect the rest of our equipment later in the summer.'

In the meantime Pardon had embarked on a hunt for the agents. On 6 July Kristian Olsen warned another of the group's contacts, Emil Ananiassen, that the Germans had obtained a fix on a transmitter and were carrying out a door-to-door search. Murmansk was warned by wireless. Six days later Mathisen saw the first troops set ashore. The group packed their transmitters and as much food as they could carry and withdrew into the mountains. After a gruelling trek lasting more than thirty-six hours they neared Løkvik, where they intended to augment their supplies, but by then it was too late: the Germans had found their hideout and stripped it bare.

'That same evening I contacted Murmansk and asked to be supplied by air. We agreed that the drop should take place beside a lake in the mountains 15 kilometres south of the Kongs fjord,' said Leif Utne in a later statement.

Circumstances now played into Pardon's hands. At about the same time that the first German patrol found the agents' hiding place in Løkvik, a woman saw a plane come in low over the Sylte fjord and release two parachutes. Knowing that the Germans had promised a generous reward to anyone providing information on suspicious incidents, she immediately phoned the *Ortskommandant* in Hamningberg to report what she had seen. This prompted Pardon to extend the scope of the operation, and he at once despatched two naval vessels and more troops to the Sylte fjord.

It had indeed been a Soviet aircraft the woman had seen. Although alerted to the impending danger a week earlier, Murmansk had nonetheless decided to drop supplies to another group, one which, since October 1942, had been holed up in a cave at the mouth of the fjord a mere 10 kilometres from a large fort. From this vantage point Oskar Johnsen, Kåre Figenschou and Kåre Øien had a clear view of the shipping lane. From this observation post too a stream of wireless reports involving German shipping found its way to Murmansk. But the group made a fateful decision. When German patrols began to come uncomfortably close, they pulled back some 15 kilometres to the east – to join the third group of Soviet agents in the same area. Håkon Halvari, Richard Johansen and their wireless operator, Vassili Jessipov, had been hiding in a cave on Segl Point at the mouth of the Per fjord since October, and from there had kept in constant touch with their three fellow agents in Syltevik.

Johnsen, Figenschou and Øien had made their escape just in time. Only a few hours after their departure, the Germans found the containers that had been dropped, along with the abandoned cave. But the Norwegians' relief at having got away was short-lived. *MPHS Kirkenes* had intercepted more wireless signals, and the bearings taken on them all pointed to the Per fjord. When, on Wednesday 14 July, the five agents made their way up on to a ridge to carry out a joint reconnaissance, a guardship came racing in to Segl Point. Everything happened very quickly. Jessipov, who had been left alone on the shore, was seen. The Germans fired warning shots and the Russian gave himself up.

In Vardø, Pardon was beside himself with glee. Only two days after the start of the operation the Germans had found three of the agents' hiding places – in the Per fjord, the Sylte fjord and at Løkvik. Large quantities of stores – wireless transmitters, weapons, provisions, clothing, letters, personal diaries, signals and wireless logs had been confiscated. The logbooks showed that many reports had been sent to Murmansk about passing German ships, minefields, gun emplacements, troop movements and other matters of military importance.

'This information has been of considerable value [to the enemy] in mounting attacks on convoys. Ships have been sunk, with a corresponding loss of human life and materials, and the troops have had to go short. Overall, the damage done to [our] coastal defences and operations in northern Norway has been very great,' wrote the judge who presided over the subsequent military tribunal.

Although Pardon was unaware of it at the time, he had dealt the whole network a mortal blow. It is true that the majority of the agents were still at liberty, but in Jessipov Pardon had found the ideal informant. 'For a Russian, he is uncommonly open and of above-normal intelligence. When asked, he immediately declared his willingness to fight on the German side, gun in hand, against the present Soviet regime. In 1939 he and his brother were sentenced to ten years' imprisonment for anti-government activities. That is why he is opposed to the regime.'

The Russian's testimony and captured material were carefully studied in Vardø by Pardon himself, *Kapitänleutnant* Axmann from Naval Headquarters in Kirkenes and *Kapitänleutnant* Bankstahl from *MPHS Kirkenes*. But in the field, the *Gestapo* had free rein. *Oberscharführer* Anton Patent, a notorious sadist and torturer, was brought in from the *Sicherheitspolizei* [Security Police] in Tromsø to help with interrogation of the prisoners.

If he isn't satisfied with an answer, he carefully selects a club and starts tapping it against his palm. If this elicits the reply he wants, he puts it down

Marked on this German map, which is from the war diary of the 210th Division, are the four hiding-places of the partisans. They range from Seglodden in the east to Nålneset in the west. Caves 3 and 4 were used by the group led by Franz Mathisen. All four hiding-places were discovered in the course of a few bloody days in the summer of 1943.

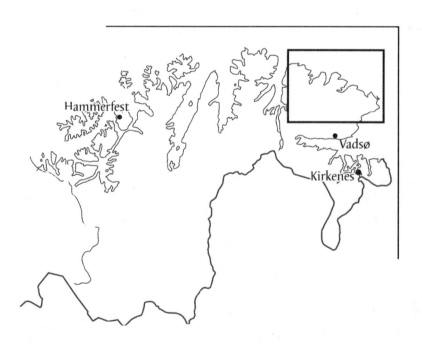

Anlage zu 210. Inf.-Division Ic
92/43 geh. Kdos.

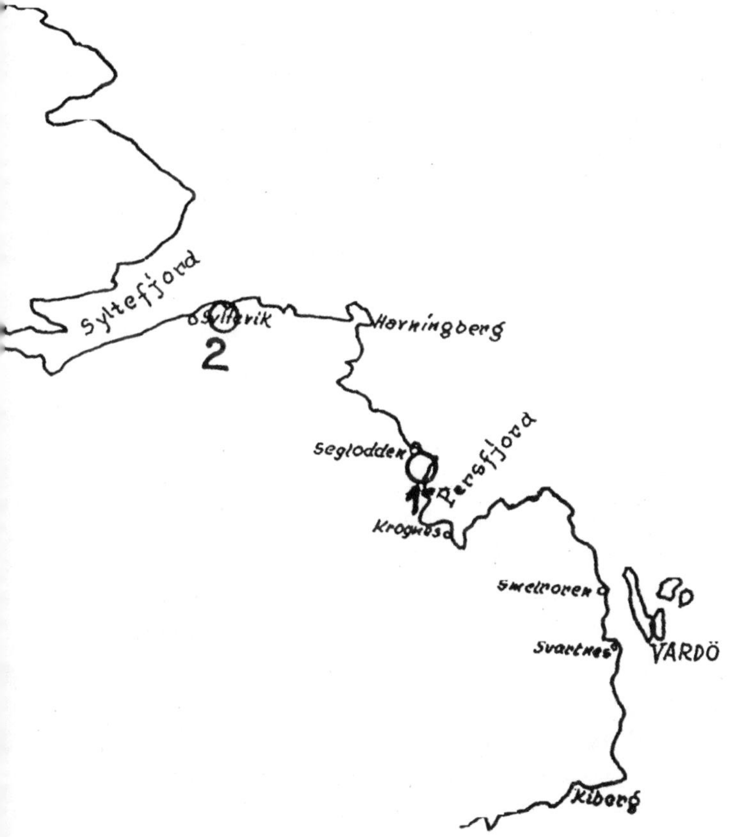

Syltefjord

o Syltevik

2

Hamningberg

Seglodden

Persfjord

Krognes

Smelroren o

Svartnes o

VARDÖ

Kiberg

M 1:300 000

on his desk to indicate that the prisoner has nothing to fear. And so the charade goes on. Hour after hour. If he loses his patience, he suddenly smashes his fist into his victim's face, knocking him off his chair. Then he puts the boot in. Only if a prisoner proves unduly recalcitrant does he have recourse to the chain. After such treatment, prisoners usually end up with several teeth missing and with broken ribs and fingers.

The first arrests were made in the area around Berlevåg on Wednesday 14 July, when neighbours and people who had rendered assistance to the Løkvik group were rounded up. On 22 July one arrestee was forced to guide the Germans to the deserted hideout on the eastern shore of the Kongs fjord. A few days later a troop of heavily armed marines again landed on Segl Point, where they immediately came under fire from a well-concealed position some 300 metres from the spot where Jessipov had been taken prisoner. The five Norwegians from the Per fjord and Syltevik had returned. They were waiting to be taken off by a Soviet submarine and had no intention of giving up without a fight. But the odds were too heavily stacked against them. After a prolonged exchange of fire, Richard Johansen and Kåre Figenschou succeeded in making their escape. Håkon Halvari, Oskar Johnsen and Kåre Øien were killed by hand grenades. The cave yielded a rich cache of arms and ammunition, two wireless transmitters, ciphers, money, provisions, maps, logbooks and diaries.

With the knowledge thus gained, the Germans adopted drastic measures against the local population. Everyone in the Per fjord area was arrested. They were taken first to Vardø, then to a prison camp. By this time, the beginning of August, four hiding places had been uncovered, three agents had been killed and one agent had been taken prisoner. In addition, more than forty of their helpers had been arrested, and many of them had been severely tortured by the *Gestapo*.

This was war, and the penalty for spying was death. Locked in a bloody war of position in northern Finland and on the banks of the Litza, Dietl's Mountain Corps was determined to make an example of their prisoners, to deter anyone else who might be inclined to help the Russians. When the 210th Division convened its first tribunal at Bjørnevatn on 17 August, the outcome was a foregone conclusion. Eleven men were sentenced to death, and three received terms of imprisonment ranging from ten to fifteen years. The German propaganda machine made much of the death sentences. The small communities of Finnmark were left reeling. Families were ripped asunder and friends and neighbours taken away to an uncertain fate. One mother lost two sons and a foster son.

Before their execution, which was set for the following morning, the prisoners were made to dig their own graves. After being humiliated and spat upon in the face, one struck his tormentor with his spade and killed him. The man's companions exacted a gruesome revenge. Instead of meeting their end before a firing squad, the helpless prisoners were beaten to death with spades.

Only ten days after this tragic incident, Franz Mathisen and Harald and Leif Utne were finally caught. They had roamed the Varanger Peninsula since their escape on 12 July with the Germans hard on their heels. They still had their wireless transmitter and repeatedly used it to summon help, but the resultant drops were seized by the Germans.

In their last few weeks of freedom they had subsisted on berries and fungi. When they were discovered and informed on on 28 August, Franz Mathisen chose to take his own life. Harald and Leif Utne surrendered.

Premierleutnant Fritz Pardon, who, by his persistence, had finally managed to destroy the whole Soviet network of agents, set out to crown his achievement with one last successful operation. The first time he interrogated Leif Utne, who had been only seventeen years old when he had accompanied his uncle from Kiberg to Murmansk, he realised that the young man was by no means a dedicated Communist. Now, at the age of twenty, Utne was exhausted and afraid. In the hands of his expert interrogators he seemed relieved at the knowledge that his days on the run were over. 'Utne must be considered to have been misguided. He is clearly glad to be free from the bonds that bound him to the other agents. Of his own free will, and with no need for coercion, he reveals all. He is willing to do whatever we ask.'

Pardon, who in these terrible autumn weeks in Varanger ruled over life and death, made Utne an offer he could not refuse. The young man would be allowed to live, provided he agreed to serve the German cause. Only one week after his arrest, Leif Utne was back in the desolate mountains of the Varanger Peninsula. With him was the wireless transmitter his captors had confiscated. The difference was that now his transmissions to Murmansk were controlled by the Germans. Like Ib Arnasson Riis in Iceland, he was a double agent – but, unlike Riis, he was working for the Germans, not the Allies. Pardon had mounted a new operation, *Operation Tundra*, the most ambitious of the many he had been responsible for since the early summer. He defined its object as follows: 'Wireless Operator Leif Utne has placed himself at our disposal to take part in a wireless subterfuge. Its purpose is to lure other agents from their hiding places and take them prisoner, and to entice to the coast and destroy an enemy submarine.'

The Russians, who had lost contact with Utne some time before he was arrested, were relieved when, on Friday 3 September, he came back on the air with the following signal: 'We had a transmitter fault. We found the supplies. Are you receiving us?' Two days later Murmansk replied: 'Receiving you loud and clear. Have you any chance of making your way over [to us] on foot or can you get a boat for transport? Sending a submarine is very dangerous.'

In the course of the next few weeks, with incredible patience and cunning, Pardon and the *Abwehr* endeavoured to persuade the Russians that it was impossible for Utne and the other agents to cross into the Soviet Union without help. In a signal sent at nine o'clock in the evening of 20 September, Murmansk indicated that they had come round. 'Do you want to be taken off by submarine from the shore of the Sylte fjord? Let us know the safest place to do so in this area.'

*

While these messages were passing to and fro between the double agent in the mountains and Murmansk, on the opposite side of the county Operation Source was nearing its climax. When Utne received the last signal, the four British midget submarines were making their way through the minefield guarding the entrance to Stjern Sound. Only two of them were in contact with each other. At 23.15 Godfrey Place on board X7 saw a familiar figure in the distance. It was Henty Henty-Creer. There he was, standing in the open hatch of X5, just discernible above the waves. The two were close friends. Only a few weeks earlier Henty had been Godfrey's best man when he married a girl he had met while in the Navy. They waved to each other and wished one another good luck and good hunting. Then they faded away, lost to view in the darkness, amid the long rollers.

Lieutenant (later Vice-Admiral) Arthur Hezlet on board the *Thrasher* had slipped X5's tow some hours earlier off Sørøy Island. Having trained together for so many months, he too was a firm friend of Henty-Creer. 'He was a delightful personality with a marvellous sense of humour while inside him burned a fire and determination to succeed. . . . When I finally said goodbye to him and wished him luck just before slipping X5, he seemed almost in a hurry to be gone and to get on with it. It never seemed to occur to either of us that we might never meet again.'

Some distance away, standing in the open hatch of X6, was Lieutenant Donald Cameron. He was already frozen to the marrow. He had seen no sign of his fellows, but he knew they were out there somewhere on the dark sea. Round about midnight he too approached the sound.

A fresh off-shore breeze had sprung up, raising a choppy sea and whipping the crests in spray. It was devilishly cold and I could no longer seek comparative shelter in the W&D. The high land ahead now showed up as a jagged black wall with the entrance to Stjern Sound a narrow grey chasm. . . . Trimmed down at this juncture, taking all possible precaution against being spotted by the enemy observation posts on Sørøy and at entrance to Ofoto fjord. . . . Still no sign of Godfrey or Henty, but expect they will turn up at the rendezvous tomorrow. Dawn came very quickly, and at 02.15, still three miles west of Stjernsund, decided to dive and end my misery. Was so stiff with cold I found great difficulty in bending to open the hatch, and my hands were quite numb.

The little craft had developed a 10° list to port, the periscope was leaking and the autopilot wasn't working. The effects of the ten-day passage were making themselves felt with a vengeance – and it would be another eighteen hours before X6 and her companion submarines reached their target. They would be long hours for the men hunched up in the four cramped steel cylinders inching their way below the surface towards the German naval base at the head of the Alta fjord.

CHAPTER TWELVE

The Attack

THE KÅ FJORD, 03.00–13.00, 22 SEPTEMBER 1943

On board the *Tirpitz* Wednesday morning dawned grey and chilly, the lowering
sky a portent of the rain to come. A westerly wind swept down from the
mountains, bringing with it a touch of autumn. The temperature was a bare
5°C. The celebration to mark the recent award of four hundred Iron Crosses was
over and the daily routine of shipboard life had been resumed. As always, 44-
year-old *Kapitän-zur-See* Hans Karl Meyer was breakfasting alone in his cabin on
an egg and two slices of bread, washed down with cups of the dark-brown
liquid that passed as coffee. His predecessor, *Kapitän-zur-See* Karl Topp, an
outgoing, hail-fellow-well-met type, had been enormously popular. Meyer was
quite different. Lean and sinewy, he was a man of few words and rarely raised
his voice. But the blue eyes that shone beneath his bushy eyebrows said it all. In
the six months he had been on board, he had earned the reputation of a hard but
just commanding officer. The arm he had lost in fighting the Spartacists in
1920 strengthened the impression he gave of self-discipline and authority. In so
far as he could, he shared the same conditions as the ship's company at large: the
same food was served at his table as in the messes of the lower deck.

'Meyer was more withdrawn than Topp: no one who had anything to do with
him could help but remark on his personal modesty and total incorruptibility,'
wrote *Leutnant-zur-See* Adalbert Brünner, who in 1943 was Meyer's adjutant.

> While I was serving under him I often had to look after his guests. They were
> usually staff officers from neighbouring units. But even generals were not given
> anything other than ersatz coffee, made from beans. It was nicely served, but it
> tasted like cat's piss. On the other hand it didn't matter much if the adjutant

passing round cigars held the box so high that no one could see how many were in it. He just laughed and never said a word about it afterwards.

In the dramatic 1930s Meyer saw little service at sea. From the time he left the torpedo-boat *T-185* in the autumn of 1931 until he took command of the *Tirpitz* thirteen years later, he spent only a few months at sea. The bulk of his time was spent in staff work ashore. The attack on Spitsbergen was his first major operation as captain of a heavy battleship, and he was happy that it had been successful. The margin between success and failure was a narrow one: his colleague, *Kapitän-zur-See* Friedrich Hüffmeier, was in disgrace, but he himself had come through without a blot on his escutcheon. For a few days he had permitted a little relaxation on board; after all, his men had won a victory and had to be allowed to celebrate. Meyer knew that it would be a long time before another opportunity for action offered. If everything went as planned, in November the *Tirpitz* would be back in Germany, and many of the men would be given leave. But her return to the Fatherland still lay several weeks ahead, and in the meantime the ship's company had to be kept up to the mark. So it was with no little satisfaction that he heard through the open ventilators that the return to normal was already well in hand. He could hear the clanking and rattling of buckets and the sound of hoses being run out – not to mention the rough voices of petty officers bawling out the men. The gun crews were busy oiling and polishing their charges. Meyer was well aware that his anti-aircraft gunners were below strength; he himself had given orders to release gunners to man patrol boats and checkpoints ashore. He was determined to do all he could to prevent sabotage. On board the *Tirpitz* the hydrophones had been manned all night long, but at 07.00 they had been switched off and their operators had turned in. Meyer was a sensible man. In daylight, an underwater attack was virtually inconceivable, as the narrow fjord was thronged with shipping of all kinds – lighters, tugs, coal barges, power-supply boats and screening ships. An intruder would inevitably be detected.

While Captain Meyer was looking forward to his morning cigar, Ordinary Seaman Karl Heinz Lohse was on his way back from the Carpenters' Shop to his sleeping quarters forward. The *Tirpitz* was a steel giant, its armoured hull almost 40 centimetres thick on the waterline; each gun turret weighed over 1,000 tons. But there was a lot of woodwork on board, too, ranging from the exquisite panelling of the captain's cabin to the well-scrubbed planks of the afterdeck. The carpenters were a close-knit bunch. Many of them were trained helmet divers and carried out minor repair work under water. They were few in number, twelve at the most, which meant that they were never short of work. Aboard a ship the size of the *Tirpitz*, there was always something that needed to be attended to.

'I was a good carpenter. I liked the rhythm of life. It was a great source of satisfaction to me to be able to put things right and keep the ship nice and tidy,' says Lohse.

The carpenters' and divers' quarters were far forward on the port side of the ship, where the bulkheads followed the battleship's clipper bow. The ventilators slanted downwards, which meant that they afforded a view of the area close to and just beneath the bow. Says Lohse:

> I happened to glance out and my attention was immediately caught by a black object moving towards the ship *inside* the anti-torpedo nets. Had it been a whale or turtle, I would have known what it was, but what I saw was a steel craft of some kind. I leaped to the phone, rang the officer of the watch and shouted, 'There's a U-boat in the net!'

*

Donald Cameron had reached his standby position in the late afternoon of Tuesday 21 September. At half-past six it began to get dark. He was some 2,000 metres due north of a small island, Tømmerholmen, the outermost of a group of rocks and islets at the head of the Alta fjord. From these heathclad islands it was a mere 10 kilometres to the mouth of the Kå fjord to the south. The crossing from Scotland had taken exactly ten days. Now X6 had reached her first objective.

> Came to low buoyancy and took all round sweep through night periscope. All clear. Decided to open hatch and investigate. Air of great tension in the craft. Opened up and crawled on to casing. Beautiful evening, atmosphere clear and everything still. Leading lights at Alten [now Alta], Boss[e]kop and Lieffshavn burning brightly. As yet no sign of surface traffic, so motored close inshore to a small brushwood cover to start charging.

When X6 was only metres from Tømmerholmen, Cameron received his first shock. On the shore, the door of a fisherman's cabin suddenly opened, to release a shaft of light. He heard the sound of voices, then the door was closed and again silence reigned. 'Swallowed very hard and found my knees trembling.

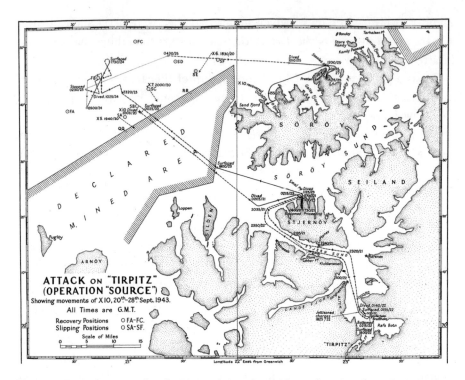

This map shows the route taken by *X10* and the other midget submarines from the spot where they slipped their tows outside the mined area, through Stjern Sound, to the Kå fjord, in the inner recesses of the Alta fjord. *X10*'s track is the only one plotted. This is because technical problems forced the submarine to abort and return to a position off Sørøy (marked on the map as 'X10 recovered'), from where all its crew were rescued one week later.

Carried on charging. Next alarm as small coasting vesssel came round point keeping close inshore. Broke charge and dived out of it.'

Only half an hour later *X6* was again surprised by a vessel sailing in the opposite direction. Below deck, John Lorimer was busy preparing a meal of boiled eggs, chocolate, cheese, sardines and biscuits.

Suddenly the hatch crashed down – 'Cut engines, dive, dive, dive! A torpedo boat!' said Don. Her searchlight went right across us. Ten feet down we could hear her coming nearer – straight towards us – 20 feet. Nearly on us – had they seen us? Thud, thud, thud of the twin propellers – 40 feet. We waited for the crushing effect of depth-charges. None came, and gradually the noise died away. 'Periscope depth . . . up periscope. OK,' said Don. 'Surface.'

So much for the eggs – John squeezed forward and looked at the mess on the deck and cleared it up. Just cheese and biscuits now and sardines.

To preclude more unpleasant surprises, Cameron took his small craft into the 500-metre-broad basin between the three islands of Tømmerholmen, Brattholmen and Skarvskjæret, where the submarine captains had agreed to rendezvous the night before the attack. When the Scotsman again opened the hatch, the fjord was in darkness. To port lay Brattholmen. Circular in shape, the island resembled nothing more than a black steel helmet. In the distance an anti-aircraft battery suddenly opened up. Tracers climbed lazily into the sky and searchlights pierced the blackness of the night. Cameron strained his eyes to see what it was all about, but where he was, all was quiet. None of the other submarines had reached the meeting-place and Cameron felt a sudden stab of loneliness.

Sat on casing and watched lights go by on both sides. Boom at entrance to Kaafjord brilliantly floodlit. Saw headlights of a car twisting and turning along shore road till it finally disappeared in direction of Kaa. Wondered if it might carry German admiral and speculated on his reactions tomorrow if all went well. Moon rising above mountains and everything brushed with silver. Wondered if Eve would be seeing it at Salterns and if Iain was behaving himself, and felt very homesick indeed. Elation of sitting in middle of enemy's fleet anchorage vied with feeling of a small boy very much alone and wanting to go home and be comforted. Was not conscious of fear, just of wanting someone to talk to.

*

Donald Cameron wasn't really alone. One of the other midget submarines, X7, had reached Tømmerholmen at about the same time as X6, but in the darkness the two had missed seeing each other. After a hair-raising start Lieutenant Godfrey Place had spent thirty hours negotiating Stjern Sound. The transit crews had just been relieved and the towline was about to be cast off when the lookouts in the tower of the mother submarine Stubborn broke into a cold sweat. A floating German horned mine had caught on the bow of the midget sub. The telephone cable between the two submarines had been disconnected, making it impossible to warn Place, who in any case had more than enough to do getting X7 ready to sail. 'Everybody's nerves were as taut as piano wire, expecting any minute to see mine, side-charges, X7 and possibly Stubborn as well, go up in a sheet of flame. After five minutes bumping on the part of the mine, up came Godfrey on to the casing to see what was amiss.'

Dark-haired and lightly built, 23-year-old Lieutenant Godfrey Place was greatly liked by all for his generous nature, dry sense of humour and relaxed attitude towards the wearing of correct military dress. But his carefree exterior concealed both strength of character and a seemingly inexhaustible source of energy. Place now demonstrated the iron nerve that, a year earlier, had earned him the Distinguished Service Cross and the Polish Cross while serving on board the submarine *Sokol*. Without a moment's hesitation he strode resolutely to the bow and put his foot first on the rope in which the deadly steel sphere was entangled, then on to the mine itself. 'He spent seven minutes shoving the mine clear with his foot. When she was finally clear – *X7* having drifted quite near to us – Godfrey shouted cheerfully, "And that's the first time I've ever shoved a mine clear by its horns."'

The voyage through Stjern Sound had passed off without incident, apart from the moment when, through his periscope, Place had seen a large warship off the island of Årøya, in the middle of the sound. It was the *Scharnhorst*, which was preparing for the next day's gunnery practice. The atmosphere on board the submarine was tense when, late on Tuesday evening, it lay to in the shadow of Brattholmen. Little was said as the men checked their equipment for the last time.

'At last Godfrey turned to the others, looking them full in the eyes, as if to pass on to them all his own determination. But there was also a slight smile playing round his thin lips, the smile of a mischievous schoolboy about to play a good trick on someone. "Ready?" he asked.'

'Ready.'

It was nearly three in the morning. The pygmy 'Pdinichthys' set out on her attack against the giant *Tirpitz*.

*

At the Admiralty in London Rear-Admiral Barry had known for some hours that the heavily armed battlecruiser *Scharnhorst* would be patrolling the fjord at the precise moment the midget submarines were due to pass through. The British wireless monitoring service had intercepted a signal to the effect that the battlecruiser was intending to carry out firing practice against sea targets on Tuesday and Wednesday. It was disquieting news. The ship's hydrophones would be manned and anti-submarine precautions heightened. The only positive thing about this news was that it confirmed what aerial photographs had indicated – that the three big ships were still in Alta.

Tension rose when the news reached the Admiralty. It was but one of a succession of worries that Barry had to contend with. On Sunday 19 September there had been a new contact with the wireless station codenamed Upsilon in Tromsø. London urgently needed more details of the anti-torpedo barrage surrounding the *Tirpitz*. The station's wireless operator, Egil Lindberg, had replied: 'The barrier at Straumsnes consists of *three rows* [author's italics] of buoys. The distance between each row is three metres, apart from in the opening towards the shore, where there is only a single row of buoys.' The battleship was protected by a triple barrage. Each net consisted of linked steel rings with a diameter of 30 centimetres. It was a formidable obstacle. If the divers were forced to cut their way through it would take a long time, and the risk of detection would greatly increase. The attempt to disable the German battle fleet might well fail less than 100 metres from its objective. The hope was that the nets did not quite reach the bottom. If they didn't, the midget submarines would be able to get through by worming their way under the steel curtain. All concerned had known from the outset that the attack was foolhardy, to say the least, but now the risks seemed to be mounting. In London, Barry was powerless. The attack was about to enter its final phase. All depended upon the resoluteness of the submarine crews. There was no going back. In a report Barry wrote after the operation he said that he resolved not to tell the submarine commanders that *X9* was missing, in order not to dishearten them. Nor did he make any change in the plan of attack, although this meant that no attack would be mounted on the *Lützow*.

*

X10 under the command of Lieutenant Ken Hudspeth had been chosen to attack the *Scharnhorst*, together with *X9*. But *X9* had been lost, and by Monday Hudspeth was already experiencing severe difficulties. His midget submarine, which he had named 'Excalibur' after King Arthur's legendary sword, had performed perfectly during the crossing, but in the minefields of the treacherous stretch of ocean known as Lopphavet things started to go wrong. First of all the electric motor that powered the periscope short-circuited, and not long after-wards the gyro compass packed up. To make matters worse, the chronic leakages in the hull were steadily ruining the submarine's electrical equipment. Without a compass it was impossible to navigate under water. The Australian, in civilian life a teacher in Tasmania, made a snap decision. He set a course for the uninhabited Smal fjord on the seaward side of Stjern Island and brought his craft to rest on a sandy beach at the head of the fjord. Ten hours later all the defective equipment had been dismantled, dried out, lubricated and reassembled.

To make up for lost time, Hudspeth taxed his engines to the utmost. He had agreed with his fellow captains that the attack should go in between 07.00 and 10.00 on the morning of Wednesday 22 September, and that the charges they carried should be set to explode simultaneously at 10.30. With a delay of, for example, one hour, this would give the submarines a fair chance of getting clear of the fjord before they went off. But the enforced repair work had delayed Hudspeth by almost twelve hours. If he were to reach the target by the agreed time, he couldn't afford to stop off Tømmerholmen but would have to proceed straight to the Kå fjord.

Round about 03.30 on Wednesday morning success seemed to be in sight. The approach had passed off without incident. He was only 5 nautical miles from the 1,000-metre-long boom that had been laid across the mouth of the fjord when he was forced to dive to avoid a ship coming straight at him. He was just about to raise his periscope to size up the situation when a loud crackling sound was heard; a shower of sparks shot out from the electric motor and the submarine started to fill with choking fumes. The motor had not only broken down, it had also burned out.

'Surface,' Hudspeth ordered.

He opened the hatch. Day was rising over Kaafjord, about 5 miles away. A milky dawn, whitening the sea and the mountains all round. He thought he could see smoke in the south, towards the fjord. Calm and practical, he wasted no time in recriminations. Without a compass, with no means of raising his periscope, he was incapable of carrying out any sort of attack – he was blind.

'Day's coming. We'll have to do our Smalfjord job all over again. We'll go south-east of Tommerholm Island, bottom there, and try to make good the defects. Nothing else to be done.'

*

At about the same time as Ken Hudspeth was bringing *X10* to rest at a depth of 60 metres off Tømmerholmen, Godfrey Place was in the conning tower of *X7* with his chart spread out before him. The first to do so, he had left their

Above: The *Tirpitz*, photographed from the western shore of the Kå fjord in the summer of 1943. Straumsnes Point can be seen in the background to the right. *Below:* The *Tirpitz* at anchor off Straumsnes Point after her move to the eastern side of the fjord in the summer of 1944. In the top right-hand corner of the photograph, rising sheer from the waters of the fjord, is Mount Sakkobadne.

Above: Kapitän-zur-See Hans Meyer (far left) is welcomed on board his new command by a fanfare of trumpets. *Below:* For the 2,300 officers and men of the *Tirpitz* the eighteen inactive months they spent cooped up in the Kå fjord were a great strain. Their yearning for home was especially intense at Christmas.

Above: The *Tirpitz*, the 'Lonely Queen of the North'. *Below, left:* The daily round was characterised by routine. Captain Meyer was a stickler for discipline and demanded that his ship be kept spick and span at all times. *Below, right:* The battleship's heavy guns in action against Barentsburg, Spitsbergen, September 1943.

Facing page: The men manning General Dietl's mountain fastness enjoy a day's skiing on the slopes above the Kå fjord. The photograph was probably taken in the spring of 1943. The pocket battleship *Lützow* can be seen in the background. *Above:* A unique photograph of X5 being towed out into the open sea by her mother submarine, *Thrasher*. *Below:* The midget submarine under way, her captain clinging tightly to the periscope.

Above: Lieutenant Henty Henty-Creer (right) together with a shipmate (probably Sub-Lt J.J. McGregor), photographed while training a few weeks before the attack on the *Tirpitz*. *Left:* Godfrey Place (left) and Donald Cameron, the two midget-submarine commanders who were awarded the Victoria Cross.

Two unique photographs of the midget submarines' attack taken from the deck of the *Tirpitz* by one of the battleship's float-plane pilots, *Leutnant* Wilhelm Rosenbaum. The photograph above shows shells bursting close to the target raft (visible on the left, with SS *Stamsund* silhouetted behind it) beneath which *X7* disappeared. The other photograph (below) shows smoke and spray drifting across the surface of the sea close to the spot where *X5* was sighted. The dark wall of rock in the background is Mount Sakkobadne. *Left:* One of the men from *X6* or *X7* who were taken prisoner, photographed by Rosenbaum on the deck of the *Tirpitz* shortly after the attack. His identity is uncertain, but he is thought to be John Lorimer.

Above: The following day, Thursday 23 September, the Germans made a photographic record of the attack. *X7* disappeared at the spot marked 2, *X5* at that marked 9. *Below:* The hull of *X7* after its recovery and beaching at Straumsnes Point.

Above: The German generals in the north: Eduard Dietl (centre), Ferdinand Schörner (right) and Georg Ritter von Hengl (left). *Below: Major* Heinrich Ehrler (left), who was unjustly blamed for the loss of the *Tirpitz*, and Robert Ehrhardt, Zeiss representative in Norway.

Above: Henty-Creer's younger sister, Pamela, and her husband, Gerard Mellor, on a hillside overlooking the Kå fjord in 1974. *Left:* Henty-Creer's elder sister, Deirdre, and Police Sergeant Georg Johnsen on board the police boat *Broder* in Hammerfest harbour in the summer of 1950.

Above: A groundstaff member of the *Luftwaffe*, Hans Moos, in front of a Messerschmitt Bf 109 fighter at Høybuktmoen airfield, near Kirkenes. *Below, left:* Regina and Werner Brand on their wedding day in the autumn of 1944. *Right:* Hein Hellendoorn as a young lieutenant on board the *Tirpitz*.

Above: A convoy carrying supplies for General Dietl's Mountain Corps approaching Kirkenes. Enormous quantities of food and equipment had to be shipped along the Norwegian coast to sustain the Litza front. *Below:* Buildings in Barentsburg ablaze after the German attack of 8 September 1943.

Above: Booty from Barentsburg is taken aboard destroyer *Z29*. *Below:* A shell from a Norwegian shore battery pierced the destroyer's hull.

Above: A view of Loch Cairnbawn, where the midget submarine crews trained for the attack. *Below:* HMS *Bonaventure*, the submarines' mothership (foreground) and, in the background, the *Titania*, the towing submarines' mothership, photographed shortly before the attack was launched.

Opposite: Above: General Dietl's floating headquarters, the *Black Watch*, photographed in the Kå fjord, probably in the winter of 1942. The *Black Watch* was later employed as a depot ship for U-boats in Hammerfest harbour. *Below:* With temperatures as low as -40°C, winters on the Litza front were a gruelling experience.

BRING HOME SUB SUNK IN TIRPITZ RAID, SAYS MP

By *JOHN OWEN*

A CONSERVATIVE M P yesterday demanded a full inquiry into the exploit of a wartime Naval officer who piloted his midget submarine through a heavily defended Norwegian fjord to tackle the German battleship, Tirpitz, in its lair.

The submarine was later sunk, and Mr David Mudd, M P for Falmouth Camborne, is to ask the Ministry of Defence to meet any request for help from the Imperial War Museum, which wants to raise the sunken submarine and bring her back to England.

This could mean sending a Navy salvage ship to Norway.

Mr Mudd acted within a few hours of *The Daily Telegraph's* exclusive report that British divers seeking the midget submarine, the X5, in the Kaafjord, northern Norway, had found X-craft wreckage.

It is being identified as the X5 following examination of the different positions in which the other two X craft involved in the mission went down.

' Full resources '

Mr Mudd is to write to the Navy Minister, Mr Frank Judd, suggesting that the divers, all experienced members of the British Sub-Aqua Club, should make their evidence available for examination and that "full Ministry of Defence resources" should be used to see what actually happened.

"The fact that the hull is recognisable would suggest that the submarine was not subject

Lieut. Henty Henty-Creer

to an explosive charge of a size consistent with the Amatol mines the X5 carried into the fjord," he said.

"This seems to indicate — if this is, indeed, X5—that she must have laid them so successfully before she was heavily shelled by the Tirpitz."

Such a conclusion, if verified by an official inquiry, would vindicate the belief of the family of the X5's commander, Lieut Henty Henty-Creer, 23, that he would have pressed home his attack and placed his mines with those of the other X-craft under the hull of the German battleship.

Both of the other two commanders, who survived to report their success, were awarded the Victoria Cross. But Lieut Henty-Creer, with the fate of X5 unresolved, received only a mention in despatches.

One of the major issues which would have to be considered by an official inquiry is the certainty of proof that the wreckage found has come from the X5.

Mr Mudd said: "The wreckage was reported by the divers to be some 400 metres from the Tirpitz anchorage. The official records of the time put her at 700 metres, when she was shelled, so, in one respect at least, it would appear there has been inaccuracy."

The Ministry of Defence (Navy) said yesterday that it had, as yet, received no official reports on the operations of the expedition, which is privately backed by the Imperial War Museum, the Sir Winston Churchill Memorial Trust and industry.

"Any representations anyone wishes to make will be sympathetically heard," said a spokesman.

If it can be proved that Lieut Henty-Creer and his crew of three showed valour of a degree higher than previously realised, presumably the possibility of a belated gallantry award, even after 30 years, would not be ruled out.

But the Ministry spokesman would only comment: "We will consider any fresh evidence that is put before this Department."

Service circles, however, yesterday considered that the posthumous award of a V C so long after the event would pose many difficulties.

An X midget submarine of the type used in the raid on the Tirpitz.

The Kå fjord expeditions of 1974 and 1976 received wide press coverage. *Right:* Henty-Creer's elder sister, Deirdre, an artist, seen here with a Sámi reindeer herder, painted many fine pictures when she visited Alta in the summer of 1950.

standby position at 03.00 and set a course for the illuminated boom between Auskar Point and Mount Hjemmeluft.

The chart contained all the information Intelligence had so painstakingly garnered over a period of many months from interpretation of aerial photographs, topographical information supplied by the Norwegian Intelligence Centre in London and the observations of Torbjørn Johansen. It gave what was in the circumstances a detailed picture, but there was something that the agents had been unable to help with. As they had no means of knowing what lay below the surface of the fjord, they couldn't say how far down the steel mesh of the nets went.

At 05.50 Place saw through his periscope the dark bulk and characteristic outline of Auskar Point. Marked on his chart was a dangerous submerged rock right in the middle of the 1,000-metre-wide fjord. For this reason ships entering the fjord were directed to the eastern side, where the water was deep; here the Germans had installed a boom, which in- and outgoing craft had to pass. The boom was guarded by an armed trawler, but it was cold and still rather dark. Place reasoned that the men on watch would be tired and in consequence less observant, and decided to take a chance. He surfaced. 'Surface! – the boom was there. Place was just in front of the entrance, which was wide open. He went through it. In the half-light of the dawning day he saw the German control vessel to starboard. It was a million to one against anyone in that noticing a dot slowly moving on the surface of the water. But here was a mine-layer, straight ahead, outward bound.'

Place crashdived and waited tensely to see whether they had been spotted. But the noise of the minesweeper's propellers gradually faded into the distance. He was over the first hurdle: they had penetrated the Kå fjord without being detected. What is more, they had covered over 2,000 kilometres since setting out eleven days earlier, and now there were only 3,500 metres left. There was just one problem: the electric motor was taking X7 into the head of the fjord all right, but Place didn't dare use his periscope. He was blind.

'Those minutes under the water, seeing nothing, knowing nothing, seemed endless. The craft was 75 feet down. Suddenly he felt certain that he was caught in a net, he had had the experience a hundred times in exercises. The craft could not move, the net was stopping her.'

*

At the same time, some distance astern, Donald Cameron was slowly nearing the same goal. He had waited as long as he dared for the other midget

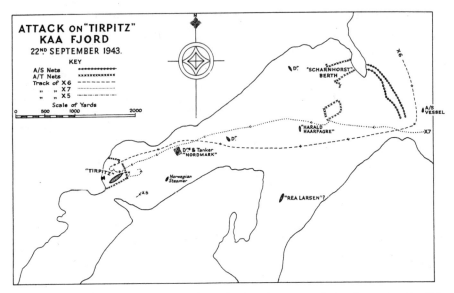

X6 followed X7 through an opening in the anti-submarine net on the south-eastern side of the Kå fjord early in the morning of Wednesday 22 September. X7 then became enmeshed in an anti-torpedo net and was passed by X6, which hugged the north-western shore of the fjord en route to the place where the *Tirpitz* lay at anchor. There were many more vessels in the fjord at the time than are shown on this wartime map.

submarines to join him off Tømmerholmen. As senior captain he had wanted them to make their way to the Kå fjord together and lay their charges in a joint and closely coordinated operation. But time had passed and there had been no sign of the others, so shortly after midnight he decided to proceed alone. By this time 'Piker' was in a bad way. The list was becoming increasingly marked, as water had penetrated the starboard charge. As if this were not enough, the clock that controlled the timer on the port side had short-circuited and was stuck at six hours. Moreover, the periscope was leaking and the lenses were obscured by condensation, making it impossible to see anything other than blurred greenish shapes. And air was leaking from one of the pressure tanks, which meant that X6 left a trail of bubbles on the surface that might easily be seen by an alert lookout. Cameron set out his alternatives in his notebook.

If I went in to attack and was successful, only one of my charges might explode, but the gaff would be blown and the enemy on the look-out for Godfrey and Henty.

If I waited for a day, the others could make their attacks, and I could limp around and perhaps do a little damage. If the others were in the fjord and in a fit state to operate, I would not compromise them. *If* the others were in the fjord? They had not turned up at the rendezvous. They might be in a worse plight than I.

If I waited any longer, my periscope might be completely unserviceable and attack out of the question. What was I to do?

Shut the hatch, went below, and headed for Kaafjord and the *Tirpitz*.

Cameron changed into dry clothes and heated up a few cups of cocoa in a saucepan. He wanted to make sure that everyone was as fit and wide awake as possible on the last decisive stretch. But when, at 06.00, he found himself midway between Tømmerholmen and Auskar Point, he discovered to his consternation that he could hardly see a thing. More water had seeped into the periscope. There was nothing for it: the eyepiece would have to be dismantled and cleaned, so he hove to and set to work.

Cleaned eyepiece as best I could and replaced. Look of dejection on everyone's face finally decided me. We had waited and trained for two years for this show, and at last moment faulty workmanship or bad joss was doing its best to deprive us of it all. There might be no other craft within miles, for all I knew we were the only starter. Felt very bloody-minded and brought her back to her original course. It might not be good policy, it might spoil and destroy the element of surprise, we might be intercepted and sunk before reaching our target, but we were going to have a very good shot at it.

Only a quarter of an hour later the electric motor suddenly began to emit showers of sparks. Acrid smoke filled the control room and the lenses of the periscope grew dark with soot. After a new provisional repair had been made, Cameron finally caught sight of the rusty buoys that marked the anti-submarine net that barred the mouth of the fjord.

Suddenly they heard the noise of a ship's propeller going from port to starboard across the X-craft's bows. Without worrying too much, Cameron raised the periscope. Through the eyepiece he could see a blurred, indistinct shadow preceding 'Piker' on her course. 'Good-oh!' he exclaimed. 'They're opening the boom to let her through . . .' and ten seconds later 'Full ahead! Starboard 20! Midships! Surface! We're right astern of her.'

With the diesel engine running at top speed, *X6* tore through the boom in the wake of the vessel just ahead of it. The time was 06.45. The second midget submarine had also penetrated the Kå fjord undetected.

*

Three kilometres away, *Admiral* Oskar Kummetz had risen to a grey day. The wind was coming from the west and during the night had driven heavily laden clouds in from the sea. There was rain in the air. Kummetz, who had spent twelve months in northern Norway, knew that it was a good sign: as long as humid air from the Atlantic lay over the base there would be no risk of snow, which meant that the winter he feared, with its frost mist, near-perpetual darkness and storms from the north, would be shorter. The Kå fjord was a well-sheltered anchorage, but the weeks of bitter cold were a trial. Temperatures had been recorded down to -30°C, making watch duty a freezing hell. For Kummetz himself changes in the weather meant little – his application for extended leave had been granted and he was scheduled to leave the *Tirpitz* and spend the winter with his family in Berlin. His officers had received the news with disappointment, but Kummetz knew something they didn't. He was only an advance party. Some units of the 1st Battle Group were to return to Germany for drydocking and overhaul. The *Lützow* would be the first to go, and would in all probability be followed by the *Tirpitz* in November. This meant that in the most severe period of the winter, the weeks immediately before and after the turn of the year, the battlecruiser *Scharnhorst* and her attendant destroyers would be left alone in Alta. This occasioned Kummetz no anxiety, as he didn't expect his ships to see action as long as winter darkness reigned. The British had brought radar-controlled night gunnery to a fine art, but the 1st Battle Group had nothing approaching the same technological standard. German radar research lagged far behind that of the British and gunners were forced to rely on optical instruments, for which they needed daylight. In the Arctic it was dark around the clock until well into February, for which reason Kummetz felt able to leave his ships with a clear conscience. The decisive blow against the Russian convoys was to be delivered when he returned with his newly overhauled ships in the new year. It irked him, however, that not all his officers shared his opinion. To relieve him the German Naval High Command had appointed a destroyer commander, *Konter-Admiral* Erich Bey. Bey, for his part, was far from pleased at being allotted the role of caretaker in the absence of the Group Commander, and insisted on retaining the Battle Group's operations officer, the highly capable *Kapitän-zur-See* Hansjürgen Reinicke, in Alta. This was not at all to Kummetz's liking, as he had wanted to have his chief-of-staff by his side in Berlin.

'I think Bey harbours exaggerated hopes as to the level of activity in the next few months,' was his laconic comment.

Just before 08.00 on Wednesday there was a knock at the Admiral's door and a messenger came in with the first teleprinter message of the day. It was from the *Admiral Nordmeer*, Otto Klüber, and consisted of only one word: 'Hansa'. Kummetz knew immediately what it meant. It was the codeword to indicate that the *Lützow* was to return to Germany the very next day, Thursday 23 September. After some discussion, the admirals agreed that the destroyer *Erich Steinbrink* should form a part of the pocket battleship's escort, as it had been having trouble with one of its propeller shafts and needed docking. Kummetz ordered a message to be despatched to *Fregattenkapitän* Otto Teichmann on board the destroyer, which was moored alongside the quay in Bukta. While the *Erich Steinbrink* was casting off and setting a course across the Kå fjord to take on extra oil, Kummetz donned his riding breeches and went ashore. The Admiral stabled his personal horse not far from the anchorage and began each day with a ride among the slagheaps that dotted the landscape, a reminder of the area's copper-mining heyday.

From the ridge, Kummetz had a magnificent view of the entire fjord. He had many times gazed with pride at the armada that was his Battle Group. The *Tirpitz* itself was anchored with its stern close to Straumsnes Point, surrounded by a triple anti-torpedo barrage, two tugs, a supply ship to provide it with electric power and a coal barge. In the middle of the fjord, only 800 metres distant, lay the legendary 23,000-tonner *Nordmark*, which had kept Hitler's battlecruisers supplied with oil and provisions on their forays into the Atlantic and had time and again successfully evaded the enemy forces. She was one of four special-purpose vessels built by the *Kriegsmarine* towards the end of the 1930s, ships designed to carry both wet and dry cargoes. Her tanks could take 10,000 tons of fuel oil, 300 tons of lubricating oil, aviation fuel and large quantities of fresh water. Beneath her reinforced forward deck lay the ammunition store, which was packed with steel crates containing shells of every description. Kummetz had close on 10,000 men under his command, and the *Nordmark* was a key factor in keeping them properly fed. Her refrigerated holds were piled high with tons of tinned and other foods. On her port side, her stern securely moored to the shore, lay the first destroyer of the flotilla, Z27, under the command of *Korvettenkapitän* Günther Schultz. Further out, in the lee of

Auskar Point, could be seen the guns of the commandeered Norwegian armoured vessel *Harald Hårfagre*. Renamed *Thetis*, she had been converted into an anti-aircraft cruiser. On the other side of Mount Sakkobadne, in Kvænvik Bay, lay the oil tanker *C.A. Larsen* and the repair ship *Neumark*, a 16,000-ton steamer that had once belonged to the Hamburg-Amerika Line. Seven more destroyers were anchored round about. Together with advance guardships and lighters, there were nearly twenty vessels grouped in the fjord, a tempting target for the British.

Under the Admiral's watchful eye, considerable resources had been expended to make the Kå fjord an impregnable fortress. Like most of his men, Kummetz expected the greatest danger to come from the air. Aircraft taking off from a carrier off the coast could reach the fjord in an hour. As an extra precaution, in addition to the anti-aircraft guns on board the ships, which were manned day and night, a number of 88mm batteries and searchlights had been installed on the shores of the fjord. There were smoke generators all over the mountains and on board a fleet of hired fishing-boats that the Germans called *Nebelkuttere* (fog cutters). It would take only a few minutes to enshroud the fjord in smoke and thus make accurate bombing well-nigh impossible.

Kummetz was aware that the British had taken a leaf out of the Italians' book and trained an elite corps of 'Charioteers'. Two such 'human torpedoes' had attempted an attack on the *Tirpitz* when she lay in the Trondheim fjord, but without success. The torpedoes had been lost in a storm, the men who manned them escaping across the border into Sweden. However, one man had been captured and 'persuaded' to talk, after which he was executed. It was a long way from Britain to western Finnmark, and few believed in the possibility of an attack by frogmen. Nonetheless, a great deal of care had been taken to perfect the anchorage's underwater defences. Despite this, the anti-submarine boom blocking the broad mouth of the fjord was by no means all it should have been. The steel net was only 600 metres across, the last 400 metres consisting of nothing more than a string of buoys linked by a wire. The boom was primarily intended to fool the men and women whose task it was to interpret aerial photographs. What is more, for most of the time the boom was open, as there was traffic day and night between Bossekop and the anchorage at the head of the fjord. It was at Bossekop, near the centre of Alta, that the Germans maintained their vast stores of coal and other supplies. Here too lay the Field Post Office, whose smooth functioning meant so much to the morale of the fleet, and many other staff units. It was about five nautical miles from the *Tirpitz* to the wharves below Mount Bossekop, which meant that countless tugs, lighters, launches, advance guardships, destroyers and hired motor cutters were constantly passing to and fro between the two points. With so much shipping in the fjord, in practice it had proved impossible to keep the boom permanently closed. If a tug were to have towed the heavy buoys backwards and forwards each time a vessel needed to pass through, the result would have been prolonged delays and overworked tug crews. This had forced Kummetz to agree that the boom should be closed only when the adjacent hydrophones picked up suspicious noises and the submarine alarm was given. In other respects it was the task of the guardship, which was rarely to be found more than 50 metres from the opening, to attend to security.

The anti-torpedo barrage protecting the *Tirpitz* was a far more sophisticated obstacle. A triple curtain, it reached right down to the seabed. A 15-metre-wide entrance north-west of the battleship was, like the boom, intended in principle to be kept closed, but here too it had proved difficult to observe the rule in practice, and at times of heavy traffic the entrance was left open. *Admiral* Kummetz and *Kapitän-zur-See* Meyer had therefore agreed to station a *Nebelkutter*, manned by armed men from the *Tirpitz*, close by to cover the gap.

On a peaceful September morning such as this, with a light rain falling over the fjord, the war seemed far away. It was hard to believe that anything could go wrong, but as Commander-in-Chief Kummetz was duty bound to consider every eventuality. The recent destruction of a network of agents in eastern Finnmark had revealed that Soviet partisans were active far behind the German lines. Towards the end of August a combat group led by *Korvettenkapitän* Claus Kühl of the *Abwehr* in Tromsø had become involved in a firefight with a Norwegian-Soviet group in hiding on the island of Arnøy in the north of the county of Troms. The leader of the group, Ingolf Aspås from Tromsø, the Russian wireless operator, Volodyna Omsk, and Aspås's girlfriend, Jørghild Rotvåg, had held two hundred German soldiers at bay for many hours. When Anton Bössler, a *Gestapo* man stationed in Tromsø, who was notorious for torturing his captives, was killed, the Germans brought in flamethrowers. None of the three in the besieged mountain cave survived, but twenty-four of their helpers were arrested and taken to a prison camp near Tromsø.

As the unequal struggle neared its end, 39-year-old Jørghild, the mother of four, had written on a scrap of paper:

We are in a terrible situation, but we are prepared for it. We know that we may die at any moment. We have knelt and prayed to the Almighty Father

for help. We all hope that Jesus will forgive us our sins and grant us eternal
life. We shall do all we can for our motherland. *Alt for Norge!* ['All for
Norway', a wartime watchword that still lives on]. Oh, how I keep thinking
of my four little ones back home, my tears are making the paper so wet that I
can hardly write. May God preserve all at home.

The trio's heroic stand and willingness to sacrifice their lives compelled
respect even from the most hardened of the German officers involved. From the
island the agents had reported on shipping movements in Lopphavet, but one of
their associates had in April been in Alta gathering information on the German
naval base there. Although in the course of the last three months the Soviet
network had been destroyed, from Varanger in the east to Tromsø in the west
the Germans had reason to fear that new groups were preparing to take its
place. Kummetz took it for granted that he would be warned if there was any
immediate danger. *Korvettenkapitän* Kühl had in civilian life been a pilot in
Bremen and had served as a U-boat officer in the First World War. Before
taking command of *Abwehrstelle* Tromsø, he had been head of the organisation's
Alta branch. Kühl was a man who could be relied upon. He knew how things
stood in the Kå fjord region and also what was at stake.

Only three days had passed since Berlin had finally called off the *Lützow*'s
long-planned sortie into the Kara Sea. Kummetz's reaction had been a strong
one. 'After the Spitsbergen operation there was reason to hope that the curse of
inactivity that had lain over the Battle Group was a thing of the past, especially
with the *Tirpitz* at the Group's disposal. With this decision that hope is
shattered,' he wrote in the war diary. Now he was under orders to despatch the
veteran pocket battleship in the opposite direction, back to the Baltic. But,
loyal officer that he was, the Admiral stifled his protests. As soon as his ride was
over, he intended to prepare the necessary papers.

*

While Kummetz was cantering towards the Mathis valley, X6 was rapidly
nearing a course which would take the submarine along the north-western shore
of the fjord. Nerves were tense. The list had markedly increased and the periscope was leaking to such an extent that it was almost useless. At a few minutes
past seven Donald Cameron had passed the empty net barrage off Auskar Point,
oblivious of the fact that X7 was caught in its steel rings 25 metres below the
surface. Lagoon-like, before him lay the fjord and, for the first time, in the

silver-grey of the morning light he could see the formidable bulk of the *Tirpitz*. It was an electrifying moment: another 2,000 metres and they would reach their target. But Cameron could see something else: a confusion of warships large and small that seemed to fill the fjord on both sides. He gave the order to dive and took his craft down to a depth of 20 metres. When he again attempted to survey the scene with the aid of his periscope, all was dark.

'Once more, the last time, Kendall dismantled the periscope. Silence reigned in "Piker". After what seemed a long ten minutes to them all, he finished the tricky operation. "Periscope depth," Cameron ordered.'

He regained his vision only just in time, as *X6* was dangerously near the *Nordmark*. The supply ship had a crew of one hundred and thirty – and her guns were manned. But no one saw the dark shadow gliding by immediately beneath her stern. Only a few minutes later Cameron was forced to make another emergency change of course to avoid collision with the moorings of *Z27*. The heavy hawsers hanging between the destroyer's bow and a buoy threatened to slice off the midget submarine's periscope. On board the little craft time had ceased to exist. They were only 500 metres from the *Tirpitz*, close to the north-western shore of the fjord. In the houses bordering the road that wound its way along the fjord, people had left their beds and smoke was rising from some of the chimneys. From the slipways and workshops lining the shore came the sound of hammering as the day's work began. The situation grew more nerve-racking with every passing moment.

'More draining of periscope, atmosphere a trifle tense, but crew behaving very well. Dicky doing his best both as helmsman and periscope brake. Brake had seized up to add to our troubles and needed kicking whenever I wanted to operate periscope. Trim-pump also showing signs of packing up.' With all the care he could muster Cameron took *X6* in the direction he believed the battleship to lie. Through the narrow ventilators he suddenly caught sight of a dark shape. Then came a horrible scraping sound.

Stopped motors and investigated. Could see the bank rising on my starboard hand and a few fish. Overhead was a black shape like a pontoon with wires hanging from it. Hadn't foggiest idea what this was, but it looked rather nasty. Did not appear to be caught up in anything, so decided to go ahead slowly. Scraping and scratching we drew clear, so stopped and trimmed up. Periscope very fogged, but could just make out dark blobs which I took to be the flotation of the A/T nets, and pushed forward towards a space in this chain.

Cameron and his crew had performed a masterly piece of navigation under extremely difficult conditions. They had made their way to the north-western part of the net enclosing the *Tirpitz*. Dead ahead lay the 15-metre-wide entrance. Now, in the very last phase of the attack, it seemed that luck was still with them. The entrance was wide open, just as it had been all night on account of the many small vessels passing to and fro between the battleship and the other ships in the fjord. Cameron didn't hesitate: he made straight for the opening. The time was 09.05 on Wednesday morning. It had taken X6 two hours to cover the distance from the mouth of the fjord to her quarry – and now they were over the last hurdle. They were inside the net barrage that from the air, and judging by the Norwegian agent's sketches, had appeared an impassable barrier. On board the little submarine the crew huddled together, hardly daring to breathe. Inside the barrage the water was a mere 30 metres deep. Dead ahead of them loomed the battleship, a mountain of steel. The deck was crowded with men, which meant that they could be discovered at any moment, but Cameron remained unperturbed. He planned to place one of the side-charges aft, beneath the rudder and exposed propellers, and to this end continued to follow the shoreline on a course more or less parallel to the battleship. He was just about to turn to port and make straight for the after end of his target when there was a sudden jolt. 'Piker' gave a great bound and, out of control, shot upwards, throwing Cameron against a bulkhead. It was some seconds before he realised what had happened. They had sailed too close to the shore and collided with a submerged rock.

*

On board the *Tirpitz*, 22-year-old Bo'sun Hans Schmidt was on watch on the upper deck. Having just finished scrubbing the teak planks aft, the men were in a cheerful mood. There had been no reports of enemy aircraft in the vicinity, so the anti-aircraft gunners were busy dismantling their weapons for lubrication and inspection. The Spitsbergen raid had been like a shot in the arm for all on board, and now there was a grapevine rumour that something even bigger was in the offing. Some of the men were said to have seen papers saying that the *Lützow* was going to Gotenhafen, and others thought the *Tirpitz* was likewise scheduled for docking. If the rumours were true, it was good news. For the first time in years everyone would be able to celebrate Christmas at home in Germany.

I was in the Watch Office on the port side aft when a seaman came bursting in. 'Bo'sun,' he cried, 'there's a U-boat inside the net.' I looked at him unbelievingly. 'That's impossible,' I said, 'it's closed. You must have seen a porpoise or something.' But he was insistent that it was a U-boat. Although still sceptical, I told him that I would have to report the observation.

By then it was 09.10. Several of the men had seen the black-painted upper hull of X6 when she broke surface a mere 20 metres from the shore, but were confused by the fact that where there would normally have been a conning tower, all that could be seen was a low platform and what looked like a few pipe ends. No one knew what to think. It had been but a momentary glimpse, then whatever it was had vanished. Men rushed to the rail, but there was nothing to be seen but an empty expanse of sea.

On a deck higher up, an anti-aircraft gunner had also seen the dark shape that had suddenly erupted from the sea like a whale surfacing to blow. But when *Leutnant-zur-See* Hein Hellendoorn trained his binoculars on the spot the gunner pointed out, 150 metres distant, there was nothing to be seen. 'You must have been mistaken,' he said. 'A U-boat can't possibly have managed to get through the net.'

In the meantime Bo'sun Schmidt had got hold of the Officer of the Watch, *Leutnant-zur-See* Alfred Walluks, the battleship's logkeeper. Walluks was reputed to be jinxed, as things so often seemed to go wrong when he was on watch. However, this time he was determined not to allow himself to be carried away. 'Don't be silly,' he said to the bo'sun, 'it must have been a turtle.'

For several precious minutes the deckhands and petty officers alternated between fear and scepticism. They were completely at a loss until the surface of the fjord was again broken – this time much closer, only 100 metres or so from the ship. Now the characteristic platform and night periscope were clearly visible. It was a submarine, but of a type none of them had seen before. Some 10 metres of the hull were visible above the surface. It looked like a giant waterpipe and was heading for a tugboat and a lighter carrying water that were moored to the forepart of the battleship. Hubbub ensued. One of those who saw the submarine and reported it was Karl Heinz Lohse, a carpenter who was on his way to his berth; another was *Leutnant* Herbert Leine, who was about to relieve Walluks.

'We were dumbfounded. No one really knew what to do. The U-boat was too near for us to bring our guns to bear, and in any case the tug and lighter were in the way. Instead, I broke out rifles and hand grenades from their lockers and began handing them to the men who were nearest,' said Bo'sun Schmidt.

The time was almost 09.20. On the bridge the ship's First Officer, *Kapitän-zur-See* Wolf Junge, had just been informed of the incident when the first alarm sounded, five piercing blasts of the siren. It was an unusual signal, one normally used only in peacetime, and meant that all watertight bulkheads were to be closed. Junge hurried to the Commander's cabin, where Meyer was still having his breakfast.

'I'm sorry to disturb you, Captain,' he said, 'but there's a report of an object inside the net. A small U-boat, they say.'

Meyer displayed no sign of emotion. All he said was: 'A small U-boat?'

'It may be a false alarm.'

'Well, if it is, it's proof that the men are keeping a good watch.'

As Meyer hurriedly put on his coat, there was a second blast of the siren. This time it was the general alarm. From the port side of the ship came the chatter of machine-pistols. There was no doubt about it: they were firing at something in the water.

Meanwhile, on deck, *Leutnant* Leine had resolutely assumed command. He jumped into one of the launches moored by the gangway, taking with him Bo'sun Schmidt and a handful of armed seamen. As they approached the submarine, which by then was right under the port bow, the men threw hand grenades and loosed off a number of rounds. But the rifle bullets had little effect, as on impact they merely glanced off the hull to fall harmlessly into the water. Schmidt was at the tiller when the launch reached the submarine. A sailor leaped on to the submarine's casing and made fast a towline. Leine ordered full speed astern with the intention of pulling the submarine away from the *Tirpitz*.

The battleship's war diary affords a vivid picture of the ensuing duel:

The U-boat has a 12-metre-or-so-long, one-metre-wide and 50-centimetre-high casing on top of the pressure hull, where are to be seen a periscope, a hatch and a glass dome of the kind fitted to aircraft. The pressure hull appears to extend for a couple of metres on both sides. The craft probably weighs some thirty to fifty tons. It is heavily loaded forward. . . . It is clear that the vents have been opened. The launch is unable to retain its hold on the submarine, which sinks after a twenty-metre tow. By then it is about fifty metres from the stem.

Just before the midget submarine sank, Leine, Schmidt and the others in the launch received another shock. 'The hatch in the monster opened. A number of bearded and weary looking men clambered out with their hands above their heads. I counted three men, plus the captain, who emerged last. It was quite something,' Schmidt recalls. Without a word, the four British sailors jumped from the submarine into the launch. Donald Cameron and his men had reached the end of their long journey.

*

The grounding half an hour earlier had been catastrophic for 'Piker'. The periscope jammed and the gyro compass was knocked out of kilter. The submarine was almost impossible to control. When Cameron had recovered from the shock he had immediately given orders to fill the tanks. 'Piker' dived slowly and stabilised at a depth of 25 metres. The men held their breath: they had broken surface and expected to come under fire at any moment. But nothing happened, and Cameron slowly began to work his way towards the battleship. He was blind and had to proceed by guesswork. What seemed endless minutes passed, then the submarine again found herself trapped – this time in a net. Cameron ordered full speed astern. They wrested themselves free, but again broke surface, to be greeted by a hail of machine-gun bullets.

'[They were] not lethal,' Cameron later wrote, 'but they made a helluva noise. Like a lone dockyard riveter. Hand grenades were also thrown down from the deck high above but thanks to the overhang, most of them plopped harmlessly into the water and exploded well out of effective range.'

He and his crew had achieved their object: their penetration of the net had come as a complete surprise to the men of the *Tirpitz*. But now they had been seen, and with their craft damaged they had no chance of escape. There was nothing more they could do: the time had come to leave the submarine. With no little coolness, Cameron backed his craft up against the bow of the German battleship and gave the order to release the charges. 'Piker' gave a lurch when the side-charges were freed and slid down into the mud beneath the stem of the *Tirpitz*. With a hammer Cameron then smashed the most sensitive instruments. He opened the hatch and looked about him. Only a few metres away, the battleship's hull reared above him like a steel wall. From the nearby launch came the sound of guttural shouting. The vents were opened and the submarine quickly filled with water. One by one the men climbed out until they were all on the casing with their hands up. From there it was only a step or two into the launch.

'[W]e were very sorry to see X6 go,' wrote John Lorimer. 'It was like parting from an old and very dear friend.' As skipper, Cameron came last, the water by then having risen to the top of his boots. "I forgot my pipe and baccy," he said.'

*

On board the *Tirpitz* confusion reigned. On the bridge, Captain Hans Meyer and First Officer Wolf Junge were at a loss. 'We were taken completely by surprise and had no idea of what to expect. We feared that an attack was imminent employing torpedoes, conventional mines and limpet mines,' Junge later explained.

The ship's Intelligence Officer, *Korvettenkapitän* Rolf Woytschekowsky-Emden, was despatched to the upper deck to interrogate the four prisoners. He spoke reasonably good English, but Cameron and his three companions refused to provide any information other than rank, name and number. However, Emden noticed that Cameron kept looking at his watch, as though expecting something out of the ordinary to happen.

'From the prisoners' attitude it appears that the U-boat has already done what it came to do. For this reason steps are being taken to inspect the hull, at the same time as the ship is being readied for sea with the utmost despatch. The netted enclosure is to be vacated before any time bombs explode,' read the war diary.

One of the divers called upon was Lohse's friend from the Carpenters' Shop, 21-year-old Ordinary Seaman Helmut Simon from Lindau in Bavaria. He had volunteered for service with the *Kriegsmarine* and had trained as a diver in Wilhelmshaven: 'It created quite a stir when we were ordered to muster at the Diving Station. No one knew what we were going to do, but we put on our diving suits, boots and helmets as quickly as we could and made our way to the gangway. While compressors and hoses were being made ready, a pal of mine and I were embarked in a light boat. Fully equipped, there we remained, waiting.'

In the boiler rooms in the bowels of the *Tirpitz*, sweat was pouring off Werner Brand and the other engine-room staff as they strained to raise pressure in the twelve steam boilers that powered the battleship's three turbines. The turbines delivered a total of 150,000 horsepower to the propeller shafts, giving the giant a maximum speed of 30 knots. 'Most of the boilers had been extinguished on our return from Spitsbergen. The machinery was extremely complicated. Time would be needed before we could get under way,' says Brand.

In the Admiral's quarters all work on plans for the *Lützow*'s transfer had come to a halt. Kummetz, who had broken off his ride when the alarm sounded, had just returned to the ship and was still wearing his riding breeches. According to Able Seaman Max Krause, 'A petty officer came running in, shouting that a submarine had been sighted. "Pipe down, it's only an exercise," he was told. "Oh no, it's not," he replied, "I've just seen the thing about 13 yards off the port bow. They were throwing hand grenades at it."'

Another rating came rushing in. 'Have you ever seen an Englishman?' he asked, 'because there are four standing outside the Regulating Office at the moment.'

Krause bounded up the companionway and found Cameron and his three companions under guard on the main deck. According to his later statement the prisoners were quite calm. The only thing he noticed about them was that they kept looking at their watches, as if they were expecting something to happen.

At 09.36 the watertight bulkheads were closed and within a few minutes all hands were at action stations. Meanwhile, Meyer had hurriedly drafted an urgent signal for the Naval High Command in Berlin with copies to the admirals in Kiel, Narvik and Tromsø. 'EMERGENCY EMERGENCY MIDGET UBOAT DESTROYED 09.30 INSIDE THE NET SURROUNDING TIRPITZ. FOUR BRITISH TAKEN PRISONER. MORE [INFO] TO FOLLOW.'

While Meyer and Junge on the bridge impatiently awaited news from the engine-room that the ship was ready to sail, the situation took an unexpected turn. The time was 09.40 when there was a cry from the foredeck. Another midget submarine had been spotted 100 metres ahead of the *Tirpitz*, just outside the barrage.

*

When, shortly after 07.00, *X6* passed the empty netted enclosure where the *Scharnhorst* was usually berthed off Auskar Point, Godfrey Place on board *X7* was engaged in a desperate struggle to free his craft from the steel rings 25 metres below the surface of the sea. He finally succeeded in escaping their clutches and continued deeper into the fjord to where the *Tirpitz* lay – probably no more than a couple of hundred metres astern of his companion submarine.

Two hours later, not long after Cameron had run aground and for the first time been observed by the German lookouts, Place too had reached the barrier surrounding the battleship. At 09.10 he set the time fuses on both side-charges to go off after an hour and took the submarine down to a depth of 25 metres. Shortly afterwards he again found himself entangled in a net. He blew his tanks and ordered full speed astern. *X7* managed to extricate herself, but broke surface and remained lying beam-on to the buoys.

Without hesitation, Place again dived. He was afraid of getting the stern of his craft caught, as, because of the rudder and screw, it was very vulnerable there. At a depth of a little more than 30 metres he again found himself stuck, and it took him a good five minutes of violent manoeuvring before X7 wrenched free. The compass needle swung wildly to and fro and he had no idea of how close to the shore he was.

'By some extraordinary lucky chance we must have either slipped through the boat passage or, less likely, through a gap where the anti-torpedo nets did not overlap, for on breaking surface the *Tirpitz* with no intervening nets was sighted right ahead not more than 30 yds away.'

By this time the main deck of the *Tirpitz* was in an uproar. Rifles and hand grenades were handed out and the barrels of the ship's light and medium guns depressed to their maximum. All attention was riveted on X6, which was closing the *Tirpitz* from a position diagonal to the bow. By a miracle, no one noticed X7, which at that very moment was approaching the battleship from ahead, some degrees off her port bow. The midget submarine was only 10 metres below the surface when Place ordered full ahead and ran his craft right in under the armoured hull below 'B' turret.

'We struck the *Tirpitz* at 20 feet on the port side approximately below B turret, and slid gently under the keel, where the starboard charge was released in full shadow of the ship.'

When the port charge was released 60 to 70 metres further astern, Place heard explosions nearby. The time was 09.22. They were the first hand grenades hurled at X6 from a distance of some 30 to 40 metres. The next half-hour was a nightmare for Place and his men. On their way out they again became caught in the net on the starboard side of the *Tirpitz*.

Without his compass, Place had no idea of where they were. What is more, the repeated trimming of the submarine and the struggle to extricate her from the net had used up most of the air: 'At sixty feet we were in the net again. . . . Of the three air bottles two had been used and only 1,200 lb. were left in the third. X7's charges were due to explode in an hour – not to mention others which might go up any time after 08.00 [10.00 local time].'

At the last minute, with hardly any air left, Place and his crew unexpectedly benefited from what seemed a second miracle, as the submarine suddenly slipped between the rusty buoys and across the net. The time was 09.40. In the control room Place heard a fusillade of bullets hammering the hull. Without stopping to check if the hull had been damaged, he opened the valves and allowed the submarine to sink to the bottom, 40 metres below the surface.

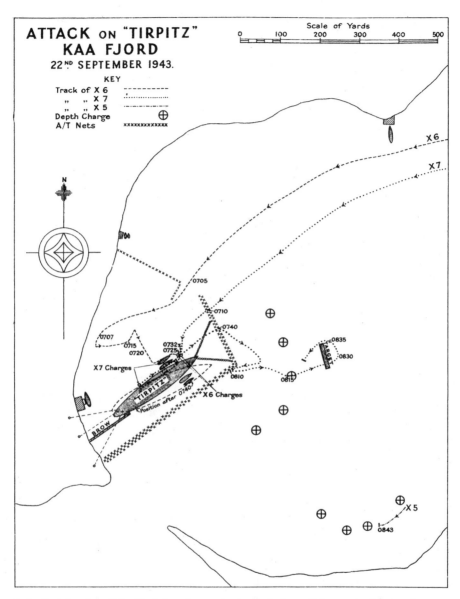

**ATTACK ON "TIRPITZ"
KAA FJORD**
22ND SEPTEMBER 1943.

KEY
Track of X 6   ----------
  "   "   X 7   ················
  "   "   X 5   —·—·—·—·—
Depth Charge   ⊕
A/T Nets   xxxxxxxxxxxx

Scale of Yards
0   100   200   300   400   500

A detailed drawing of the *Tirpitz*'s anchorage in the final phase of the attack, showing the routes assumed to have been taken by *X6* and *X7*. The first midget submarine, *X6*, laid charges to port of the battleship's bow and was then scuttled. At about the same time the other, *X7*, laid its two charges beneath the battleship's keel. When they exploded, *X7* was hurled over the anti-torpedo net and sank near a target raft (marked TARGET on the diagram). A few minutes later *X5* was sighted some 700 metres to starboard of the *Tirpitz* and came under heavy fire, before being attacked by a launch from the destroyer *Z29*, which dropped five depth charges.

In the fire-control centre the moment had come that *Leutnant-zur-See* Hellendoorn had so eagerly been awaiting. The moment X7 was spotted, he ordered all the guns that could be brought to bear to let fly with all they had. 'The U-boat was visible for only an instant. The range was short, barely a hundred metres. But our 20mm and 37mm guns got off several rounds,' Hellendoorn says.

On the bridge Meyer and Junge immediately grasped the danger they were in:

As there's at least one more U-boat outside the net, there can be no question of leaving the enclosure. We must now assume that explosive charges may detonate at any time close to the sunken U-boat. The bow must therefore be turned as far as possible away from where it [the U-boat] went down. Orders are given to slacken the chain on the port side and tighten that on the starboard side.

On board the other ships in the fjord it was generally realised that something extraordinary was afoot on board the flagship. *Korvettenkapitän* Günther Schultz on *Z27*, which was moored on the north-western side of the fjord, had heard the firing, but it was not until 09.43 that he managed to read the first, vague signal sent by flag from the *Tirpitz*: 'UBOAT AHEAD'. The alarm was sounded when the Morse signal U-U-U was flashed across by lamp and Schultz understood that the situation could be serious. On board the *Erich Steinbrink*, which had arrived from Bukta that same morning, the alarm sounded at almost the same time. But although *Fregattenkapitän* Teichmann had lain to beside the *Nordmark* at 09.27, it took half an hour for the destroyer to move clear.

'They're firing from the *Tirpitz*. A just about recognisable part of a U-boat shows above water, but immediately disappears.'

Repair work on board Flotilla Commander Rolf Johannesson's flagship, *Z29*, had still not been completed and it would take time before the destroyer could cast off from the *Neumark*. But that same morning the launch was on its way to the *Tirpitz* on a routine errand under the command of the destroyer's torpedo officer, *Leutnant-zur-See* Eberhard Schmölder. As it neared the net surrounding the battleship, Schmölder found himself centre stage.

'As I approached the *Tirpitz* I saw that they were firing their secondary guns at a target to starboard. I reported to *Korvettenkapitän* Schlüter, who immediately ordered me to turn about and fetch depth charges from *Z30*, which was the ship nearest to where we were,' Schmölder wrote in his report the following day.

The only ship in the fjord that was not a part of the 1st Battle Group was the cargo vessel *Stamsund*, which lay at anchor only 350 metres from the *Tirpitz*. A newly built 1,400-tonner, she was owned by a Norwegian company, but had been commandeered by the Germans shortly after the invasion. Now the *Stamsund* was sailing under charter for the *Kriegsmarine* between Oslo and Kirkenes. She was carrying an assorted cargo of motor transport and the day before, despite the protests of her captain, Sven Hertzberg, had been sent to the Kå fjord for unloading.

> Not long after breakfast, about nine o'clock it would be, I was on deck when I saw people crowding to the rail on board the *Tirpitz*. Suddenly every available gun opened fire against something inside the net. The alarm was given by flags and sirens. The firing ceased after a time, only to be redirected at a target just outside the net. I saw several small submarines surfacing here and there. One of them passed so close to us that we could estimate its length at about ten metres.

By this time several destroyers had got up steam and begun slowly to make their way towards the head of the fjord with their hydrophones in operation. But Meyer refused to allow any of them to come closer to the *Tirpitz* than 1,000 metres, as he had no wish to expose them to danger unnecessarily. Nor did he want them to get in the way of the battleship's own guns. A duel of sorts was in progress between the *Tirpitz* and the midget submarines, an unknown number of which were outside the net. That battle he intended to fight alone – until the launches were ready with their depth charges.

On the bridge the seconds ticked slowly by. At 10.03 the engine-room reported that they had the burners going under four of the ship's twelve boilers. The bow had in the meantime been swung some 60 metres to the south-east by alternately slackening off and hauling in the moorings. Meyer was still hesitant. He was waiting for information from the prisoners, who were being subjected to intense interrogation.

Korvettenkapitän Woytschekowsky-Emden had, however, made no progress at all, except to assure himself that the men were British, not Russian. He prepared to change his tactics. While Kendall and Goddard were placed under guard in a passageway near 'X' turret, Cameron and Lorimer were taken to an office. Says Lorimer:

> The Germans behaved correctly, but the situation began to get very unpleasant. They were very much on edge and some of the guards were very threatening. We were seated on chairs before the officer conducting the

interrogation. The charges could go off at any moment. We hadn't told them anything, but we had protested when the Germans wanted to send down divers. We tried to convince them that it was pointless.

The Intelligence Officer opened with a strangely formulated question, asking: 'You was born, was you?'

'It was a peculiar question, but I took it that he wanted to know when I was born. I was just about to answer when the charges went off. I felt as though I'd been kicked by a horse. We were all thrown out of our chairs and slammed against the bulkhead.'

Waiting in the corridor outside, Robert Kendall was suddenly brought to his knees.

My knees buckled as the explosion hurled the ship out of the water. Complete darkness in the alley as all the lights shattered. Fire-sprinklers showered foam on us, I was grabbed by the guard and pushed through the door into the bright sunlight. What a change in those few moments! The ship started to list rapidly to port. Steam gushed from broken pipes. Seamen ran in all directions. Oil flowed from the shattered hull covering the water of the fjord. Injured men were being brought up on deck. Bursts of machine-gun fire were interspersed with the loud crashes of the secondary armament firing wildly. It was impossible to take it all in. All around was confusion.

In the Admiral's quarters, Max Krause fumbled for a flashlight. He was convinced that the *Tirpitz* was sinking and wanted to collect some of his belongings.

[T]here was an exceptionally heavy explosion. The whole great ship heaved several feet out of the water and bounced down again with a slight list.

All the electric lights went out immediately. Doors jammed, gear of all sorts fell all over the place. Fire extinguishers fell from the bulkheads and started belching foam. The officers' quarters[,] in which there were a number of fire extinguishers, were lathered in what looked like beaten white of egg. Glass from broken mirrors and scuttles was everywhere.

Ratings who had been standing up were flung off their feet and fell as often as not on their faces on the deck. The whole ship was in an uproar. Men rushed about with blood streaming from surface cuts, not knowing what had happened or what to do.

On board the launch by the gangway Helmut Simon and his friend were still awaiting orders when, without warning, the sea about them gave a tremendous heave. 'To this day I don't know what happened,' he says. 'Everything went dark. When I came to, we were floating in a battered boat on the fjord. My friend was unconscious and lying half underwater. I pulled him towards me and signalled for help.'

In the engine-room, where Werner Brand and the rest of the staff were watching the needles of the pressure gauges climb slowly upwards, the explosion had a disastrous effect.

'The burners under the boilers suddenly went out. The metal grilles on the floor were slung up to the roof. It was pitch dark. Water and oil came pouring in. It's a wonder that more people weren't injured.'

The visible effects of the explosion were less than most people had expected. *Korvettenkapitän* Schultz had his binoculars trained on the *Tirpitz* when the charges went off. 'A heavy explosion occurs on the port side of the *Tirpitz*, creating heavy waves. They broke several times on the shore. I sincerely hope that the explosion was caused by the depth charges thrown into the net barrage from the launches. From our position the *Tirpitz* does not appear to have suffered much damage,' he wrote in the war diary.

*

For X7, which again found itself caught in the net 100 metres from the *Tirpitz*, the explosion struck like a shock wave. 'This shook us out of our net, and when we surfaced it was tiresome to see the *Tirpitz* still afloat. This made me uncertain whether the explosion we had just heard was our own charges or depth-charges, so X7 was taken to the bottom.'

But when X7 surfaced outside the barrage a few minutes later, discipline on board the *Tirpitz* had been restored. Her gunners were all at their stations and the little craft was peppered with gunfire. Water poured in from holes in the hull and the submarine sank ever deeper. 'We can't go on,' said Place. 'Stand by to abandon ship.'

As X7 was subjected to intensive fire whenever the casing showed above water, Place decided that he should be the first to chance his luck. He opened the hatch and climbed out, waving a white sweater. Moored right in front of him was a raft that was used for gunnery practice. That would be their salvation – provided he could survive long enough to get himself and his crew on to it. But X7 was still moving forward. Realising that the submarine would slide under the raft and plunge to the bottom unless he did something, just before leaping on to the raft, Place took a desperate decision: he turned and kicked the hatch shut.

'X7 had so little buoyancy that she was forced under the target raft. I didn't realise what was about to happen. I was right behind him and tried to push open the hatch. A trickle of water came in. X7 lost what little buoyancy was left and sank to the bottom. The hatch-cover was forced tightly shut by the pressure of the water and with the help of Godfrey's foot,' recalls Robert Aitken.

The *Tirpitz* was still firing and two motor-boats were rapidly approaching. They were the launches from *Z27* and *Z29*, each of which was armed with ten depth charges.

'I was halfway back to the *Tirpitz* when I saw the submarine surface near the raft. The conning-tower hatch opened and an arm waved a white cloth. Shortly afterwards a man in a white shirt and white socks climbed on to the raft. The U-boat was still under way and glided under the raft and disappeared. When another motor-boat approached the raft from the opposite direction and opened up with a machine-pistol, I had to turn away,' Schmölder wrote in his report.

The unfolding drama had been closely followed by the men of the *Stamsund*, where the situation was chaotic. The freighter was right in the firing-line and richochets criss-crossed her deck. One man was mortally wounded, but despite numerous appeals it proved impossible to get hold of a doctor. The *Stamsund* had to warp to the *Nordmark* to get help. 'It was a miracle that the *Stamsund* wasn't sunk and that only one person was seriously wounded,' said the steward, Leif Remme, in a statement he made later.

Midway between the *Stamsund* and *Tirpitz* there was a target raft. Between each salvo we crept out to see what had happened. I saw clouds of spray, and a man climb on to the raft. He immediately came under a hail of fire, but wasn't hit. When the firing stopped he lit a cigarette and started to pace backwards and forwards on the raft. A motor-boat came and took him off.

*

The time was approaching 10.20. On the bridge of the battleship Captain Meyer had been badly shaken and First Officer Wolf Junge, battered and bleeding after a bad fall, had to be taken to the sickbay. The situation was utterly chaotic. The ship was listing to port and a patch of oil was streaming with the current towards the mouth of the fjord. The deck was strewn with broken glass and all electrical and optical instruments appeared to have been put out of action by the violence of the explosion. The ship was in darkness. Damage reports poured in. In a moment of aberration Meyer, normally so calm and collected, ordered the prisoners to be shot. 'Someone pointed out to him that they were soldiers who had merely done their duty. That persuaded him to change his mind,' said Krause.

In the darkened engine-room, deep beneath the bridge, the staff were struggling to plug the leaks. An 8-metre-long gash had appeared in the bottom of the hull under Section 8 aft. Water was flooding into the compartments that housed the diesel-powered generators, which was why the electricity had failed. Things looked bad for a time, but the men knew their jobs and the damaged compartments were soon sealed off. After only half an hour, two of them had been pumped dry. The ship was out of danger. The other and less visible damage was worse. The close on 1,100-ton main gun turrets rested on enormous bearings. They had been lifted up and thrown out of kilter, as had the turbines and propeller shafts. The *Tirpitz* was still afloat, but she was incapable of moving under her own steam. Viewed from without, the damage seemed slight, but in reality it was a near-mortal wound. The midget submarines' attack had transformed the giant into a cripple.

*

The mood on the upper deck was an angry one. No fewer than sixty-eight men had been wounded in the attack; seven of them had suffered severe head wounds. One man had been killed; knocked overboard by a recoiling gun, he had died in the sea. The Germans were enraged with their prisoners, who had now been joined by Godfrey Place. The captives were roughly pushed about and threats were hurled at them. The most aggressive of the sailors even released the safety catches on their guns.

Under such pressure, one or two of the prisoners loosened up a little and began to talk. After all, the charges had gone off, so there was no longer the same need for them to remain silent. At 10.32 *Korvettenkapitän* Woytschekowsky-Emden reported that the first submarine had laid two charges, both of which, in the prisoners' opinion, had exploded. Three minutes later he reported that three midget submarines had taken part in the attack. Meyer's response was immediate. Only two had been accounted for, so where was the third?

The answer came a few moments later. At 10.43 the third submarine was seen on the surface 700 metres north-east of the *Tirpitz*. The battleship's light and medium batteries immediately opened fire.

'I saw the spray thrown up as the shells hit the water around the craft heading towards us. It could only be one boat, *X5* with Henty-Creer and his crew. I prayed that they wouldn't be hit, but my prayer wasn't answered. I could actually see the shells striking home. So could the Germans. They cheered every hit,' John Lorimer recalls.

'It was a nasty few minutes,' says Richard Kendall. 'They didn't have a chance against those medium guns. It was with a heavy heart that I saw the submarine vanish among the spouts of water.' The nearest eye-witnesses were Eberhard Schmölder and the four seamen he had chosen to accompany him in *Z29*'s launch.

At about eleven o'clock the *Tirpitz* again opened fire, to starboard. There I saw a third U-boat break the surface. I couldn't see in which direction it was heading, or whether it was hit, as it was obscured by spray and the spouts of water thrown up by the shells. When it disappeared, firing ceased. I immediately made for the last place I'd seen it. At 30-metre intervals I dropped five depth charges around the spot where it had disappeared. The last but one left on the surface an extra-strong eddy mixed with black bubbles of oil. Afterwards more oil rose to the surface and spread to form a large patch on the sea. The submarine had most certainly been badly damaged and put out of action.

*

In the meantime, the three men still on board *X7* were undergoing a further trial 40 metres beneath the target raft. The submarine had come safely to rest on the bottom and was still more or less undamaged. Robert Aitken, Bill Whittam and William Whitley were all unhurt, but time was running out. Before they could open the hatch and make their way to the surface in their survival suits, the pressure inside the hull had to be equalised with that of the water outside. That meant that they would have to wait until the submarine was full of water. The vents were opened, but water came in with agonising slowness. Meanwhile the air grew ever fouler as the remaining oxygen was gradually used up. Aitken gave a graphic account of the course of events.

It [the water] was reaching to our knees, and it was icy. We tried to open three other vents, but they were blocked or stuck, somehow. There was nothing to be done. We waited like this – for half an hour. The water, or ice rather, was up to our thighs. We could still only wait. It reached an electrical circuit, the fuse-wires exploded. . . . Smoke, gas from the batteries, all the rest of it, you can imagine. From then on we were forced to start breathing our escape-oxygen. And it was utter darkness: 120 feet down, a coffin.

The three stayed put for a further hour. By then the water was up to their chests and they were numb with cold. Aitken made another vain attempt to prise open the hatch, but it refused to budge. When he rejoined his companions, he found them unconscious. Their emergency supplies of oxygen had run out. He opened his own emergency bottle and crept back into the W&D compartment. 'I remember scrambling back into the escape compartment for one more go at the hatch. Then things went black, and I must have fainted. But I suppose I must have somehow got the hatch open at last – and when my eyes opened I saw a stream of oxygen bubbles all round me as I sped up to the surface.'

At 13.25 Aitken was taken off the raft, the last of the submarines' crews to be rescued. Two hours and forty-five minutes had elapsed since X7 had sunk. He was taken on board the *Tirpitz* just as Captain Meyer was giving Admiral Kummetz and Operations Officer Hansjürgen Reinicke his first verbal report on the state of the battleship. By that time one of the wireless stations was back on the air and at 13.48 Kummetz transmitted his first damage report to his superiors in Kiel.

1. Not one, but two explosions fore and aft almost simultaneously.
2. The ship's fighting capability has been severely impaired as a result of the exploding mines.

This was an understatement, to say the least. His ship's ability to fight had been more than severely impaired. In the event, the *Tirpitz* was out of action for the next six months.

PART III

CHAPTER THIRTEEN

After the Attack

THE KÅ FJORD, 22 SEPTEMBER 1943 TO 15 MARCH 1944

It was 10.00 on Wednesday 15 March. The mountainsides were still metre-deep in snow, but the sun was again in the ascendant, climbing higher with every day that passed. Spring was fast approaching. For the first time since the surprise attack by midget submarines the *Tirpitz* was leaving her anchorage under her own power. It was an emotional experience for all who witnessed it. Earlier that morning two tugs, the *Arngast* and *Bardenfleth*, had dragged aside the heavy anti-torpedo net that had for so long protected her. Oily black smoke rose from the funnel. The bronze propellers churned up the mud in which, only six months earlier, those deadly amatol-packed charges had been embedded. The armour-plated hull shuddered under the pressure exerted by the ship's twelve boilers. On the bridge, *Kapitän-zur-See* Hans Meyer stood seemingly unaffected as the giant battleship glided past Auskar Point. Gradually it picked up speed as it headed for the mouth of the fjord and the open sea beyond. Unlike their captain, other watchers were unable to hold back their tears.

'Everyone was deeply moved to see the ship slowly pull away from her anchorage. Once again her bow cleft the waves, while the men of the repair ships and destroyers round about paid homage. The *Tirpitz* had been restored to life.'

In the boiler rooms, far below the waterline, the temperature was nearly 40°C. Werner Brand and his fellow artificers wore tight-fitting leather trousers and jackets to protect them from scalding steam, should a pipe burst. Though soaked in sweat, no one uttered a word of complaint. The explosion in September had snapped stays and inch-thick steel bolts. Most of the engines had been wrenched from their beds, and in the turbines, rotor blades were twisted and bent. Bearings had suffered severe damage and the propeller shafts had jammed. It had been a terrible time all round. Trapped within her defence nets, the *Tirpitz* was immobilised, a sitting duck. But now the main engine was to be put to the test. The nerves of all concerned were taut as they waited to see if the ship would withstand the resultant vibration. On the bridge, Meyer's eyes were glued to the speed indicator. If it proved impossible to extract full power from the turbines, the *Tirpitz* would never again be battleworthy. The pride of the *Kriegsmarine* would be of as little worth as a heap of scrap metal. A few happy smiles made their appearance when the speed reached 20 knots; a little later the needle crept up to 27 knots. That was 3 knots short of the battleship's top speed before the attack, but it was enough. The *Tirpitz* was again ready to take on all comers. Meyer gave the order to reduce speed. His face was inscrutable, but he was satisfied. Difficult though they were, the repairs had been carried out to perfection – and that in a thinly populated area devoid of engineering shops, floating docks and the requisite materials. The men responsible had every reason to be proud of their handiwork.

The captain would not have been quite so pleased had he been aware of the signal that was hurriedly despatched to London from a clandestine wireless transmitter, codenamed Ida, operating from Alta. '*Tirpitz* left Kaafjord at her usual speed. I heard violent gunfire in the fjord at 1600 GMT. Her net is open. The net at Auskarnes is now closed. "Stand by" for goodness sake.'

Later that same day the decrypted message was read with great interest at the Admiralty, where there was no intention of leaving the *Tirpitz* in peace.

*

The immediate crisis had passed when, at 13.25 on Wednesday 22 September, just about dead on his feet, Robert Aitken was picked up beside the target raft and taken aboard the *Tirpitz*. To be on the safe side, the launches from Z27 and Z29 had dropped two extra depth charges, causing large quantities of oil to rise to the surface and spread out across the fjord.

'There was no doubt that the submarine had been destroyed. After ten to fifteen minutes the first pieces of wreckage came floating up: tinned food, first-aid kits, what was left of a rubber suit, toilet paper and bits of wood,' wrote *Leutnant-zur-See* Schmölder in his report. The prisoners had told *Korvettenkapitän* Woytschekowsky-Emden that three midget submarines had taken part in the attack. All three had been destroyed – but were the prisoners telling the truth? On board the battleship the atmosphere remained tense. Godfrey Place claimed that X7 had released her charges *outside* the nets, in which case they had not yet exploded. He had also explained that the range of timer settings was very wide and that the delay could be anything from half an hour to twenty-four hours. But the British submariners were hardened, well-trained men, so too much reliance could not be placed on what they said. There might well still be undetonated mines on the seabed. Meyer was far from easy in his mind. He ordered the crews of the destroyers conducting a hydrophone search among the supply ships to be very much on the alert.

The violent explosion that had occurred some three or more hours earlier had silenced the battleship's wireless transmitters, as there was no electricity to power them. When the mast snapped and tumbled to the deck, it had taken with it the aerials. The first reports of the incident had thus to be signalled by lamp to the destroyers *Z27* and *Erich Steinbrink*. The *Stamsund*, which had sustained serious damage, was hounded out of the fjord and the *Lützow* was ordered to release the *Watt*, which provided it with power. Moreover, the *Scharnhorst* was refused permission to return to its net enclosure off Auskar Point, as a hydrophone had detected suspicious scraping noises close to the anchorage; instead, it was instructed to keep moving and not to anchor at any cost.

At a quarter past twelve the first of the wireless rooms was back in operation, enabling Meyer to re-establish communication with the admirals in Narvik and Kiel, who were eagerly awaiting news from the Kå fjord.

The first report of the damage made dismal reading. All three turbines were unserviceable. Only one of the ship's eight generators was working. Two of the four 38cm batteries were out of action. Fire-control rooms, optical rangefinders and radar installations were likewise unfit for use. One of the two rudders was damaged. Some 800 tons of water had penetrated the compartments in the double bottom and some of the engine-rooms were flooded. The one bright spot was that the leaks were under control, so there was no longer any danger of the ship sinking at her moorings. 'Everywhere, apparatus is out of action because there is no electricity and pipes, cables, bolts and screws are broken.'

Meanwhile, *Admiral* Oskar Kummetz had taken draconian measures to ensure that news of the attack did not leak out. Total secrecy was imposed on every vessel in the Battle Group and the fjord was cordoned off. Norwegians were not allowed to use the roads, and in the fjord the net barrages were closed and shipping movements banned. 'These directives will cause untold difficulties for traffic between the units of the Group. They are, however, essential to safeguard the base pending permanent measures,' he wrote.

But Kummetz saw no reason to retain his captives any longer. 'I have asked *Admiral Polarküste* [Admiral Polar Coast] to arrange for the prisoners to be collected, as they can no longer remain on board and the regiment in Alta has no facilities for keeping them isolated.'

Later that afternoon the first reinforcements arrived: four submarine chasers set about searching for any submarines that might be lying low in Stjern Sound. And a Blohm & Voss BV 138 flying-boat took off from Skattøra in Tromsø to search the sea off Sørøy Island.

*

All this time *X10* was still lying quietly on the bottom at a depth of 65 metres off the island of Tømmerholmen, while her commander, Lieutenant Ken Hudspeth, decided what to do. The submarine was still blind. He and his men had heard the charges go off at 10.12 and the reverberations of the depth charges that followed. They knew then that the element of surprise had been lost. To attempt an attack with their craft in the state it was would be suicidal.

'Conditions were such as to make it imperative to stay on the bottom, so that's what we did all day. I think we were all feeling a bit churned-up inside. We were glad about the bangs, but sorry they weren't ours. We were pleased that we didn't have to take our wreck of a boat into Kaafjord, but sad that we'd had such an appalling run of bad luck,' said Geoff Harding, who had just celebrated his nineteenth birthday and was the youngest member of the midget-submarine crews.

When the air on board became so foul as to be unbearable, Hudspeth surfaced and made for Stjern Sound at full speed. By this time it was 18.00 and darkness had fallen. He was hoping to make it to one of the parent submarines waiting out at sea. En route, both side-charges, which were flooded and proving a drag, were dropped.

'We went flat out down Altenfjord with the skipper on deck. We dived once or twice under patrol boats, and at these times Ken would come below caked solid with ice and refusing all offers to take over from him up top, when we surfaced again. He had to "con" us all the way out on the surface, as we had no compass.'

Following a day spent in the Smal fjord, *X10* successfully negotiated the minefields barring the way to the ocean and set a course for one of the agreed pick-up points. There Hudspeth waited for five long days – in vain. 'The days were the longest I have ever known. None of us seemed particularly worried though and we spent the time making ever more far-fetched plans for escape routes, should no-one ever turn up to claim us.'

After a night in a lonely bay beneath a rock formation known locally as the 'Lump of Steel', Hudspeth sailed to another rendezvous outside the mouth of the Øy fjord. There, at 01.00 on Tuesday 28 September, he and his crew were found by the *Stubborn*. A week later they were back in England.

On hearing Hudspeth's account of *X10*'s ill-starred voyage, Rear-Admiral Barry upheld her commander's decision to call off the attack. 'I consider Lt. Hudspeth's decision to abandon the attack was in every way correct. To have made the attempt without a compass and with an immobile periscope would have made any chance of success remote indeed. It would have been doomed to failure from the outset and would merely have been an unnecessary loss of valuable lives.'

*

Shortly after Hudspeth had begun to make his way back out through Stjern Sound, four of the German destroyers were ordered to escort the *Lützow* to Germany at 20.00 the following evening.

'This is welcome news on what has otherwise been a black day,' wrote *Korvettenkapitän* Günther Schultz in *Z27*'s war diary. 'At the hands of the British, using only a few men, contemptuous of death, and unconventional means we have suffered a particularly galling setback. . . . Like Günther Prien's penetration of Scapa Flow and all other intrepid achievements, this attack proves that boldness and determined exploitation of the element of surprise nearly always yield outstanding results.'

Admiral Kummetz had nothing but praise for the men of the *Tirpitz*:

I have myself witnessed, time after time, the men's alertness and quick response when the alarm sounds. . . . *Leutnant-zur-See* Leine's resolute action deserves special recognition. His grapple with the U-boat using hand grenades and his attempt to tow it away undoubtedly helped to ensure that the mine was not laid where the enemy intended it to be, beneath the battleship's bow. . . . I fully concur in the officers' conduct before and after the explosion. The giving of orders and reporting were characterised by calmness and assurance, despite massive technical failures, especially of the power supply. The same was the case when U-boats nos two and three were continually fired at by all available anti-aircraft guns.

The attack necessitated immediate reassessment of the plan to return the *Tirpitz* to Germany for docking. The battleship was no longer seaworthy, and in Berlin *Grossadmiral* Dönitz had his doubts about the wisdom of moving it to a yard in the Baltic. In the war at sea, priority was given to U-boats, and it was in the Baltic that new crews were trained. The presence of the *Tirpitz* would encourage the Royal Air Force to attack her with long-range bombers, and that would indirectly affect the U-boat arm. The bold decision was therefore taken to repair the ship on the spot, in the Kå fjord.

Early in October a party of specialists from the naval dockyard in Wilhelmshafen, Brown Boveri, Carl Zeiss and other relevant companies was flown to Alta. Under the code name *Kommission Paul*, the men were given a week to decide whether the *Tirpitz* could be repaired and, if it could, what would be needed to do so. The commission members were dubious about the possibility when they learned of what had happened.

'To eyewitnesses on the shore it looked as though the hull was blown several metres upwards in a jolting movement. Both ends of the ship and the mast were set *swaying* at a high frequency. Most of the movable parts were badly shaken and rendered unserviceable,' said one report. The bottom plating bulged over a length of 35 metres, but the hull itself proved highly resistant, though a few welded joins were ripped apart. The problem was that the leaks were difficult to get at, deep down as they were beneath the flat bottom. It would have been a simple matter to repair them in dry dock, but now the work would have to be performed underwater. That meant that watertight coffer dams would have to be constructed and positioned over the holes. The divers and welders would have an unenviable job. The Commission calculated that it would be several months before the ship would again be ready for sea, and that was on the assumption that sufficient numbers of workmen, raw materials and repair facilities – including a 100-ton floating crane – could be made available.

While the already hard-pressed shipyards in Germany were being readied for the task, on board the disabled ship tension had begun to relax. Everyone was granted Christmas leave, one-third of the ship's complement at a time. The first batch of 600 left on 1 November. The officer commanding the *Scharnhorst*, *Kapitän-zur-See* Friedrich Hüffmaier, had already returned home, to be replaced in October by *Kapitän-zur-See* Fritz Hintze. On 9 November Kummetz handed over command to *Konter-Admiral* Erich Bey, who made no attempt to hide his dissatisfaction with the posting, which he regarded as a step down.

'I have several times sailed with *Konter-Admiral* Bey,' wrote *Kapitän-zur-See* Rolf Johannesson, Commander of the 4th Destroyer Flotilla. 'It was sad to see the change in him. He was embittered.'

At last, on the morning of 28 November, the 24,000-ton one-time luxury liner *Monte Rosa* and a cargo ship, the *Pernambuco*, steamed into the Kå fjord, where two repair ships, the *Neumark* and *Huascaren*, were already in place. The *Monte Rosa* brought with her 700 skilled workmen, while the *Pernambuco* was heavily laden with steel plating, tools and spare parts.

Bey immediately found himself faced with an unforeseen problem. 'The man in charge of the shipyard workers says that it will not be possible to get the *Tirpitz* ready for sea in the time stipulated if the *Monte Rosa* remains anchored in Kvenvik. It is intended that the 700 workmen shall take their four meals a day on board her. As it will take an hour to reach the ship and another hour to get back, it will be impossible to finish the job in time.'

The Admiral knew he had no time to lose. The *Tirpitz* was due to make her first trial voyage on 15 March, a mere fifteen weeks away. He solved the problem by moving the *Monte Rosa* to a berth off Straumnes Point, only 200 metres or so from the battleship. Wooden walkways were then laid across the intervening narrow strip of land, enabling the workmen to pass freely to and fro between the two ships. 'Today, almost ten weeks since the battleship was damaged, repair work can finally begin. That shows how much time is needed to repair damage in remote places. . . . The arrival of the *Monte Rosa* with workmen and of the *Pernambuco* with large quantities of valuable materials must be viewed as a big and important first step on the road to realisation of *Kommission Paul*'s objective,' says an entry in the war diary of 29 November.

*

In the meantime, *Operation Tundra* in eastern Finnmark had evolved into a large-scale undertaking supported by forces from the 210th Division, the *Kriegsmarine*, *Luftwaffe*, *Abwehr* and *Gestapo*. Ever since 3 September twenty-year-old Leif Utne had moved about the Varanger Peninsula under the strict supervision of German wireless experts. The plan devised by *Premierleutnant* Fritz Pardon, who was responsible for the operation, was an ambitious one indeed. By means of spurious messages transmitted to Murmansk he hoped to inveigle the Russians into sending a submarine to an agreed rendezvous, where it would be attacked and destroyed. As Utne and his transmitter neared the coast, an attempt would also be made to lure from their hiding places any other agents who happened to be in the neighbourhood. Pardon was determined to find out as much as he could about how the Russians maintained contact with their agents in Finnmark and kept them provisioned.

On 7 October, one month after the charade had begun, a surprising signal was received that suggested that the Russians had taken the bait: 'Two comrades dropped in your area. [They] will find you and take you [to the coast].' The two were Oscar Nyström from Kirkenes and a wireless operator, Nicolai Korowin from Murmansk, who had been dropped by parachute over Hill 637 on the moor. They had with them two containers packed with supplies for what the Russians believed were three Norwegians in danger of being captured by the Germans.

'Wiskin and Labanov briefed us on what we had to do, which was to bring out *Gruppe Franz*. They told us the three were trapped in the mountains and in desperate need of food,' said Korowin in a subsequent statement. Captain Paul Wiskin was in command of Naval Group 4090, to which most of the partisans from Finnmark belonged; Labanov was the Group's parachute instructor. At their headquarters at Retinski, near Polyarnoe in the Murmansk fjord, the two men in charge had no idea that the leader of the group of partisans had taken his own life and that Leif Utne was working for the Germans.

'We are worn out from hunger and the cold. The comrades must come to us. Greetings,' Utne signalled to Polyarnoe a few days later.

From the base, Wiskin answered: 'Do not despair of receiving help. Oscar has been instructed to bring you food. We admire your courage. We firmly clasp your hands.'

Pardon's sly hand is in evidence in the deception. To begin with he had thought that it 'made things difficult' that the two would-be rescuers had been hurriedly flown to Varanger. But the potential advantage became increasingly apparent as the Germans began to piece together the Russians' operational pattern. 'Signals relating to the parachute drops were intercepted by the *Luftwaffe*'s direction-finding service and confirmed by the signals interchanged between Utne and the Russians. The planes came in low and circled for quite a time over certain points.'

A week or so later things hotted up. Leif Utne and his German controllers were by then nearing the coast. On Monday 18 October the signal Pardon had been so eagerly awaiting was received: 'Wait for the submarine every night between 2300 and 0400 commencing 19.10. Be careful.'

It caused consternation among Pardon and his *Abwehr* cohorts. From the 210th Division they had requisitioned two 7.5cm cannon, along with armour-piercing shells, three 37mm guns, a rocket battery, heavy machine-guns and two searchlights. The Navy was prepared to contribute several patrol vessels and a number of smaller craft. The intention was to lay a perfect ambush. But there was one thing Pardon had failed to take into account. 'It turned out that at the point chosen by the Russians, three kilometres west of Segl Point, the cliffs were so steep that it would be impossible to deploy the guns.'

However, by the time the submarine had nosed its way in and lain to 300 metres from the shore in the evening of Tuesday 19 October, the Germans had decided to attempt a suberfuge, albeit a rather simple one. They planned to send Leif Utne down to the beach. There, as soon as he saw the rubber dinghy approaching, he would shout to the men on board that they had to find a better landing place. Then he would withdraw into the shadows. It would be pitch dark and the Germans reckoned that he would be able to melt into the blackness and quickly disappear.

The submarine had two Norwegians on board, the 48-year-old veteran Åge Halvari, a fisherman and long-standing member of the Norwegian Communist Party, who acted as pilot, and 33-year-old Henri Normann Pettersen, who, before the war, had worked at a sawmill.

'Pettersen rowed to the shore. Shortly afterwards he returned to say that he had seen Leif Utne. He had recognised him, but Leif had said something he failed to catch, then run off, shouting for his Uncle Harald. I decided to go back with Henri. When I did so, there was no one to be seen, so we assumed that Leif had lost his way in the darkness of the cliffs,' Halvari later explained.

The Germans' ruse had succeeded beyond all expectations. When the two Norwegians got back to the submarine, Pettersen offered to row ashore again, taking with him a rucksack full of food, and try to find the five partisans they had come to collect. The KGB lieutenant in charge of the operation, a man who called himself Arkady, fell in with Pettersen's proposal and promised that the submarine would return the following evening.

Next morning Utne sent the Russians what appeared to be a desperate message but was really nothing but a pack of lies. 'Why did not the submarine wait for our return? Djin had hurt his foot in a crevice. We cannot get down to the original rendezvous. Can you collect us instead two kilometres west of Segl Point?'

Djin was Leif Utne's cover name. Polyarnoe acquiesced and answered briefly: 'Wait to be fetched at your place each night.'

This was the crowning moment for Pardon and his fellow conspirators, who, for seven long weeks, had patiently concocted a cock-and-bull story with the aid of false wireless messages. The Russians were prepared to send a submarine to rescue the reportedly starving agents fleeing from a ruthless enemy. The trap was about to close.

The following morning the guns and searchlights were hurriedly taken ashore and placed in camouflaged positions on either side of the bay in which the agents were supposed to be collected, while out in the fjord the submarine chasers took up their stations. Henri Pettersen was witness to these preparations but he was powerless to intervene. 'In the darkness I was unable to find the men I was looking for and decided to wait until the next day. When morning came, I suddenly found myself watching the Germans deploy their guns. I had to find a hiding place deeper in the mountains.'

When, at 20.00 on Wednesday, the submarine neared the pick-up point, the stage was set. The agreed light signals were exchanged and Åge Halvari rowed to the shore, expecting to find Henri Pettersen and the five partisans waiting for him. 'I started to look for Leif Utne on the rocky shore when suddenly all hell broke loose about me as the guns opened up. I'd no idea of what was happening and simply dived for cover among the rocks.'

The Germans had taken the crew of the submarine completely by surprise. There it lay, caught in the searchlights, only 350 metres from the shore; the German gunners could clearly see a group of men in the conning tower. In the course of less than two minutes 20 armour-piercing shells and 1,500 machine-gun bullets were fired at it before it slewed round and disappeared beneath the surface of the fjord. The gunfire was the signal to bring the submarine chasers racing up to Segl Point. At eleven o'clock the German sonar operators picked up the unmistakable sounds of a submarine at a depth of 60 metres, and in the course of the next fifteen hours dropped no fewer than 191 depth charges in a systematic pattern that thoroughly covered the area where the noises had come from. Bubbles of air and large quantities of oil rose to the surface, but of the submarine itself there was no trace.

Premierleutnant Pardon, who had personally followed the hunt from the deck of the patrol ship *VP 6113*, was convinced that he had achieved his purpose. 'According to the report submitted by the Commander of the 61st Flotilla, the hits sustained by the conning tower must have caused the submarine to take in water. This in turn must have so impaired its manoeuvrability that its destruction by the depth-charge attacks that followed must be deemed a certainty.'

But Pardon and the German naval officers were wrong. Information released only recently shows that the submarine was a small one of the 'M' class, *M-105*. These craft were 45 metres long and 275 tons deadweight. Built by a Black Sea yard, they were designed for operations in coastal waters. With a crew of twenty-two and carrying only two torpedoes, they had a limited range and attack capability.

M-105 left Polyarnoe on 12 October and reached the rendezvous five days later. When the Germans unexpectedly opened fire, there were five men in the conning tower – the captain, his second-in-command, the torpedo officer, the senior petty officer and a representative of the Northern Fleet, who, according to the archives, was a Lieutenant Yakovlev. All five made it safely down out of the conning tower, closing the hatch behind them, and the submarine immediately dived and headed for the open sea. The first seven depth charges smashed a few lamps and damaged the rudder, but the captain kept his head and succeeded in making his escape six hours later, at 01.45 the following morning. By that time the crew had counted fifty-five explosions close by. A few minutes later the submarine surfaced, and while the German vessels continued their depth-charging all through the morning of 21 October, sailed for home. *M-105* reached Polyarnoe that same evening, more or less unscathed.

*

Encouraged by what they thought of as their success, the Germans decided to exploit their charade for all it was worth, signalling the next day, 'The Germans opened up with cannon. Who has betrayed us? They are still looking for us. We are keeping to the mountains. We are starving.'

Containers filled with food were still being dropped by parachute as late as 1 November, but in Polyarnoe Wiskin and his associates were beginning to suspect that something had gone terribly wrong. Two days later they sent their first test question: 'Who did Artist fish with in the Vadsø area?'

'Artist' was a cover name known only to the Norwegians of *Gruppe Franz*. Leif Utne answered: 'Artist has never fished as you claim. If you are unable to help us immediately with food and batteries, we shall have to resort to stealing. We have been unable to find the provisions that were dropped.'

Their suspicions allayed, on 7 November, the twenty-sixth anniversary of the Russian Revolution, Polyarnoe sent the following signal: 'Congratulations on the 26th anniversary and [re-]capture of Kiev. Hope you are not losing heart and resolution in fulfilling your tasks.'

That same day Oscar Nystrøm and Nikolai Korowin were surprised in an outhouse. Nystrøm was killed in the ensuing exchange of fire and Korowin surrendered. More food was dropped on 10 November, but after that all wireless contact came to an end. By then the charade had been kept going for nine weeks without a break, with disastrous consequences both for the Soviet Intelligence Service's activities behind the German lines and for the partisans and their local helpers. Both Åge Halvari and Henri Pettersen, who had together rowed ashore from the submarine, had been compelled to give themselves up. Since the launching of *Operation Mitternachtssonne* early in July, four groups of agents had been wiped out. If the action on Arnøy is included, seventeen Norwegian and Soviet partisans had been killed or taken prisoner and close on seventy of the Norwegian civilians who had supported them in some way had been arrested. At a second military tribunal held on 1 December, with *Premierleutnant* Fritz Pardon as prosecutor and Stromsky presiding, three of the partisans' Norwegian helpers were condemned to death; seven received sentences ranging from five to fifteen years' imprisonment.

Pardon, the former district stipendiary magistrate, had played a variety of roles throughout the summer of 1943, having coordinated the operations, interrogated prisoners and acted as prosecutor at their trials. He had been careful, however, to distance himself from the *Gestapo*'s bloodstained cellars, where *Obersturmführer* August Haberstroh and his henchmen reigned supreme. Confessions were extracted from the helpless prisoners by systematic beatings, most of them breaking down under the maltreatment and torture to which they were subjected. The Russian Nicolai Korowin, who had on a fur-lined American jacket and trousers when he was taken prisoner, broke on the very first day and declared himself willing to perform 'any kind of service' for the Germans. He had served for two years as a wireless operator at the Radio Station for Special Purposes (RUON) in Murmansk and thus possessed a detailed knowledge of Soviet communications.

'After a few initial lies, Korowin readily tells all. He gives the impression of being extraordinarily intelligent and alert, and has a first-class memory. He will be able to tell [us] much about the Intelligence Service and wireless communication with the agents,' wrote Pardon.

The lieutenant's attention had been caught by a flaw in the Soviet communication system. The agents were in contact with RUON in Murmansk, which was staffed by twenty-five wireless operators, among them four Norwegian girls from Kiberg. But Captain Wiskin and Naval Group 4090 were stationed on the far side of the Kola fjord. This meant that RUON had to relay the messages from the partisans to their controllers by wireless, using Morse code.

'Thanks to Korowin, the frequency used to communicate between RUON and Polyarnoe is known to us. Continuation of the deception will afford us an excellent opportunity to discover the codes employed and the contents of the messages.'

In the event, 48-year-old Åge Halvari proved the Germans' trump card. He was suffering badly from shock after being captured immediately after the shelling of the Soviet submarine. Once he began to talk, after a week's softening-up, the Germans were left with an almost complete picture of the Russian Intelligence Service's organisation and methods. Halvari was one of those who had fled from Kiberg as early as September 1940. He had been recruited as a submarine pilot and had taken part in ten forays to the Finnmark coast, which meant that he knew about all the groups that had been set ashore there since early in 1942. 'Halvari is shrewd and very intelligent. He has occupied a position of trust in Naval Group 4090 and for this reason been privy to most of what went on there,' Pardon recorded.

When, in November 1943, after more than four months' sustained effort, he set out to summarise the results achieved, the lieutenant was able to say, without fear of contradiction, that eastern Finnmark had been swept clean of enemy agents: 'According to statements made independently of each other by prisoners Halvari, Pettersen and Korowin, there are now *no* groups of agents in the Varanger area.'

Towards the end of November the results of the operation that had been carried out behind the lines of Dietl's Mountain Corps reached the *Wolfschanze*, where Hitler was brooding over German setbacks elsewhere on the Eastern Front. It was *Admiral* Wilhelm Canaris, head of the *Abwehr*, who personally proposed that the men responsible should be suitably rewarded. And from his headquarters in Petsamo, *General* Ferdinand Schörner sent many complimentary letters and telegrams to the 210th Division. One read:

I commend the 210th Division and, in particular, Pardon and Stromsky, for the swift and efficient way in which they conducted the trial of those responsible for espionage in Varanger. . . . I wish to pay a special tribute to Pardon for his foresight, vigour and perseverance in leading this joint operation . . . and to *Obersturmführer* Haberstroh, who so wholeheartedly and energetically placed himself at the disposal of the *Wehrmacht*.

Only one thing marred the success of the operation. Halvari had told his captors that two new groups of agents had been landed in the west of Finnmark in October. What made this item of news so alarming was that the destination of one group was Alta.

*

The admirals in Alta, Narvik and Kiel were already greatly disturbed by the results of the investigations into the surprise attack by the British submarines.

The day after the attack, *Leutnant-zur-See* Schmölder had proposed that the three submarines be salvaged:

> U-boat A [X-6] will be the easiest to locate and raise, provided it has not been destroyed by the explosion. U-boat B [X-7] received a direct hit and is unlikely to yield much information of value. U-boat C [X-5] may be semi-intact. The spot where it went down is marked on the chart. To speed up recovery, it may pay to search the area with a drag line towed between two tugs.

At nine in the morning on Friday 24 September, two tugs, the *Arngast* and *Bardenfleth*, began their search. Divers from the *Tirpitz* stood by, ready to help should the line catch on the wreck of *X5*, which it was thought lay some 700 metres north-east of the battleship. Hydrophones had picked up the sound of hammering just there, suggesting that attempts were being made by the trapped men to carry out underwater repair work, but after twenty-four hours the noises ceased. It was a complex and frustrating operation, as every time the line caught on something on the bottom, the divers had to go down to see what it was.

'The work was supervised by Naval Diver Sachtien from Wilhelmshaven. It was tough going, and by the end of the day the divers were just about at the end of their tether,' recalls Helmut Simon, who was granted sick leave after the explosion.

Schmölder had thought *X5* would be the easiest of the midget submarines to locate, but in the area where he had dropped depth charges nothing was found. Says an entry in the war diary of the 1st Battle Group for Sunday 26 September: 'After having searched in vain for the third U-boat, it seems clear that we have found U-boat no. 2 further out. However, the line keeps slipping off, so further work will have to be postponed until tomorrow.'

The following day the first divers descended to the wreck. Their report was encouraging:

> *Arngast* reports that U-boat no. 2 has been found 350 metres away, at an angle of 40 degrees to the *Tirpitz*. The U-boat is on an even keel and has a slight list. The hatch is open. The stern is missing, probably blown off by a depth charge. The hull is fitted with heavy ring bolts. It is planned to shackle wires to them and tow the boat into shallower water.

A week later the midget submarine was beached at Straumsnes. It turned out that it was the bow that had been blown off, not the stern. Closer examination also revealed that the craft was *X7*. The bodies of the two crew members who had gone down with her were taken out and buried in Alta. A team of experts was flown in and every inch of the wreck minutely studied. Equipment of special interest was removed and sent to Timmendorfer Strand, near Lübeck, where *Admiral* Helmuth Heye was in process of building up Germany's own midget U-boat arm. The recovery of *X7* taught the Germans how the British had solved the towing problem and how the timer mechanism for the charges worked. But what most aroused their interest were the documents found on board, which disclosed that the crew possessed detailed knowledge not only of the *Tirpitz* but also of the base in which it lay. They found charts, current tables, photographs of the ship and the area round about, information on defences and a sketch of the battleship's hull with the engine-room clearly marked. In the 1st Battle Group's diary the following conclusion was drawn: 'One of the most important lessons learned is that the enemy has such accurate information regarding the base that we may assume with certainty that agents are active in the Alta area.'

*

In London, Rear-Admiral Claud Barry and his staff were following with keen interest the hectic wireless traffic between the *Tirpitz* and the German Naval High Command, from which they learned that the battleship had been badly damaged and was to be repaired in the Kå fjord. Barry knew from the decrypts that the ship's engines and guns were out of action, but it was impossible to determine quite how serious the damage was. The Upsilon station in Tromsø had transmitted its first report on the result of the attack on 29 September, though it was not entirely accurate, as it claimed that the forepart of the battleship had been badly damaged and that she was down by the bow. It also said that many men had been killed. However, it correctly stated that four members of the submarine's crew had been taken prisoner immediately after the attack.

Barry had hoped, deep down, that the twelve tons of amatol carried by the six side-charges would suffice to sink the *Tirpitz*. If he was disappointed at their failure to do so, he gave no sign of it in the report he submitted to the Admiralty on 8 November 1943:

That these three very gallant commanding officers succeeded in carrying out their intentions and pressing home their attacks to the full, I have no doubts. But what difficulties and hazards they were called on to negotiate in the execution of the attack are not known. Nor is it known how some of them (if the German wireless broadcast is to be believed) came to be taken prisoner. It is certain that outstanding devotion to duty and courage of the highest order were displayed. . . . Finally I cannot fully express my admiration for the three commanding officers, Lieutenant H. Henty-Creer, RNVR, D. Cameron, RNR, and B.C.G. Place, DSC, RN, and the crews of X5, X6 and X7 . . . whose daring attack will surely go down in history as one of the most courageous acts of all time.

Only three days later, on 11 November, a signal reached London from another clandestine transmitter, Ida, which was operated by two Norwegian MI6 agents, Torstein Pettersen Råby and Karl Rasmussen. It confirmed that the first transmitter provided by the British had been successfully installed close to the German naval base. Before long one message after another began to come in with details of the state of the German battleship. In time, Barry and his fellow admirals learned all they needed to know to set about planning how to rid themselves once and for all of Churchill's bugbear, which was still undergoing repair in the Kå fjord.

CHAPTER FOURTEEN

The Search

GERMANY, ENGLAND AND NORWAY, SUMMER 2003

I spent much of the summer of 2003 endeavouring to determine precisely what had happened in the Kå fjord on that eventful Wednesday morning of 22 September 1943. The truth proved as elusive as the wreck of *X5*. Early in May I drove 800 kilometres to the delightful little seaside resort of Heiligenhafen on Germany's Baltic coast, where, in recent years, *Tirpitz* veterans have every spring held a reunion. The numbers attending have become fewer with the passage of time, but some two hundred or more continue to subscribe to the Association's newsletter, *Der Scheinwerfer* (The Searchlight), thus helping to keep alive memories of the 'Lonely Queen of the North'.

I was lucky. Many of the men gathered in the Reception Room at the spa had been on board the battleship when the charges exploded. They were all very friendly, and willingly answered my many and searching questions. I met Ship's Carpenter Karl Heinz Lohse, Diver Helmut Simon and former *Leutnant* Hein Hellendoorn, one of the few of the ship's officers still alive. Both Lohse and Simon had seen *X6*, and possibly also *X7*, but Hellendoorn proved to be my star witness. A gunnery officer in charge of the battleship's secondary armament, he had been on watch in the superstructure, some 40 metres above the main deck, when the midget submarines made their attack and thus had a grandstand view of the fjord and the dramatic events taking place below him. Because the heavy guns had been jolted from their bearings and were tightly jammed, while others could not be sufficiently depressed because the submarines were too close to the battleship's hull, recourse had to be had to Hellendoorn's light artillery – mainly rapid-firing 20mm and 37mm anti-aircraft guns, but also the heavier 10.5cm guns located on both sides of the ship.

Tall, grey-haired and, thanks to his youthful prowess as an athlete, still impressively fit despite his eighty-three years, Hein Hellendoorn, a retired dentist, was a cultured man. Both when I spoke to him in Heiligenhafen and later, when I visited his lovely home in Bad Bentheim, on the Dutch border, where he was surrounded by painstakingly constructed model ships and a large collection of wartime photographs and documents, he did his utmost to assist me. But, as he himself pointed out:

Memory can never be relied upon. I know what it says in the war diary, but when I set about trying to remember, I can only recall *one* midget U-boat, the one we later knew as X7. I can see it in my mind's eye at the very moment it broke surface and leaped across the net forward and to starboard of us, like some black sea monster. It's sixty years ago now since it happened. I have no recollection of the other two at all.

By coincidence, two days earlier Hellendoorn had received a visit from another former shipmate, Wilhelm Rosenbaum, a retired engineer, like himself a spry 83-year-old. Rosenbaum, then also a lieutenant, had piloted one of the battleship's Arado 196 float-planes. When the attack took place, he had snatched the camera from the plane and taken a set of photographs that today may well be termed sensational. Unfortunately, though, only three of them are still extant. One is of the starboard side of the wet main deck, with the dark bulk of Mount Sakkobadne looming large in the background. A few ratings can be seen to the left of the picture, their eyes on the wood-and-canvas target raft that was Godfrey Place's salvation. In the background, right behind it, can just be made out the silhouette of the Norwegian steamer *Stamsund*, which inadvertently found itself in the line of fire, peppered by ricochets, stray shells and bullets. But in the centre of the picture is a greyish-white cloud of smoke and spray where shells from Hellendoorn's guns rained down – and thus also the spot where X7 disappeared at 10.40 on that fateful morning.

There is something very disturbing about this picture. It is not the cloud of smoke and spray drifting across the silvery-grey surface of the sea but the men standing with their backs to the camera. It is clear from the set of their shoulders and casual appearance in general that they are all at their ease. Those of them gazing out across the sea are plainly quite relaxed and in full control of their emotions; they might almost be made of wax. But they are very much alive and alert. Sixty-eight of the men at the rail were badly wounded, and one was killed when he was swept overboard from a position close by. Catching as it does one of the war's most dramatic moments, it is a unique picture, war reporting at its best.

In the other photograph, the ship's catapult is in the foreground and Mount Sakkobadne, a dark wall, again provides the background. The camera lens has caught the clouds of smoke and spray drifting across the spot where X5 was last seen. I have pored over this picture for hours in the hope of catching sight of Henty-Creer's small craft somewhere on the surface of the sea, but there is nothing to be seen apart from the greyish-white clouds drifting lazily across the fjord as though released from a source hidden in the depths. When I spoke to Rosenbaum, I asked him whether he had pointed the camera at an identifiable object or simply directed it at the spouts of water thrown up by the falling shells. 'I'm sorry, but I can no longer remember,' replied the amiable old gentleman, who had ended his working life as a senior lecturer at a technical college.

In July, I gave up. I knew I could find more eye-witnesses, but I could not expect them to remember exactly what they had seen or experienced sixty years earlier. I had embarked upon a programme of basic research into a subject that no one had attempted before me. I had set out to discover just what people had seen in the water some 500 to 700 metres to starboard of the *Tirpitz*, and what Hellendoorn's men had fired at. The midget submarines lay extremely low in the water and were difficult to see at the best of times, even at close range. Was it conceivable that the German fire had been directed at reflected light dancing on the surface of the water or at a figment of some over-excited young gunner's imagination seen through wavering binoculars? The thought entered my mind after talking to Robert Aitken in Ipswich. By a miracle, Aitken had survived after spending over two hours trapped in a steel cylinder slowly filling with chlorine gas. The last member of the submarines' crews to be saved, at a little before 13.30, he had, of course, seen nothing of what had taken place on the surface earlier in the day. As he explained, 'I wasn't there. I was clinging to life 40 metres down and only reached the surface when it was all over. But I've always wondered just what it was the Germans saw. Were they really capable of spotting a midget submarine so far away or were they simply firing at light reflected from a wave?' Aitken was over eighty at the time I interviewed him, and back trouble had left him with a stoop. But he still played golf, and as the former manager of a large engineering works, he possessed a mind trained in the art of critical analysis. 'I don't know, but I've always been sceptical about the whole thing,' he told me. 'I'm not sure that they saw anything at all.'

This had never occurred to me and it made me uneasy. I was thus greatly relieved when I found in the National Archives in Freiberg a report from

Leutnant Eberhard Schmölder that no one had referred to before. Schmölder had been at the tiller of a launch that had been much closer to *X5* than Hellendoorn, Rosenbaum or any of the other witnesses watching from the *Tirpitz*. He was no longer alive, but the report he wrote was clearly the work of a meticulous and self-respecting man who may have been expecting his efforts that day to be suitably rewarded. Be that as it may, he made no attempt to exaggerate his part in the proceedings – if anything, the reverse. It was a sober report, written the day after the attack, while the happenings were still fresh in his mind. What I liked about it was that, to substantiate his views on salient points, he had drawn on the testimony of other witnesses. He seems to have realised that he had taken part in a historical event and so had to be accurate in what he wrote. When he saw the *Tirpitz* open fire just before eleven o'clock, he raced to the spot where the shells were falling. '*Dort sah ich wiederum ein U-boot auftauchen*,' he wrote, 'There I again saw a U-boat break surface.'

This was an unequivocal statement, one I felt could be relied upon. Schmölder and the ratings with him in the launch had, at any rate, seen *X7* close to and knew what they were looking for. When, half an hour later, he made for Sakkobadne and saw what the guns were firing at, he can have had no doubt as to what the target was. Would a young and conscientious lieutenant risk overstating what he had seen in a report on which his future career as a naval officer might well depend, a report about something he had to assume would have been seen by hundreds of other watchers – the men on board the *Stamsund*, *Nordmark*, the destroyers and the *Tirpitz* itself? Not in my opinion. After having read this report, I felt pretty certain that the lookouts on the *Tirpitz*, Schmölder and the other men involved had indeed seen a third midget submarine midway between the battleship and Sakkobadne, and that this craft was *X5* under the command of Henty Henty-Creer. Even a sceptical Admiralty had acknowledged in a postwar report that Henty's craft had successfully forced the barrier between Auskarnes and Mount Hjemmeluft and entered the fjord:

[I]t remains to be recorded that at 0843 a third X-craft was sighted some 500 yards outside the nets. *Tirpitz* opened fire and claims to have hit and sunk this X-craft. Depth-charges were also dropped in the position in which the craft disappeared. This was X-5 [Lieutenant Henty-Creer, RNVR] which had last been seen off Soroy on 21st September by X-7.

Nothing is known of her movements, nor was any member of her crew saved.

When this was written the Admiralty was unaware of Schmölder's report. The evaluation was based on interrogation of the survivors of *X6* and *X7*, who had returned home after two years in a prisoner-of-war camp. Most of them had been standing on the deck of the *Tirpitz* at the time and had witnessed the same as Schmölder and the other Germans. The difference was that the British knew what a midget submarine looked like as it lay half-submerged on the surface. They knew what to look for and most probably had their eyes glued to the spot in the hope that the last of the flotilla would succeed in doing what they themselves had failed to do, that is, sink the *Tirpitz*.

I several times spoke to the second-in-command of *X6*, John Lorimer, who confirmed my opinion of what had happened.

All I can say is that I *saw* *X5* on the surface, and that I *saw* it disappear in cascades of water, having probably been hit by several shells. As soon as I got back to England, I informed my superiors of what I had seen, as did the others who were with me on the deck and witnessed the action. In my opinion there is no doubt that *X5* surfaced and was sunk by gunfire, before our very eyes.

The third of the survivors, the diver Robert Kendall, who now lives in Canada is, however, less categorical. 'I can't, of course, swear with my hand on the Bible to something I saw sixty years ago. But at the time I was convinced that *X5* surfaced and disappeared in the spray thrown up by shells hitting it. At least one heavy gun was firing. I can still see it all before my eyes.'

The Admiralty's report was undoubtedly based on the testimony of Lorimer, Kendall and the other survivors – men who had lived and talked together for two long years as prisoners of war. I felt that my investigations had not been in vain. The key German report and the British eye-witnesses agreed that Henty-Creer's *X5* had disappeared just about where Jon Røkenes and his fellow divers from Alta had found the remains of a small craft – and, some distance away, a metal object that looked very much like an intact side-charge. Maybe it was too late to solve the mystery completely, but I felt that, step by step, at least we were getting closer to a better understanding of what had happened during the attack.

CHAPTER FIFTEEN

Attack from the Air

THE KÅ FJORD, 3 APRIL 1944

The air-raid alarm sounded at 06.25. The warning came quickly, but not quickly enough, as only five minutes later the first Hellcats came screaming out of the sky from behind Mounts Haldde and Sakkobadne. The pilots held their fire until they couldn't miss, then opened up with their 12.7mm machine-guns, which fired several thousand rounds a minute. The *Tirpitz*'s anti-aircraft gunners were racing to their guns when the hail of bullets swept the upper deck. The attack was meant as an execution, and that is what it proved to be. The men had had no time to don flak jackets. Caught in the open, they were mown down in mid-stride. Before long the teak planks of the deck were running red with blood.

'We had steam up and had cast off aft. We had weighed the starboard anchor and only 25 metres of the port chain were left to bring in when everything exploded around us. I felt no pain, but completely blacked out,' says Helmut Simon, who was manning the forward windlass.

Some fourteen days had passed since the *Tirpitz* had completed her first trials after the attack by the X-craft. Now repair work was finished and she was about to undertake her final trials in the Alta fjord. Her captain, Hans Meyer, was a cautious and determined man. He had no intention of allowing the *Monte Rosa*, and the 700 shipyard workers she had brought with her, to return to Germany until he was assured that his ship was fully seaworthy. By rights, the trial run should have taken place two days earlier, but bad weather had led to its postponement. But now it had cleared up and the Kå fjord was bathed in bright spring sunshine. The temperature was eight degrees below zero and there was not a breath of wind. Conditions were ideal for testing the engines and fire-control systems. To be on the safe side, that morning Meyer had had the men roused from their slumbers earlier than usual, at 05.30. There had been a few grumbles, but the men were well disciplined, and only an hour later the battleship was ready to leave her berth. The boilers had built up a full head of steam and tugs had dragged the anti-submarine net well to the side. In a matter of minutes the port anchor chain would be secured and the *Tirpitz* would once again put to sea under her own steam. Meyer was about to issue his final orders when the air-raid sirens sounded. The Air Surveillance Centre in Alta had detected thirty-two aircraft some 80 kilometres north of the Kå fjord – and they were making straight for the base.

*

In London the planners had long been aware that repairs to the *Tirpitz* would be completed by the end of March. Director of Shipbuilding Krux, who had been in charge of the work, had estimated that it would be four and a half months before the battleship was again operational, but after an all-out effort on the part of the workmen quartered on board the *Monte Rosa*, it looked as though he would finish his task with plenty of time to spare.

'Our source in the Kå fjord has spoken to German civilian workers who had helped build the *Tirpitz*. They say she will be ready to put to sea in March,' reported a clandestine transmitter codenamed Lyra early in February. Located in Porsa, Lyra was the second of the two transmitters the British Secret Service had set up in western Finnmark in autumn 1943. The information they provided confirmed the picture presented by enemy signals intercepted and decrypted by the British. In January a heated argument had taken place between Krux and the Central Supply Depot in Kiel, which was having difficulty in meeting his many requirements. The upshot was that oil pumps had to be taken from the bomb-damaged battlecruiser *Gneisenau* and sent to Alta. A 100-ton floating crane on its way north had run into heavy weather off the Norwegian coast and been badly knocked about, but in February it was replaced by one capable of lifting 20 tons, enough to hoist most heavy pieces of equipment into place. In a summary report dated 27 January 1944 the British Intelligence Service wrote that work to restore the *Tirpitz* to a state of operational readiness was clearly well under way: '[W]hile her hull, engineering and electrical repairs would be completed by 15 March, her gunnery repairs were likely to be delayed beyond that date, and that even then she would not be operationally effective as she had not docked for two and a half years.'

But on 3 March people living on the shores of the Kå fjord were startled by a succession of loud bangs. A signal from Ida that same day explained what had caused them: '*Tirpitz* still at anchor in her old position fired salvos with her two forward guns at a floating target to-day 3.3.44 at 1000 GMT.'

Rear-Admiral Henry Moore realised that he had to get a move on. As Second-in-Command of the Home Fleet, a few weeks earlier he had set to work on the planning of a large-scale air attack on the *Tirpitz*, an attack that had been accorded top priority. Two of the Navy's biggest aircraft carriers, the *Victorious* and *Furious*, were to spearhead the operation, which was codenamed Tungsten. They would be accompanied by a further three carriers, the *Emperor, Pursuer* and *Searcher*. Under cover of darkness they would sail to a position 60 nautical miles west of the island of Sørøy and fly off two waves of 42 Barracuda dive bombers and 88 Corsair, Hellcat and Wildcat fighters, which would then make a beeline for the Kå fjord.

Writing on 19 March, Admiral Andrew Cunningham, the First Sea Lord, opined that 'we had a very strong force provided we could find *Tirpitz* and time our operations well. A very great deal would therefore depend on the soundness of our reconnaissance and intelligence to enable the C-in-C Home Fleet to judge his time for sailing.' Meanwhile, on the northern coast of Scotland the Fleet Air Arm had found around Loch Eriboll a stretch of desolate countryside similar to that their planes would be flying over in the Alta region. Anti-torpedo nets, smoke generators and anti-aircraft guns were quickly dispersed round about, and while Rear-Admiral Moore waited impatiently for the *Victorious* to leave the dockyard where she was undergoing a few minor repairs and modifications, day after day the bombers and fighters thundered across the loch. The plan was for the Barracudas to hug the mountains for cover, then dive down on the battleship and release their 800-kilogram bombs – after the fighters had knocked out the anti-aircraft batteries. It was a bold and complex operation that depended for success on strong nerves and hard training.

On 17 March the British wireless monitoring service intercepted a signal from *Kapitän-zur-See* Hans Meyer to Kiel in which he reported on the results of the trials carried out two days earlier. It was far from encouraging. 'Hull, guns and power installation were from a material point of view fully operationally effective,' he said, only to add that communication facilities were still incomplete and that there was 'unacceptable vibration in midship cruising turbines'. This meant that the faulty machinery had to be flown all the way to Mannerheim for repair, while electricians set about bringing communications up to scratch. Two weeks later another signal advised that the next trials would start early in the morning of Monday 3 April. When the news reached Rear-Admiral Moore he was already on his way north from Scapa Flow in the *Victorious*, where the pilots and their observers were engaged in studying a large-scale relief model of the Alta fjord area, including the Kå fjord, constructed in the utmost secrecy from plywood and plaster at RAF Medmenham. Nothing was left to chance. According to one Barracuda observer, who attended ten hours of concentrated briefing, the model showed 'light and heavy flak positions, air-landing strips etc. . . . Photos and maps were plentiful.'

In the meantime Tungsten had evolved into what was destined to be the greatest naval operation ever undertaken in the Barents Sea. The C-in-C Home Fleet, Admiral Bruce Fraser, had decided to attack the *Tirpitz* in the lee of the outward-bound convoy JW58, which was scheduled to pass Bear Island on Tuesday 4 April and was sure to occupy much of the Germans' attention. The convoy comprised no fewer than fifty merchantmen and nearly thirty escort vessels. The Home Fleet, which was responsible for both the convoy's escort and the Alta-bound strike force, had at sea a further two battleships, six aircraft carriers, four cruisers and fourteen destroyers. When this armada of more than one hundred ships reached a point between Jan Mayen and Bear Island, Fraser made a brilliant move. He ordered Moore to bring the attack forward by twenty-four hours and hit the *Tirpitz* before she left on her trials. Weather reports transmitted by Ida at two-hour intervals revealed that the sky was clear over western Finnmark and that there was next to no wind – perfect conditions that Fraser intended to exploit to the full.

At 05.15 in the morning of Monday 3 April the first Corsairs took off from the flight deck of the *Victorious*, to be followed in the course of the next fifteen minutes by all the sixty or so aircraft taking part in the first attack.

They 'left the carriers' decks in the greatest heart, and brimful of confidence,' said the ship's captain, M.M. Denny. At 05.36 the last to take off disappeared eastwards, where a pale sun was beginning to light up the horizon. The Kå fjord was less than an hour's flying time distant.

*

At the German naval base some of the former optimism returned when, in March, officers and men saw that the flagship could again put to sea under its own steam. The trial run brought a gleam of light to what in other respects had been a grim winter. With the *Lützow* back in Germany and the *Tirpitz* disabled, the only one of Hitler's capital ships capable of attacking the Allied convoys was the battlecruiser *Scharnhorst*. But the German admirals knew that an attack in the Arctic darkness by only one ship would have little chance of success. The consensus was that what remained of the winter would pass without incident and that nothing would happen until the *Tirpitz* was again fully operational and *Admiral* Kümmetz back in command. But on the Eastern Front the army was hard-pressed and *Grossadmiral* Karl Dönitz had promised Hitler a devastating blow against the Allied supply lines through the Barents Sea. When, shortly before Christmas, a convoy was detected west of Trondheim, halfway up the Norwegian coast, Dönitz had ordered the *Scharnhorst*, along with the 4th Destroyer Flotilla, to attack it. It was a fateful decision. On 26 December 1943 the German battlecruiser had sailed straight into an ambush and been battered to bits and sunk by a superior British force off the North Cape. In the darkness and icy sea, only 36 of its complement of 1,972 were saved and taken to Britain as prisoners of war. Among the many who lost their lives were *Konter-Admiral* Erich Bey, the Battle Group's Intelligence Officer, Rolf Woytschekowsky-Emden, and some thirty officers and ratings who only a few days earlier had been transferred to the *Scharnhorst* from the *Tirpitz*.

When the 4th Flotilla's five destroyers returned from this ill-starred venture on Monday 27 December, something not far short of panic seized the men of the *Kriegsmarine* cooped up in the Kå fjord. Hans Meyer, the *Tirpitz*'s captain, and six hundred of his men were in Germany, enjoying Christmas leave, with the consequence that *Kapitän-zur-See* Rolf Johannesson, who had commanded the destroyer force and had lost contact with the *Scharnhorst* in the confusion and bad weather, had temporarily to assume command of what was left of the 1st Battle Group. He immediately issued an order designed to bring the ships under his command to a state of instant readiness. As he wrote in the war diary, 'The loss of the *Scharnhorst* has weakened the Group. With strong enemy forces present in the Arctic Ocean, material, psychological and military-political circumstances would appear to favour a surprise attack on the Kå fjord.'

The decision of the U-boat commander in Narvik, *Kapitän-zur-See* Rudolf Peters, to exploit the loss of the *Scharnhorst* by demanding the return of the repair ship *Huascaren* aroused much dissatisfaction. With twenty-four U-boats in the Barents Sea, the backlog in their maintenance was an ever-present problem. Peters reasoned that with the *Scharnhorst* gone there was no longer need for *two* repair ships in the Kå fjord. The *Neumark* should suffice, he thought. Johannesson disagreed: 'The *Neumark*'s capacity is fully absorbed by the *Tirpitz*. The *Huascaren* is needed for running repairs and maintenance of a repair ship, four tankers, three water tankers, three power-supply vessels, eleven tugs, two floating flak batteries, five to eight destroyers and twelve other special-purpose vessels.'

It was thus apparent that the Kå fjord still sheltered a formidable force, one which, in its present critical state, made a tempting target for the British Home Fleet. The base's defences had been tested, with alarming results. Theoretical exercises revealed that a British force could easily penetrate the inner reaches of the Alta fjord and send not only the *Tirpitz* but also the auxiliary vessels attendant upon it to the bottom.

'The coastal defences are incapable of offering serious resistance to big ships forcing their way in. The six 35.6cm guns on the foredeck of battleships of the Duke of York class will very quickly knock out our own unprotected 10.5cm and 15.0cm batteries.'

The prospects were indeed dismal, but the new year dawned without any attempt having been made by the British to seize the opportunity thus open to them. As January gave way to February, the tension once more eased. But things had changed.

'Morale on board can safely be described as bad for following reasons. First, the attack on *Tirpitz* and the sinking of the *Scharnhorst*. The bombing of Germany, and the long hours of darkness and other reasons. An ordinary seaman (probably drunk) said, "What else can one do except drink, while one awaits capture?"' stated a message received from Ida at the end of January.

In his war-diary entries Rolf Johannesson gave expression to much of the same bitterness and frustration: 'Not many words are needed to describe the highly unsatisfactory situation we are in. Valuable convoys are taking supplies to the Eastern Front only 100 nautical miles from our coast. Owing to our numerical inferiority it has not yet proved feasible to attempt to intervene with destroyers and torpedo boats,' he wrote on 29 February. His frustration is also in evidence in the following *cri de coeur*:

As we are never in action, we are slowly becoming increasingly like the French fleet in the Napoleonic Wars. The enemy's ability to fight continues to improve. He is constantly engaged, for which reason his morale continues to improve too and he gains operational experience. Is it not possible to scrape together all we have and despatch a couple of destroyer and torpedo-boat flotillas north?

Johannesson's plea fell on deaf ears. Germany was in retreat on every front and there were no ships to spare. Every effort had thus to be made to restore the *Tirpitz* to operational readiness. In the meantime, it was up to the destroyers to hold the fort.

*

The first wave of aircraft from the *Victorious* crossed the Norwegian coast at 0608, half an hour after take-off. The weather was still perfect – there was no wind to speak of and the sun shone brightly from a near-cloudless sky. From an altitude of about 3,000 metres the aircrews had a magnificent view of Loppen Island and the Øksfjord glacier. The wide expanse of mountain moorland was criss-crossed with ski tracks left by German sailors on their time off ashore. Lieutenant-Commander Richard Baker-Faulkner, who led the first wave of Barracudas to the target, reported that the weather was exceptionally good and that visibility could not have been better.

Not long afterwards Mount Halldde hove into view beneath them. All was quiet. Not an enemy fighter was to be seen and the anti-aircraft batteries remained silent. There was nothing to suggest that the attackers had been detected. Just before 06.30, Baker-Faulkner gave the signal. The bombers put their noses down and went into a dive that would take them in a swoop over the last mountain crest and bring them out above the Kå fjord and their target.

*

Twenty-four-year-old *Leutnant* Hein Hellendoorn was on watch in the main anti-aircraft fire-control room 40 metres above the deck when, at 06.24, the first warning was received from the Air Surveillance Centre in Alta: 'Thirty-two approaching aircraft detected 80 kilometres to the north.'

'If the observation was correct, some time would elapse before they reached us – perhaps twenty minutes. But I had no idea how long the report had taken to get to us. The consequence was that I acted instinctively and sounded the alarm,' says Hellendoorn.

He was only just in time. The warning had been badly delayed. When the alarm-bells rang throughout the ship, sending men hurrying to their action stations, the leading aircraft were less than 20 kilometres away. The fast Hellcat and Wildcat fighters had 'hedge-hopped' through the valleys and defiles beneath Mount Haldde, to come roaring in at tree-top height. At 06.28 the first streams of bullets raked the battleship's deck.

'We whistled down over forested hills . . . [and] shot across the fjord in a straggling line abreast shooting into the battleship. . . . Various missiles appeared to be whizzing in all directions. . . . Very exciting,' said Lieutenant-Commander J. Cooper, who commanded 882 Wildcat squadron.

Hellendoorn's quick response had afforded the *Tirpitz* a breathing space, albeit a brief one — only four minutes. 'We were taken completely by surprise,' he says. 'The planes dived straight down on the ship from the mountains round about. Before we knew, it they were right on top of us.'

The attackers' machine-guns transformed the battleship's upper deck into an abattoir. The men manning the forward windlass were slaughtered where they stood. Many of those racing for their stations were hit by splinters and ricochets. The 20mm and 37mm anti-aircraft guns were located on open platforms on both sides of the ship. Unshielded, the gunners suffered appalling losses. The fighter attack was intended to spread death and destruction and to leave the Germans shocked and demoralised, and in that it was highly successful. When the twenty-one Barracuda bombers of the first wave swept in over the *Tirpitz* one minute later, the smoke generators were only just coming into action. There was a certain amount of ragged fire from the ship, but it proved largely ineffective.

'[The] fighters had shot up target very well and undoubtedly spoilt *Tirpitz*'s gunnery,' Baker-Faulkner reported.

Six minutes elapsed from the sounding of the alarm to the moment when the first high-explosive bombs struck the upper deck at 06.30. One of the very first hit forward of the bridge, sending a rain of red-hot splinters in every direction. The steel door between the control room and chart room had been left open, with the result that the helmsman and officer of the watch were killed instantly, their faces badly burned. The control panel, engine telegraph and other instruments on the bridge were shattered and fire broke out. *Kapitän-zur-See* Hans Meyer, who was on the wing, was flung violently against the bulkhead and fell to the floor, bleeding from both ears. The explosion had burst his eardrums and he had also sustained internal injuries, leaving him in a state of shock. For a few fateful minutes the *Tirpitz* had no one to command her. The battleship's new and untried navigating officer, *Fregattenkapitän* Hugo Heydel, had to take over until, three-quarters of an hour later, the first officer, *Kapitän-*

zur-See Wolf Junge, managed to make his way to the bridge. A hail of bullets swept the anti-aircraft fire-control positions in the upper turret. Hein Hellendoorn was wounded in the back by a shower of splinters, with the consequence that command of the guns had to be transferred to the aft control room. 'It was feared for a time that some of the splinters had pierced a lung,' Hellendoorn says. 'Fortunately, it wasn't that bad.'

The attack lasted for three minutes. After that, the planes were lost to sight above the smoke that was slowly enshrouding the ship. For a time, chaos reigned. In the last sixty seconds of the attack eight bombs had found their mark on the upper deck, though none had penetrated its armour to damage the engines or disrupt other vital functions below. Despite this, the external damage was considerable. One bomb had blown in the funnel and sent a cloud of soot billowing across the superstructure. Another had exploded in the Officers' Mess, wreaking havoc and destroying the grand piano that a former first officer, Hans Assmann, a gifted musician, had somehow managed to procure. A third smashed a launch, bored its way through the deck and wrecked all about it. The damage extended from stem to stern. Dead and dying men lay everywhere, and the deck was red with blood.

'I came to outside one of the gun turrets. I had been thrown several metres across the deck and was unable to move. But I was lucky. A hatch opened and strong arms dragged me to safety inside the turret,' says Helmut Simon.

While Hans Meyer was being carried away from the shattered remains of the bridge on a stretcher, men who were unhurt set about tending the rest of the wounded. Temporary bandages were applied and the most seriously injured men taken to the sickbay. But the battleship's surgeon had been killed in the attack and another doctor was away on leave. Only Dr Bailloff was available to treat the casualties, with the result that the line of men waiting outside the operating theatre for treatment grew ever longer. Some men ran out fire hoses with the aim of preventing the fires spreading to the oil tanks and magazine. Many were badly shocked, however, and simply wandered aimlessly about, black with soot and bleeding. To add to the noise and shouting, one siren defied all attempts to switch it off and continued with its mournful wailing.

In the meantime the battleship had drifted back into the net cage and come to rest broadside to the fjord, its bow almost on the shore. The engines had to be started to prevent it running aground. But no sooner had the first two tugs appeared out of the smoke, at 07.25, when the air-raid warning sounded for a second time. The fjord was by then almost completely covered in smoke from the generators, but the battleship's foretop and aft mast remained visible above the grey carpet. The anti-aircraft guns opened fire, but their targets were invisible. All the gunners had to go by was the terrifying howl of engines as the dive bombers hurtled down to release their lethal loads. One bomb ploughed its way into the float-plane hangar, while another penetrated to the upper 'tween-deck, destroying the adjacent cabins and storerooms. To make matters worse, the hose used to pump aircraft fuel to the hangar burst, starting more fires.

Out in the Alta fjord, waiting for the *Tirpitz* to join him, *Kapitän-zur-See* Rolf Johannesson on board the destroyer *Z38* watched through his binoculars as the drama unfolded. As he sped into the smoke-blanketed base he passed to starboard the flaming bulk of a former whale factory ship, the *C.A. Larsen*. Just after nine he received the first desperate signal from the battleship: 'All doctors and surgeons to *Tirpitz*.'

'Through the smoke emerges the shape of the *Tirpitz*. The ship seems to be lying broadside on to the fjord and to be listing slightly,' he wrote in the war diary. At 09.30, together with the destroyer's doctor, he boarded the battleship by the stern and made his way to the bridge.

> The *Tirpitz* is on fire in several places and there are numerous dead bodies on the upper deck. Casualties are undoubtedly very high. The captain is lying on a stretcher in the Control Room and First Officer Wulf Junge has assumed command of the ship. The engines and rudder are undamaged. . . . The fire on board *C.A. Larsen* can be clearly seen through binoculars from the battleship's bridge. It looks to me as though the flames on the upper deck have died down a little, but on the other hand the fire appears to have spread to the inside of the ship. I have signalled *Z34* to fight the fire. I myself am returning to *Z38* to help. If at all possible, some attempt must be made to save the 9,000 tons of fuel.

At about eleven o'clock, as the two destroyers lay to alongside the burning *C.A. Larsen*, the first ambulances from Alta Hospital reached the scene. Junge had put every available man to work. Some carried the wounded ashore, others fought the fires, while the remainder did what they could to clear blocked passages and companionways. No fewer than 113 men had been killed and 284 wounded, and it was a most distressing task, as Junge fully understood:

> The way the men, most of them young and inexperienced, mastered the task before them is truly deserving of praise. My own impression, which is

confirmed by the reports I have received, is that the work was performed both swiftly and correctly. They did not lose heart, despite having to deal with more than four hundred [*sic*] dead and wounded as the day progressed. Although, regrettably, we were on the receiving end, the attack seems to have called forth something extra after many months wihout an engagement.

On board the *C.A. Larsen* the fire had developed into a raging inferno. Barrels of oil and wooden sheds on the foredeck had gone up in flames. The fire spread to the flensing deck, which was soon filled with oily black smoke and became almost impassable. The heat was intense. The crew had abandoned ship and the men from the destroyers had difficulty in finding their way in the maze of smoke-filled corridors below deck. Johanneson wrote:

After a time the crew returns. Some of them can be set to work removing oxygen and gas cylinders, others to act as guides on the lower decks. Often, however, reports of extra-dangerous spots prove contradictory and cause a lot of trouble. The ratings tackle their tasks with enthusiasm after many months of idleness. For the first time they are having to fight a real fire and put their theoretical knowledge to the test. Until we are able to get through to the burning rooms on the starboard side of the tank deck, all windows and portholes are being staved in. It is intended to flood the tank deck with water to prevent the fire reaching vital storerooms in the bowels of the ship.

Later that same evening the fires on board both the *C.A. Larsen* and the *Tirpitz* were at last under control. The factory ship was partially burned out, but its cargo of oil was safe. All the wounded were by this time under proper medical care. Later, 142 of them were flown to hospitals further south, while a further 37 were transferred to the hospital ship *Humbold*, which had been hastily summoned from Tromsø. One of those who found himself on the operating table was Hein Hellendoorn.

'They were armour-piercing bullets and the splinters had gone deep. The man who operated on me was actually an eye-specialist. He tried to draw the deepest splinters out with a magnet, but without success. The jackets were made of copper. Then he simply gave up and closed the wounds. The splinters are still there,' Hellendoorn told me when I met him in the summer of 2003.

Although discipline was maintained throughout, the men were deeply affected by the loss of so many of their comrades. As the evening wore on, the bodies were collected and covered with sheets and blankets. Karl Heinz Lohse, who had come through the ordeal unscathed, was shocked to learn that Werner Brand was among those killed.

'There were several men on board with the same name, so I made the rounds of the corpses, lifting the blankets to see if I could find Werner. We had become close friends and I wanted to bid him a proper farewell. Suddenly a voice behind me said, "What are you doing?" I spun round, and there was Werner, large as life. He'd been in the engine-room and had come through without a scratch.'

Some weeks before the attack Regina Looft had returned to Wilster after a year spent in Alta and Hammerfest. Werner had proposed and she had accepted. They planned to marry as soon as he could get leave.

In his next letter, which was dated Friday 7 April, Werner made no mention of the attack, but to anyone able to read between the lines it was plain that something out of the ordinary had occurred.

My dear little Gina,

First of all, greetings and a tender kiss from your Werner! You must forgive me for making you wait for this letter, but I couldn't write before for reasons that have to do with my service. . . . Yesterday, looking out across the water, I caught sight of a Looft barge and I was immediately overcome with a longing for your presence. You are not here, but even so, Gina, my dear, for a brief moment I was happy. After all, the men on the barge are people I know from my new home. Oh, Gina, can you find us a small house in Wilster? How marvellous it would be! . . . Before I close, there is something I hope you can do for me. That big photograph I had of you has been slightly damaged. It would make me very happy if you could send me a new one.

Lots of kisses
Your Werner

That same day *Kapitän-zur-See* Rolf Johannessen wrote in the war diary: 'After having succeeded in repairing the flagship by long and sustained effort, coupled with exemplary cooperation among all concerned, the Battle Group has suffered a serious setback. I feel a strong bond with the men of my old flagship and am convinced that, with the thought of their fallen comrades before them, with faith and resolution they will soon overcome this reversal.'

Karl Heinz Lohse ought by rights to have gone home on leave in mid-April. But there was an urgent need for skilled carpenters and mechanics, with the result that all leave was cancelled. It was a hard blow for the two friends, who were thus forced to remain on board. Says Lohse: 'I had many days' leave owing that I had intended spending together with my fiancée. As it was, I had to wait till the autumn before I was able to see her again. I was terribly disappointed, but looking back now I see things differently. Fate had intervened.'

CHAPTER SIXTEEN

The Kå Fjord is Abandoned

THE KÅ FJORD, FRIDAY 15 SEPTEMBER 1944

A *Luftwaffe* NCO stationed in Kautokeino was the first to spot the incoming planes, wave after wave of heavy four-engine Lancaster bombers flying serenely westwards at an altitude of 5,000 metres. He counted forty before grabbing the phone and alerting the Air Surveillance Centre in Alta. A massive new attack on the Kå fjord base was all too clearly about to begin.

Kapitän-zur-See Wolf Junge on board the *Tirpitz* was not unduly perturbed. The battleship had been towed to the eastern side of the fjord and was now well sheltered beneath the beetling brow of Mount Sakkobadne. Air-raid warnings had long been a daily occurrence. Since the lightning attack of 3 April, the Fleet Air Arm had tried no fewer than eight times to put paid to the *Tirpitz* once and for all, but without success. The anti-aircraft defences surrounding the base had been reinforced and observation posts set up on the mountainsides. The lack of radar stations had been made good and the number of smoke generators greatly increased. On such occasions as the weather had not compelled the British to call off the attack, they had found the battleship invisible beneath a blanket of dark-grey smoke. All the attacks been beaten off with only minor damage to the base and ship.

On this particular day the first warning reached Junge at 12.46. Shortly afterwards a carpet of smoke began to roll across the fjord. By the time, twelve minutes later, that the throb of the Lancasters' heavy engines was heard, the *Tirpitz* was already largely invisible from the air and every gun in the vicinity was blazing away for all it was worth.

*

Although the *Tirpitz* had been restored to operational readiness and had recovered its firepower, Junge, like everyone else in the know, realised that Germany's defeat was drawing ever closer. In March 1943 the High Seas Fleet had been transferred to western Finnmark with the sole aim of cutting the Allied convoy route through the Barents Sea to the Eastern Front. The mere presence of the Battle Group in the Kå fjord had forced the British to maintain large naval forces in the North Atlantic in order to protect the convoys from attack. But this was little consolation for the German admirals: in a wider sense, their strategy had been a failure. On the rare occasions when an attack had been attempted, it had ended in disaster. The *Hipper* and *Lützow* had been ignominiously put to flight and the *Scharnhorst* sunk. In the past eighteen months the *Tirpitz* had put to sea only three times, twice on exercises and once to attack the Allied bases on Spitsbergen. The Battle Group had failed to sink a single merchantman. What is more, the convoys were sailing more frequently than ever, transporting thousands of tons of invaluable supplies to the Red Army from Scotland and Iceland to the Soviet ports on the Kola Peninsula.

Now, in autumn 1944, the results of this material aid were becoming increasingly apparent. On the central front, further to the south, the *Wehrmacht* was relentlessly being pushed back, suffering appalling losses as it retreated. The Normandy landing had afforded the Allies a foothold on French soil and in August Paris had been liberated. As Eisenhower's armies closed on Germany's borders from the west, Soviet troops entered Poland from the east. It was only a matter of time before Berlin would be under siege.

In the north, the Finns had proved themselves to be unreliable brothers-in-arms, unwilling as they were to go down together with Hitler. The attack on Murmansk and the railway running south had ground to a halt in the autumn of 1941. Not strong enough to break through to the White Sea, General Dietl's Lapland Army had for three years been locked in a bloody war of position. As early as the autumn of 1941 the Finns had regained Karelia, together with other territory lost to the Soviet Union in what has become known as the Winter War. The Finns were gallant fighters, dedicated to their cause, but they had half a million men under arms and had lost more than 150,000 soldiers killed and wounded since 1939. For such a small country the strain was proving unsustainable.

In late 1942 many of the nation's military and political leaders came to the realisation that the alliance with Nazi Germany might well prove their downfall. The pragmatic commander-in-chief, Marshal Carl Gustaf Mannerheim, finally declared his unwillingness to shed more blood to achieve

Germany's aims and said that no further attempts would be made to cut the railway from Murmansk. The surrender of von Paulus's Sixth Army at Stalingrad in February 1943 proved a turning point. Realists in Helsinki realised that a German defeat would have disastrous consequences for Finland's independence. Under diplomatic pressure from the United States, peace talks were initiated; but Moscow refused to consider a separate peace until the Finns accepted its terms, which were incredibly harsh. Finland would have to return all the territory it had reconquered, intern the German troops in the north of the country and pay heavy reparations. The Finns initially rejected the Russian terms, but by late 1944 pressure, both from Berlin and from countries endeavouring to mediate between the warring nations, had considerably increased. In the event, it was not until Stalin launched a massive offensive against the Finnish forces in Karelia in June that serious negotiations were entered into. An armistice was signed in September 1944 and Finnish resistance ceased. The Finns agreed to sever all ties with Nazi Germany and to drive all German troops from Finnish soil in the course of two weeks.

'I regard it as my duty to take my people out of the war,' Mannerheim wrote in an explanatory letter to Hitler. 'As long as I am free to do so, I neither can nor will turn the weapons I have received [from Germany] against Germany. Although you may deplore the step I have taken, in common with all other Finns I hope that termination of our relationship may take place without retribution of any kind.'

Hitler was furious and never replied to the marshal's letter. To his closest associates he simply declared: 'Mannerheim is a great soldier but a poor politician.'

In the meantime Hitler's favourite, Mountain General Eduard Dietl, had joined the long roll of the fallen. The man who had been despatched northwards to Nazify the Arctic was dead – dead not on the field of battle but in a plane crash in the mountains near Salzburg.

When the Führer personally placed a wreath of edelweiss and rhododendrons on the general's bier at an impressive ceremony at Schloss Klessheim in Graz, he took the opportunity to deliver yet another of his perverse speeches.

It is very hard for me to speak on an occasion that has not only deprived me of one of my best soldiers but also of one of my most faithful friends. The military achievements of *Generaloberst* Dietl will go down in history. His personal qualities can be appreciated only by those who have had the pleasure of knowing him for many years. . . . In all that he did he was the very epitome of a National Socialist officer, an officer who does not hesitate when faced with a challenge and the need for action, a man who, in the present struggle, knows that no sacrifice is too great or too costly, yet who, at the same time, is like a father to his men. Not a National Socialist in words alone, but also in his strength of will, his indomitableness and his heart. When, today, I bid farewell to my friend, it is not only with a grievous sense of loss but in the deepfelt certainty that this sacrifice on the altar of the Fatherland places us all under a new obligation.

Implicit in Hitler's eulogy was an injunction to the man who had been appointed to take Dietl's place in the Arctic, *Generaloberst* Lothar Rendulic, a grey-haired sixty-year-old. Rendulic arrived at the 20th Mountain Army's headquarters in Rovaniemi well equipped to live up to Hitler's image of a Nazi officer. As commander of the 2nd Panzer Army, the year before he had remorselessly hunted down and eradicated guerrilla forces in the Balkans and in so doing secured Germany's south-eastern flank. The Finns might be wavering, but Rendulic's orders were crystal-clear: cost what it might, the Northern Front had to be held.

At the time of the Lancaster attack against the *Tirpitz* the situation was still confused. On Thursday 14 September the Finnish delegation appointed to negotiate the final terms of a separate peace had held its first meeting with Foreign Minister Molotov in Moscow. Rendulic was as tough as they come, but he was also a military realist. He knew that if the Finns accepted the Soviet demands, the situation might well take a critical turn. To evacuate 200,000 men and 60,000 horses in a mere two weeks was an impossibility.

*

Few of the civilians behind the front had any conception of what was to come. In Hammerfest, Lohmann & Co.'s fish-filleting factory continued to work its normal two shifts. Since it was opened in 1942 the factory had taken delivery of more than 40,000 tons of fresh fish, which, at a handsome profit, it had processed to provide frozen and tinned field rations for the German forces. Although the factory possessed two up-to-date Bonex filleting machines, its freezing process was a relic of the past, the fish being packed in watertight aluminium moulds and sprinkled with atomised calcium chloride-based brine. The liquid was both ice-cold and caustic, which made it hard on the hands and clothing of the four hundred Ukrainian girls who kept production going. Anny, the girl who had been sent from Dnepropetrovsk to Hammerfest in the summer of 1942 wrote:

Compared with the way the Germans treated ordinary [Russian] prisoners of war we weren't too badly off. We were never beaten or mistreated in any way, but German guards with dogs patrolled the camp area. We were not allowed to be out of doors after seven o'clock in the evening in winter and ten in summer. The food was poor, soup and bread, but we used to steal fish, which we cooked in our quarters, so we managed all right. The work was hard and monotonous. We packed fillets in two shifts. We were paid ten kroner a week and now and again were thus able to buy a little soap and other necessities. Fraternisation with the local population was forbidden, but we used to sneak out and converse with them anyway. On Sundays we went for walks, all of us together, or were taken to the cinema to see German propaganda films. Some of the girls fell ill because of the hard work and harsh climate. But most of us were young and strong. We survived.

Pretty and hot-blooded, the Ukrainian girls inevitably attracted the attention both of the town's young men and of the men who manned the U-boats lying alongside the *Black Watch*, their mothership. Bleak and dangerous as the times were, a little human warmth and female company could make a big difference to the lives of lonely men. Unbelievably, even as late as the winter of 1944 such matters as fraternisation continued to occupy the minds of the men of an *SS* 'hygiene unit' sent to Norway to uphold the sanctity of pure Aryan blood.

'In Hammerfest there is a fish-filleting factory that employs among its workers Ukrainian women. These women are housed in a hutted camp. The men serving on board the *Kriegsmarine*'s sea-going units are forbidden to fraternise with the Ukrainians. Nonetheless, it transpires that in practice this prohibition is very difficult to enforce,' wrote an *SS* doctor named Riess in a report dated 8 February 1944. The local naval commander wanted to have the ban lifted and had sought the opinion of the *SS*. 'Despite severe punishment, infractions continue to occur. As it is men of good standing who get into trouble in this manner, ultimately it is the U-boats' fighting capacity that is affected,' he wrote.

The *Gestapo* in Tromsø had interviewed some of the men and ascertained that the prohibition was a cause of much disgruntlement.

The Ukrainian girls say that they cannot understand why the soldiers should not be permitted to fraternise with them. In the Ukraine both officers and other ranks enjoy close relations with the civilian population, whose brothers and fathers are fighting side by side with German soldiers against the

Bolsheviks. Accordingly, it is difficult to understand that in Norway such relations should be forbidden. Officers posted from the Eastern Front to northern Norway agree that the ban is incomprehensible.

As a provisional measure the head of the *Gestapo* in Tromsø had ruled that the Ukrainians should bear a clearly visible distinguishing mark, a strip of cloth stitched to the back of their work clothes proclaiming that they had been 'freed from the East', i.e. from the Bolshevik yoke. 'We shall have to see if that serves to change the way the soldiers regard these workers from the East,' he wrote. 'The medical officer on the spot says that if the ban on fraternisation is lifted, an increase in both venereal disease and [illegitimate] births must be expected.'

No right-thinking member of the *SS* could fail to be horrified by such a prospect, with the consequence that Dr Riess was prompted to propose a radical solution. 'The Navy always argues that Hammerfest is the first port the men put into after patrols of several weeks' duration involving little physical activity and proper food, and that in consequence their misconduct is understandable. In the matter of their unacceptable relations with Ukrainian girls it may therefore be appropriate to suggest to the *Wehrmacht* that a brothel be opened in Hammerfest.'

A senior medical officer in Oslo, Dr Paris, viewed the situation in the world's northernmost town with greater equanimity, declaring: 'In my view we should not make things difficult for fraternising soldiers. It is quite out of the question to open a brothel up there.'

To Anny, the controversy was of no concern. She had fallen in love with an eighteen-year-old lad from Hammerfest, Jacob Evensen, who also worked at the factory. 'I was very much in love with her,' Jacob said many years later. 'We saw each other whenever we possibly could.'

*

Although she had long been back in Germany, Regina Looft, who in the autumn of 1943 had lived for three months in one of the filleting factory's bed-sitters while Tiefbaumfirma Looft completed their work on the wharves and harbour installations on Fuglenes Point, had left her heart in the north. Despite the distance that separated them, the love she shared with Werner Brand had continued to grow, and they were determined to marry as soon as he could obtain leave. But on board the *Tirpitz* there was still a pressing need for engine-room artificers of Werner's calibre and he had no idea of when he would be allowed to leave for Wilster, where the wedding was to take place. His friend

Karl Heinz Lohse was more fortunate. He had been due for leave in early April, but as a carpenter had had to stay on to help patch up the *Tirpitz* after the devastating attack of 3 April. Now the damage had been made good and he had been issued with a leave pass and travel warrant. He was due to set off from Alta in the first week of September.

As August drew to a close, Werner penned another loving letter to his fiancée:

My dear Gina,

Here comes another sign of life from me, my darling. I know how you long to hear from me, so first let me thank you for your wonderful letter, No. 87.

Today I too am thinking back to 1943, a year of so many wonderful memories, [memories] that help me to get through many burdensome moments. Karl Heinz dropped in yesterday. He is off home next week to see his beloved. I am really sorry that I am unable to go too, but I know that soon it will be my turn. . . . Tomorrow is Sunday and I plan to go out and see if I can find some mushrooms and bilberries. They aren't as plentiful as they were last year and this time I shall be on my own. . . . Leave and our great day are, and will continue to be, the primary considerations. Tell me, Gina dear, what would you like me to get you as a wedding present? Please let me know if you have some special wish. It would make me happy if I could fulfil it.

Many kisses from your loving Werner

In Jena, fourteen-year-old Inge Ehrhardt was delighted to have her father home on holiday for the first time for many months. The job the Zeiss factory had sent him north to do after the midget-submarine attack was nearing completion when, on 3 April, the *Tirpitz* was again attacked, this time from the air. For a second time the battleship's rangefinders had been damaged and Robert Ehrhardt had had to stay on to repair them. But now he was home. Inge was overjoyed.

I loved my father and we always made it an occasion whenever he could get home. It was wartime and we were badly off for food. I remember how he used to bring with him a small barrel of salted herrings, which we thought was marvellous. The local farmers always had a little more food than the rest of us, but herrings could be exchanged for a few eggs or a little pork, flour and potatoes. Bartering with them was often difficult. I thought it most embarrassing and used to hide behind my mother and father. My father loved gardening. Sometimes we would visit relatives, but my father was an easy-going sort. In summer he used to wear *lederhosen*. In our village bare knees were looked upon as most improper and immoral. I remember our being told [by relatives] that we needn't bother to come again if Father insisted on wearing such short trousers.

*

The men responsible for security at the naval base had been angered by the intensity of the air attack, which left behind nearly 400 men dead and wounded. The documents recovered from the wreck of X7 had convinced the senior officers of both the Battle Group and the 230th Division that Alta had been infiltrated by enemy agents. The *Abwehr* chief in northern Norway, 54-year-old *Fregattenkapitän* Claus Kühl, had once been in charge of the organisation's offices in Kirkenes and Alta, so he was well aware of the success achieved against the Soviet partisans in eastern Finnmark by *Premierleutnant* Fritz Pardon. Together with the 230th Division's intelligence officer, *Premierleutnant* Ewald Vierhaus, he too set about relentlessly hunting down the agents who had directed the British planes to the *Tirpitz* with such horrendous consequences. Alta and Talvik had a combined population of about 4,000, to which number had to be added a large number of Russian prisoners of war and German soldiers. This made it impossible to conduct searches like those that had been made in eastern Finnmark, which was so sparsely populated that agents could remain undetected for long periods in remote mountain hideouts. For this reason reliance had to be placed in modern technology. Even the *Abwehr*'s head office in Berlin, which was noted for its scepticism and which had originally erred in rejecting the findings of *MPHS Kirkenes*, appeared to have had second thoughts, as they confirmed that wireless transmitters were operating from the area. The distance was too great for them to be able to locate the transmitters with any accuracy, however, so they contented themselves with stating that they were constantly picking up signals from a transmitter located somewhere between Tromsø and the North Cape. This was by no means good enough for Kühl and Vierhaus, who then set about combing the area surrounding the naval base with the aid of direction-finding equipment installed in vans and ships. In May they felt certain that they had found what they were looking for. There *was* a transmitter in Porsa, on the shores of Varg Sound – and living in Porsa were only ten families. Information provided by an *Abwehr* agent, an engineer working at the Porsa power station, appeared to confirm that all was not as it should be in the little community midway between Alta and Hammerfest. The time had come for drastic action. *Premierleutnant* Pardon's house-to-house search in Varanger had paid off, so it was resolved to carry out a similar operation in Porsa to ascertain whether the bearings were correct. The *Gestapo* in Tromsø and Hammerfest were alerted, and after some discussion it was decided that the matter was of paramount importance to Germany's security and strength at sea. To the head of the *Gestapo* in Hammerfest, the one-time hatmaker Hans Otto Klötzer, a man who had never before resorted to violence, the message was plain: if they did find signs of traitorous activity, all possible means were to be employed to stamp it out. 'The way I saw it,' he said when interrogated after Germany's defeat, 'we were to stop at nothing to put an end to the enemy transmissions. The *Tirpitz* was too important for that.'

Early in the morning of 6 June 1944 the Allies landed in Normandy. That same morning several vessels equipped with direction-finding apparatus approached Porsa. On board were men from the 230th Division, the Gestapo and the Naval Commandant's headquarters in Hammerfest. As the German ships entered the small bay, the signals they were tracking grew stronger. There was a transmitter close by – and it was transmitting at that very moment! 'The wireless operator had just finished transmitting when the first ship drew alongside the quay and German soldiers leaped ashore. When I saw Klötzer making straight for us, I knew the game was up,' said Rolf Storvik when he was interviewed after the war.

Klötzer and his men didn't use half measures. The entire population of Porsa was rounded up and herded into a building used for storing ice. Storvik and his wireless operator, Trygve Duklæt, were beaten and tortured until they broke down and confessed. It later transpired that the raid had been so unexpected that they had had no time to destroy incriminating evidence, with the result that when the Germans left they took with them a rich haul of codes, copies of signals and lists of cover names. The Germans had captured the SIS transmitter codenamed Lyra.

It was a proud Claus Kühl who made his way on board the *Tirpitz* on 11 June to give an account of the raid to her captain. Less than eighteen months from the battleship's arrival in the Kå fjord he had brought about the capture of a pair of enemy agents. 'He reported that they had found in Varg Sound a transmitter working for the British navy. Nearly all the signals that had passed to and fro between Norway and England had been seized, but some of them had not yet been decrypted,' *Kapitän-zur-See* Wolf Junge noted in the ship's war diary. He continued:

Judging by this material and the *Abwehr* officer's verbal account, it has been established that the enemy is taking an excessive interest in the *Tirpitz*. He is well informed in regard to some matters, though not quite as well as I had thought. From the questions asked [by the British] it is quite clear that the operator exaggerated the damage resulting from the attack on 3 April. The station has been especially active in the matter of weather reports.

At that time Junge was under the impression that Lyra was the only clandestine transmitter in the area. He was wrong. In the course of the next two days two more British transmitters, Ida and Vali, the former in Alta, the latter in Hammerfest, were located, together with a Russian station operating from just outside Hammerfest. With four enemy transmitters in their hands, Kühl and Vierhaus set about planning their next move, which was to emulate Pardon and use the transmitters for their own devious purposes.

For that we shall need to work closely together with the Battle Group, the *Tirpitz* and the *Abwehr*, to procure appropriate items of intelligence. It will be necessary to make the ship appear to be in a worse state than it really is and to exaggerate the extent of the damage, as well as to provide guarded weather forecasts. This will be especially important when the ship again puts to sea, which will be in the near future. It will also be very important to ascertain what is being done about the agents' helpers. If one of their accomplices gets across to Sweden, it will be both pointless and dangerous to continue the deception, as to pursue it we shall have to release credible information.

One of the men Klötzer had arrested was 21-year-old Aksel Bogdanoff. At the time of his capture in a mountain hideout on the island of Kvaløy, not far from Hammerfest, Bogdanoff had been suffering from exposure and was in a state of near-exhaustion. A few days earlier he had parachuted from a Russian plane, bringing with him a wireless transmitter and provisions to last for several months. When Klötzer learned Bogdanoff's name, he needed only a brief search of the files to complete the picture. In Kirkenes, a few months earlier, Fritz Pardon had filed a report on his interrogation of Aksel's mother, Signe, who was fifty-one and had three other children besides Aksel. She told him that she had been at home one dark December evening in 1943 when she had heard noises outside the house. Opening the door to investigate, she had found herself confronted by five men, who were holding her son Aksel captive. They were strangers to her and spoke Russian.

'They said I was to go with them to Russia. I refused and said that I was not going to leave my two youngest children alone. They threatened us with their machine pistols and said they'd be back. Then they went away, taking Aksel with them.' Pardon had believed the woman's story and noted that she had made 'a very favourable impression'.

Now Signe Bogdanoff's son was in prison in Hammerfest. Klötzer and his thugs had made good use of their clubs and blood-stained chains, and it hadn't taken them long to persuade Duklæt and young Bogdanoff to fall in with their plans. It may have been the way the war was going for the Germans that induced Vierhaus to propose a more merciful course than that resorted to by Pardon in eastern Finnmark eight months earlier. Instead of a military tribunal and the threat of a death sentence for the men who had contributed to the attack on the *Tirpitz*, he made a pragmatic agreement with his two hapless captives. If they were willing to continue their transmissions under German control, the lives of those who had helped them would be spared.

*

On the bridge of the *Tirpitz*, *Kapitän-zur-See* Wolf Junge could barely see the British bombers through the swirling smoke from the generators. But when the first bombs fell at 12.59 he had no difficulty in hearing the resultant explosions; they were much heavier than those made by the bombs dropped in previous attacks.

'A succession of extremely strong tremors ensued as a result of exploding bombs in the forward part of the ship and close to the hull. The ship is not yet fully obscured by smoke. It is clearly visible from the air,' he wrote.

A quarter of an hour later it was all over and the bombers disappeared to the south-east. When the smoke dispersed, Junge realised that the battleship had been under attack from an entirely new weapon. A bomb that had fallen on Straumsnes Point had left a crater almost 40 metres wide and 10 metres deep. The bombs dropped by the Fleet Air Arm had rarely exceeded a few hundred kilograms. Those dropped by the Lancasters were something else entirely. Known as Tallboys, they each contained 5.6 tons of high explosive. The *Tirpitz* was fortunate to escape a direct hit, but one bomb penetrated the foredeck and hull, to explode in the water, close under the starboard bow, leaving a gash nearly 50 metres across. Two thousand tons of seawater flooded into the forward section of the ship, five men were killed and fifteen wounded. Closer inspection revealed extensive internal damage too. Frames had buckled and broken and bulkheads had been blown in. On the starboard side, only the undamaged steel plating surrounding the hole still held the bow and the rest of the hull together.

Some of the vessels anchored close by had also suffered badly. Three had been sunk – the steamer *KHZ57*, a trawler, the *Kehrwieder*, and a lighter, *Nord 29*, newly arrived from Oslo with 200 tons of supplies. It was the *Kehrwieder* that, in the winter of 1942, had transported *Abwehr* agent Ib Arnasson Riis from Hamburg to Heligoland, where he had transferred to the U-boat that took him to Iceland. The lighter, which was Dutch, had been sunk by a direct hit forward. Suffering badly from shock and immersion in the icy water, her 39-year-old engineer was rescued. His 24-year-old Norwegian girlfriend, Astrid, was less fortunate and disappeared without trace. She had been in the forward cabin when the bomb hit.

For Junge, who only a few months earlier had taken over captaincy of the *Tirpitz* from Hans Meyer, the conclusion was all too evident. The tenth air attack had achieved its object. Although the giant was still afloat and its engines and armament were undamaged, for fear that its weakened bow would give way, it would never again dare to brave the open sea.

'The attack has confirmed that the defences are not good enough to ward off high-altitude attacks by heavy bombers,' Junge wrote. 'The ship can no longer remain in the Kå fjord.'

CHAPTER SEVENTEEN

Defeat

TROMSØ AND OSLO, NOVEMBER/DECEMBER 1944

The room was still when *Generalrichter* Dr Reuter declared the court martial in session. During the night, Oslo had had its first snowfall of the winter and the streets were deep in slush. It was Sunday 17 December 1944 and the three judges would very much have preferred to be elsewhere. But Hitler, ensconced in his western headquarters, the *Adlerhorst* (Eagle's Eyrie), had personally taken command of his last great offensive in the Ardennes and was in no mood to be gainsaid. The court martial had been accorded maximum priority and for that reason required the presence of a trio of high-ranking officers. That explained the profusion of gold braid and decorations among the judges, who had been specially flown in from Berlin. Foremost among them was one of the *Luftwaffe*'s veteran pilots, *Generalleutnant* Karl Angerstein, a First World War fighter ace who was now in charge of the Air Force's Fighter and Reconnaissance Training Establishment and also responsible for liaison with the *Kriegsmarine*. Beside him sat another of Göring's close associates, *General der Flieger* Karl-Heinrich Schulz, for many years Chief of Staff of *Luftflotte 4*, which was fighting on the Eastern Front. *Grossadmiral* Dönitz had also sent a senior officer, *Konter-Admiral* Gerhard Wagner, former head of the Naval High Command's Operations Staff.

These three highly distinguished officers were in Oslo that dark December morning for a very important reason. They were there to decide the fate of one of the *Luftwaffe*'s greatest heroes, 27-year-old *Major* Heinrich Ehrler, holder of the Iron Cross of the Knight's Cross with Oak Leaves, an honour he had been awarded for shooting down a total of 199 enemy aircraft in the north.

Ehrler was in a very tight corner indeed, having been blamed for failing to prevent the sinking of the *Tirpitz* outside Tromsø a few weeks earlier with the loss of more than a thousand lives. He risked being sentenced to death for dereliction of duty.

*

The Finns signed an armistice with the Soviet Union on 19 September 1944 and immediately severed all ties with Berlin. This left the new commander of the 20th Mountain Army, *Generaloberst* Lothar Rendulic, in a parlous position. Two hundred thousand of his men were entrenched between the Fisherman's Peninsula in the north and Salla in the south. He had been ordered to hold the Litza front, but under the terms of the armistice the Finns had committed themselves to expelling the Germans if they failed to withdraw within two weeks. Many of the German officers involved did not believe that their erstwhile companions-in-arms really would turn upon them after having fought alongside them for so many years, but in that they were mistaken. Only ten days after Helsinki had agreed to the terms of the armistice, Finnish troops under General Hjalmar Siilasvuo opened fire on Rendulic's forces, who had begun to fall back on well-prepared positions in Lapland. Early in October a number of bloody skirmishes occurred around the towns of Torneå and Kemi. But the Finnish attacks were only the beginning of Rendulic's problems. Early in the morning of Saturday 7 October, his 2nd and 6th Mountain Divisions, which for three long years had remained dug in on the banks of the Litza and Titovka, found themselves under a concerted artillery barrage backed by screaming rockets from multiple launchers known as Stalin organs. When, after two and a half hours, the bombardment finally ceased, the Soviet infantry rose from their trenches and stormed the German positions. This heralded the start of a major offensive involving 135,000 men of the Soviet 14th Army and Northern Fleet. When marines landed in the rear of the German forces, Rendulic immediately grasped the gravity of the situation. It was going to be a decisive battle. Only by frantically mobilising 1,000 lorries to transport the 63rd Division across the 500-kilometre-long Arctic Highway from Finland to Pasvik on the Norwegian border did the Mountain Corps succeed in extricating itself from the enemy's rapidly closing jaws. In Berlin, Hitler realised that there was no longer any point in fighting over the mountainous landscape of the Kola Peninsula and agreed to the withdrawal of Rendulic's hard-pressed army to a new defensive line at Lyngen in the northern part of the county of Troms. *Festung Kirkenes*, the naval base in the Kå fjord and the remainder of Finnmark were all to be evacuated.

*

The *Kriegsmarine* followed the progress of the fighting in the east with growing concern. 'Under Bolshevik pressure Finnish regiments are doing all they can to harry our forces in northern Karelia and Lapland. Since the Finns began their attacks north of Torneå, there have been some heavy engagements. West of Murmansk the Bolsheviks have launched strong attacks. Heavy fighting has flared up around our strongpoints along the Finnish-Soviet border,' said a communiqué issued by the *Wehrmacht* on Sunday 8 October.

'It looks to me as though, after nine months at anchor, the flotilla will at last be allowed to do something,' wrote the commander of the 4th Destroyer Flotilla, *Kapitän-zur-See* Rolf Johannesson. He was delighted when, a few days later, the order came to go the aid of the Mountain Corps. 'It is with no little joy that I welcome this order. What have I not written, said and proposed to get us away from the soul-destroying atmosphere of Alta? In such circumstances people inevitably grow slack. Speaking for myself, I would cheerfully throw myself into battle rather than lie idle somewhere, ignorant of the enemy's morale and tactics,' he wrote.

Johannesson's destroyers had one last task to fulfil before they were free to set a course eastwards for Varanger. The bomb that had gone through its forward deck on 15 September had left the *Tirpitz* a near-cripple. It was feared that if she were to exceed a speed of 10 knots the bow would tear away. As a seagoing battleship she was out of action for good. Instead, it was resolved to capitalise on what remained of the ship's firepower. She was to make her way to Tromsø, where she would be transformed into a floating artillery platform. Her heavy guns would protect the western end of Rendulic's new line of defence through Lyngen.

Sunday 15 October was a sad day for the once so proud *Kriegsmarine*. The disabled battleship left her net enclosure in the Kå fjord for the last time and set a course for Tromsø. Her speed was a mere 8 knots; in case of need, six tugs and auxiliary vessels followed in her wake.

'Despite the severe damage she had suffered, her manoeuvrability remained unaffected. The fear that she might be difficult to control proved unfounded. She reached Tromsø under her own steam,' said a despatch to the Naval High Command.

This was no consolation to the admirals. They had come to the Kå fjord eighteen months earlier with the avowed intention of delivering an annihilating blow against the Allied convoys sailing through the Barents Sea, but had achieved very little. And now the illustrious Mountain Corps was engaged in a bloody retreat from the River Litza. Worse, the 1st Battle Group was no more and its advance base had been abandoned.

Admiral Oscar Kummetz never returned to Alta. In June 1944 command of the Battle Group was taken over by *Konter-Admiral* Rudolf Peters, who until his transfer had been U-boat Commander in Narvik. When, for the last time, Peters mustered the ship's company for a farewell address before the *Tirpitz* left for Tromsø, he made a brave attempt to boost their morale.

'We are living in momentous, but difficult, times,' he said. 'They demand much of a man – enterprise and tenacity. I feel assured that, in these changed circumstances, all the men who till now have been under my command will, with undiminished vigour and determination, do their duty until victory is ours!'

In the war diary he struck a more sombre note, however, writing: 'Notice has been received from the Naval High Command that the 1st Battle Group will be disbanded with effect from 20 October. As the Group's last commander since 6 June, I have not been able to lead it into battle against the enemy, despite the Group's having consisted of capable, well-trained men eager to fight. That is the tragedy of this command.'

In Tromsø an anchorage had been prepared for the *Tirpitz* off the island of Håkøy, a few kilometres away from the town itself. It had been chosen with care, as the sea round about was shallow, which meant that there was no danger of the ship capsizing. In fact, at low tide there would be only about a metre of water beneath the keel. It was reasoned that if the battleship were again to be hit by a bomb, she would settle on the bottom instead of turning turtle. However, soundings revealed that there was a deep depression in the seabed amidships, which Junge ordered should be filled in. In the course of the work, which commenced on Wednesday 1 November, 14,000 cubic metres of sand and gravel were dumped into the hole. In the meantime, the ship's complement was halved, although the men thus rendered surplus were not permitted to leave Tromsø. Instead they were set to work installing anti-aircraft guns, smoke generators and the anti-torpedo nets that had surrounded the battleship in the Kå fjord. An armoured turret aft was converted to hold a Würzburg/Dora-type radar, which could detect an aircraft at distances of over 100 kilometres.

'We kept all the anti-aircraft gunners on board, as we expected air attacks to continue. There was thus no question of reducing our state of readiness,' says

Hein Hellendoorn, who had meanwhile been promoted to *2. Flakoffizier* and made second-in-command of the ship's anti-aircraft defence, in which capacity he reported to 1st Gunnery Officer Willi Müller and the senior flak officer, *Kapitänleutnant* Alfred Fassbender.

'*1. Flakoffizier* Friedrich Spies was a man of considerable experience, but he had been badly wounded in the air attack of 3 April. Fassbender was posted to the *Tirpitz* as his replacement in the spring, so he had been on board for about six months when we got to Tromsø,' says Hellendoorn.

Although there were many replacements among the senior officers, the old hands felt safer in Tromsø than they had in the Kå fjord. This was because of an item of good news that had been announced by their new commander, *Kapitän-zur-See* Robert Weber when he took over from Wolf Junge on Saturday 4 November. There was a fighter squadron stationed at Bardufoss, only a quarter of an hour's flying time from the anchorage.

'We felt relieved,' Hellendoorn remembers. 'We hadn't seen a sign of the *Luftwaffe* since we arrived in northern Norway. Allied bombers were able to attack without fear of German fighters. We had been forced to defend ourselves with the weapons we had to hand. All of a sudden things looked brighter. We were very pleased.'

*

It was because of a dramatic turn of events in the north that there were fighters nearby. Under relentless pressure from Soviet and Finnish forces, Rendulic's orderly withdrawal had gradually deteriorated into a headlong retreat. As October drew to a close, endless columns of soldiers, motor vehicles and horses wound their way westwards along rutted, unmade roads. The Mountain Corps fought a stubborn rearguard action, while the men of the supply and transportation services laboured to empty the abandoned depots. Thousands of tons of ammunition, provisions and fuel were stored in Varanger and Lapland, and Rendulic was determined that nothing should fall into the hands of the Russians. Moreover, he intended to take as much as he possibly could back to Lyngen. What could not be transported there by road or sea was to be burned.

In northern Finland, an orgy of mass destruction had already begun. More than 100,000 civilians had been evacuated, and as the German rearguard withdrew westwards they blew bridges, mined roads and torched every large building. Rovaniemi, once home to Dietl's command headquarters, was razed by a firestorm that started on the night of 13/14 October. It took only a few days to reduce the town's picturesque old wooden buildings to heaps of smoking ruins.

'Standing in the station was a heavily laden ammunition train. But it had no engine, so I ordered up a tank to haul it into a siding. Shortly afterwards I received a phone call from a desperate stationmaster. The train had rolled back into the station and he was afraid that it would blow up at any moment,' wrote *SS-Oberführer* Schreiber, commander of the 12th *Jäger* Regiment of the 6th *SS* Division North. As Schreiber was trying to get back to the railway, a wagon did blow up, one of its wheels landing a bare two metres away from him.

'For the next few hours ammunition continued to explode, turning the centre of the town into a raging inferno. The air was full of flying glass and baulks of timber. Many soldiers were killed. About three hundred of the most seriously injured were housed in a school, but that was heavily damaged too. There was nothing we could do.'

Having suffered more than 300 air raids, Kirkenes was already in ruins. Everything that room couldn't be found for on the last convoys was blown up and set on fire, as were houses, docks, bunkers and mines. When the first Russian troops reached the town late in the evening of Tuesday 24 October, only a handful of private houses were still standing.

'The storming of the fortified defences took several hours during the night between Tuesday and Wednesday. When day dawned, the whole town was wreathed in smoke. The mines were on fire, as were factory buildings and harbour installations. . . . There was some savage street-fighting in the southern outskirts of the town. The Russians fought their way into the town, block by block, street by street. By noon, the 5,000-strong garrison was forced to admit defeat.'

The local Quislings knew that the hour of reckoning was fast approaching. Few of them were in doubt as to what their fate would be if they remained behind when the Germans withdrew. Together with their families, the first of the fellow-travellers to leave had set off for the comparative safety of the south early in the autumn. When the front began to crumble in October, both the German High Command and Nazi officials found themselves faced with yet another problem, and that an acute one. If Finnmark were to be left as it was, it would provide the Russians with a bridgehead from which to mount further attacks on the Lyngen Line. And a free county in the north under legitimate Norwegian control would be a thorn in the side of the Quisling government in the south. Rendulic, Quisling and *Reichkommissar* Josef Terboven decided to resolve the problem by adopting the Russians' own scorched-earth policy. Finnmark was to be laid waste and its population of close on 75,000 evacuated. To Rendulic, this made military sense. Finnmark and northern Finland were to be left a vast no-man's-land in order to slow down the Russian advance. Or, as he put it in his first order, which was dated 15 October 1944: 'Throughout the whole Finnish-Norwegian region . . . in the course of the retreat all buildings are to be destroyed to deny the enemy a base in the winter.'

Terboven and his Norwegian henchmen viewed the situation from a political standpoint. They knew that Germany was doomed to defeat. Evacuation, coupled with wholesale destruction of Finnmark, would afford the regime a breathing space. 'If large numbers of people remain behind, an assumption of power in the abandoned area by the Bolsheviks or the Norwegian government-in-exile will create major political problems in Norway as a whole . . . with [resultant] industrial sabotage . . . and impairment of [our] military strength,' he wrote.

Police Chief Jonas Lie and the Minister of Social Affairs, Johan Lippestad, were appointed 'governors of Finnmark' and charged with the task of overseeing this cold-blooded operation from their headquarters in Alta and Hammerfest. When, on Tuesday 17 October, Lie issued his first appeal for voluntary evacuation, he invoked the spectre of Red terror.

Norwegian women and men! I have seen for myself what things are like in Bolshevik Russia and know what the consequences will be for a superior people like the Norwegians. The result will be murder and pillage, terror and despotism, rape, atheism and moral degeneracy. And the fighting may leave the people to face the winter without a roof over their heads. Think of your children's future in such circumstances! As earnestly as I can I urge you, one and all, to avail yourselves of the opportunity to leave that is now open to you. Seize it without delay. One day it may be too late, leaving you to reproach yourselves and bear the responsibility. This is a matter of the utmost gravity.

Only a few people heeded Lie's warning. They knew that liberation was imminent and were not prepared to leave their homes. Terboven therefore turned to Hitler and asked his permission to evacuate the population by force. The result was Hitler's tragic decree of Saturday 28 October authorising the *Wehrmacht* and their pro-Nazi helpmates to destroy the northernmost region of Norway.

Because the people of northern Norway are not willing to leave of their own volition, the *Führer* has agreed to the *Reichkommissar*'s proposal and ordered that, for its own safety, the entire Norwegian population east of the Lyngen fjord be forcibly evacuated and all dwellings burned down or [otherwise] destroyed. The Commander-in-Chief in northern Finland is responsible for ensuring that this *Führerbefehl* is ruthlessly carried out. . . . There is no room for compassion.

Thus sanctioned by Berlin, the retreating Germans then embarked on a programme of systematic destruction. From that time onwards, until the depredations came to an end in February 1945, more than 16,000 buildings were burned down and some 50,000 people evacuated; about 25,000 sought refuge in the mountains.

In my own town of Hammerfest, Lippestad set about evacuating people two days before Hitler's order came through. On Friday 27 October a start was made on dismantling industrial properties. But one business, Lohmann's fish-filleting factory, was destined to be spared. 'Everything of value was stripped down and loaded into cargo ships. We were then evacuated to Svinøya in the Lofotens, where it was planned to start afresh,' says Anny Evensen.

My parents were permitted to take with them only what they could carry: two suitcases, a milk pail and a cardboard box. They were herded on to a fishing boat, which took them southwards, together with the rest of the townspeople. One week later, on Saturday 11 November, Hammerfest was deserted – except for the German fire-raisers, Norwegian Nazis and a handful of others who, for various reasons, remained behind. In the course of the next few months the town was systematically demolished. All the houses, which were of wood, were burned down and telegraph poles and foundations blown up. The dock installations so painstakingly built by Tiefbaufirma Looft were completely destroyed.

The municipal engineer, Johannes Kummenje, who had been kept back by the Germans, recorded in his diary:

The systematic destruction by fire engulfed quarter after quarter, after houses and warehouses had been emptied of their furnishings and goods of every kind. As a parting gesture, even doors and windows were removed, along with stoves, electric cookers and the like. After that, anything that happened to have escaped the flames was meticulously sorted out and thrown into the burning buildings; and when the ruins had sufficiently cooled off, the foundations were blown up to ensure that not as much as a corner was left standing over which a roof could be laid for shelter.

The first of the townspeople to return after this act of wanton destruction were horrified by the sight that met their eyes:

Two men went ashore and made their way towards the ruins. A boat was then launched and four other men rowed slowly along, parallel with the shore, to what remained of the steamer quay. There they made the boat fast and clambered ashore. They were expecting ruins, but nothing had prepared them for what they saw. The town had gone. It had been levelled to the ground. Only a few jagged foundations stood out above the rubble. Streets and open spaces were full of broken glass, tortured metal and the remains of what had once been walls – mute testimony to the manic destruction wrought upon a defenceless town.

Lie and Lippestad relied on terror to cow their compatriots into submission. One of their victims was Ragnvald Wærnes, the 46-year-old printer from Vadsø, who had seen the paper for which he worked, the *Finmarken*, turned into a Nazi propaganda sheet. Its end came in August 1944, when Soviet bombers reduced much of nearby Vardø, where the paper had its offices, to ruins. The newspaper ceased publication and was amalgamated with the *Finnmark Folkeblad*, which was published in Hammerfest. The *Finmarken*'s printers were thrown out of work, but Wærnes found himself a new job as a steward on board a small coal-fired steamer, the *Hornøy*, which had been commandeered by the *Wehrmacht* and operated a regular service between Alta and Kirkenes. He had seen at first hand the chaos that reigned in Finnmark. In Varanger, the Germans were in full flight, their convoys constantly harried by Soviet aircraft and torpedo boats. When, on Thursday 26 October, the *Hornøy* docked in Hammerfest with a full cargo of soldiers and civilians, Wærnes came up with a bright idea, which he confided to his crewmates. He suggested that on their next trip eastwards they should choose a course that would take them out of sight of German patrol vessels. Then, when they were far enough east, they would hoist a white flag and surrender to a Russian or an Allied ship.

Unfortunately for Wærnes, a German sailor overheard him and reported the matter to the *Gestapo*. Wærnes was arrested and taken to Alta, where Jonas Lie immediately realised that here was a golden opportunity to make an example that would put the fear of God into the population. A special court was quickly convened, but the legal proceedings were a travesty. Wærnes claimed that the sailors had been having a party and that he had only been joking, but to no avail: the verdict was a foregone conclusion. He was sentenced to death and on the morning of Sunday 29 October executed in a pine forest as a warning to others. A Norwegian Nazi, Gard Holtskog, Lie's adjutant, Karl Sommerfeldt, and three Norwegian military policemen were responsible for this despicable crime. Wærnes was allowed no defence counsel, no right of appeal and no visiting clergyman. 'When the order was given to fire, the prisoner was leaning back against a steep bank. He crumpled up and fell to the ground, whereupon Sommerfeldt strode over to him and shot him in the head with his pistol.'

*

To the very end the pilots of the Arctic Squadron continued to fight bitter and bloody battles in the skies above the Varanger Peninsula. On 9 October, with Soviet troops only 10 kilometres from the airfield in Petsamo, a tremendous battle between Russian and German fighters raged above the front. *Major* Heinrich Ehrler who, two months earlier, had been promoted to *Kommodore* and placed in command of *Jagdgeschwader 5*, reported that that day his pilots had shot down 85 enemy machines. This brought the total number of kills claimed by the squadron since its arrival in Kirkenes to more than 3,000. Ehrler was at the peak of his career. He wore the ribbon of the Knight's Cross of the Iron Cross with Oak Leaves and a number of other decorations. As squadron commander he had to spend a great deal of time behind a desk, a chore he hated; he much preferred to lead his men from the cockpit of his yellow-painted Messerschmitt. He was popular with pilots and ground staff alike. 'His boldness and contagious fighting spirit make him both an example and an excellent teacher,' says a *Luftwaffe* assessment compiled that same autumn.

On a sortie he flew on Sunday 22 October Ehrler brought down a Soviet Il-2 fighter-bomber over Kirkenes harbour to bring his total number of victories up to 199. But time was running out for the major and his men. Kirkenes was blazing and the squadron's airfield at Høybuktmoen was under Soviet mortar fire. Some of the squadron's auxiliary units had already been evacuated to Banak and Bardufoss.

'A sense of impending doom hangs over Kirkenes. There is nothing left of the town but ashes and ruins and it is under constant attack by the Russians from the air,' says an entry in the squadron's history. The next day, Monday 23 October, Ehrler took off from the badly cratered airfield for the last time and headed west. Three days later Høybuktmoen was in Soviet hands.

*

A week later the *Tirpitz*'s anti-aircraft gunners beat off the first heavy British air attack. Thirty-seven Lancasters took off from Scotland, crossed the North Sea, cut across neutral Sweden and launched a surprise attack from the south-east with 5.6-ton Tallboys. The weather had been unseasonably fine and sunny ever since the battleship's arrival in Tromsø. When, at 09.00 on Sunday 29 October, after a flight of several hours, the bombers droned in over their target, there was little wind; a layer of cloud had, however, formed at an altitude of 2,000 metres above the town. The smoke generators were not yet in place, but the anti-aircraft guns were, and they immediately opened fire.

Egil Lindberg, who was still operating a clandestine transmitter located in the municipal hospital, signalled to London that the explosions were so heavy that the earth shook. But the cloud cover made precision bombing difficult and no damage was done to the *Tirpitz*. Her men were jubilant when the bombers turned for home and disappeared over the island of Senja. 'We put up an effective barrage. A lot of bombs fell close by, but none of them scored a hit,' says Hein Hellendoorn, who had directed the ship's anti-aircraft guns from his position in the main turret, 40 metres above the deck.

Robert Ehrhardt, the Zeiss representative, who had been kept busy working on the lenses of the battleship's rangefinders ever since the midget-submarine attack in September of the previous year, was looking forward to being home in Jena for Christmas. In a letter dated Friday 3 November to his daughter Inge he wrote:

Up here, winter has not yet really got a grip. How things are further south I do not know, but here, only the tops of the mountains are white. That suits me fine, because of my work, but the men don't like it. They all long for storms and clouded skies, so that the 'four-engined' [bombers] can't get to us. It's not too bad when a town is attacked, but up here we know for certain that we alone are the target of the eight-ton bombs. When they hit the water, they send up a spout 200 metres high! It's a wonderful sight. But it's not so wonderful when you think about what would happen if one were to land on your head. I shall be finished with my work tomorrow. I shall then spend a day or two in Tromsø before setting off for Horten [a small town on the western shore of the Oslo fjord, then a naval base]. You ask me when the next ship leaves. I don't know, all I know is that I may need to possess my soul in patience for a few days. In the meantime I shall have to remain on board. I will write you again as soon as I get to Horten. Thank you for your nice letter.

Many loving greetings to Mother and yourself
Your father

The next day Wolf Junge was replaced as captain of the *Tirpitz* by Robert Weber, who continued the work of safeguarding the anchorage against further air attacks. He had been notified in strict confidence that some twenty to thirty fighters of the renowned Arctic Squadron were to be stationed at Bardufoss. This made it vitally important to establish good lines of communication between the battleship, *Hauptflugwache Tromsø* and the duty officer of *Jagdegeschwader 5*.

'We laid an underwater telephone cable from the *Tirpitz* to the Air Surveillance Centre in the town, which in turn had a wireless link with Bardufoss. The earlier all concerned were alerted to an impending attack, the better the chance of averting it. At all costs we needed to gain time, to avoid being caught napping. It would be a great advantage if we were able to call on the fighters for assistance,' Hellendoorn says.

Air-raid warnings in the region between Tromsø and Narvik were the responsibility of the 42nd company of *Luftnachrichtenregiment 251*. The company commander was a former *SS* man, a one-time shopkeeper from Stuttgart, 28-year-old *Premierleutnant* Walter Härer, holder of the Iron Cross 2nd Class and War Merit Cross with Swords. He had been highly praised by his superior officers for his accomplishments on the Eastern Front. 'A dedicated and honourable officer who is a convinced National Socialist. An ever-reliable and enterprising company commander who, in a spirit of optimism, overcomes all difficulties and is capable of improvisation, [he] has an excellent knowledge of wireless and has made every effort to familiarise himself with the air-raid warning system. [He is] physically fit and strong.'

Under Härer's command was an extensive network of observation posts whose duty it was to report every incursion by an enemy aircraft to *Hauptflugwache Tromsø*, which operated from a building in the centre of the town. Most of these posts were located at fortified points on the coast, where soldiers maintained a visual watch. They were backed by radar stations equipped with new FuMG 402 Wassermann and FuMG 80 Freya sets, which were able to detect aircraft at distances of up to 190 kilometres. But because of Hitler's fanatical belief in an Allied landing in northern Norway, most of them were so sited as to scan the open sea. There was next to no surveillance of the air space over Sweden, and a radar chain in the hinterland was still only halfway to completion.

Despite these shortcomings, Härer was optimistic the first time he conferred by phone with *Kapitänleutnant* Alfred Fassbender on board the *Tirpitz*, early in November. Between the main observation centre in Tromsø and the satellite centre at Bardufoss there was a duplex wireless link to which the *Tirpitz* was indirectly connected via the underwater cable. Härer assured Fassbender that all reports of approaching aircraft would be passed on to Bardufoss, be they from the *Tirpitz* itself or from the land-based observation posts. 'My principal task is to ensure that the fighters are alerted in time. There is no cause for anxiety,' Härer said.

On Friday 10 November an informal meeting took place between the *Tirpitz*'s 1st Gunnery Officer, Willi Müller, the 2nd Flak Officer, Heinrich Hellendoorn, Walter Härer and 24-year-old *Leutnant* Leo Beniers, who occupied a key position at Bardufoss. The subsequent enquiry into the course of events gave Beniers, the tall, slim son of a teacher, a good reference. 'Beniers is extremely knowledgeable and possessed of sound judgement. He is ardent, keen and proud, expresses himself well orally and is highly conscientious.' Beniers' eloquence and other qualities were just what he needed as fighter controller and the officer in charge of the airfield's report centre, as he was responsible for ensuring that the stream of observations coming in reached the men who had to act on them in a readily comprehensible form. What this meant in practice was that he was one of the men who had to see to it that the fighters took off in time. Says Heinrich Hellendoorn:

The first British attack had been unsuccessful, but we were quite sure that they would try again. The weather was still perfect, all cloudless skies and no wind. But in Tromsø the sun disappears below the horizon at the end of November. There were only three weeks left until the onset of the Arctic night, which would preclude attack from the air. For that reason we were eager to ensure that communications were in order and that we were properly prepared. We knew that if the fine weather continued we could be attacked again at any time.

On Saturday 11 November Beniers was invited on board the *Tirpitz* by *Korvettenkapitän* Müller and shown over the ship. This enabled him to see for himself that the battleship's anti-aircraft guns were ready for action. The same was true of the batteries ashore and those on board the flakships *Thetis* and *Nymphe*, which lay at anchor some distance from the ship they were there to protect. The snag was that the land-based smoke generators were not yet operational. Admittedly, the Naval Commandant in Tromsø had provided seven fishing boats, which had been converted to add to the smoke screen, but they were meant to be employed only after dark.

'The Kå fjord was narrow and could quickly be blanketed in smoke. The basin between Tromsø and Håkøy was different, and much wider. The smoke boats wouldn't be enough to blot out the *Tirpitz* completely. We reasoned that all the smoke would do would be to make things difficult for the anti-aircraft gunners. We had to place most of our reliance on the fighters,' says Hellendoorn.

Major Heinrich Ehrler had in the meantime landed at Bardufoss in his Messerschmitt Bf 109, together with his somewhat younger adjutant, *Leutnant* Kurt Schultze, *Hauptmann* Franz Dörr, *Premierleutnant* Werner Gayko and other Arctic Squadron aces.

'We had just left the front, where, at constant risk of his life, Ehrler had led us in battle until the Russians were on the verge of overrunning the airfield. We had seen for ourselves the bloody chaos and knew exactly how matters stood,' says Schulze.

At the headquarters of *Luftflotte 5* in Oslo it was decided to break up the squadron and disperse it about the country. One flight would go to Sola, near Stavanger, while the bulk of the squadron's aircraft would be divided between the airfields at Banak, Alta and Bardufoss. After having fought for long without reinforcements, the squadron suddenly found itself re-equipped with new machines – 56 Messerschmitt Bf 109G-6s and 22 brand-new Focke-Wulf 190 A-8s. Heavily armed and with a top speed in excess of 700 km/h, the Fw 190 is recognised as one of the best and most versatile of all Second World War fighters.

Ehrler was only in transit, as it was the intention that he should push on to Alta, where he would establish a temporary base at Elvebakken. However, when, on Thursday 9 November, he made a tour of inspection at Bardufoss, he found the situation untenable. 'Most of the pilots were totally unacquainted with the Focke-Wulf 190; none of the flight commanders had flown one before. Worse, the young pilots who had recently arrived to replace men who had been shot down had no front-line experience at all. Not only that, they were ignorant both of weather conditions and of other characteristic features of war in the north. Nor had they had any training in formation flying.'

As one of the *Luftwaffe*'s most highly decorated officers, Ehrler got his own way. When he informed commanders in the area that until further notice he intended to take personal charge of the fighters, there was not a word of protest. He immediately set about organising a training programme for the new recruits: the Focke-Wulfs were to be 'flown in' and their pilots given training in formation flying.

'Ehrler prolonged our stay by three days and decided that we should go on to Alta early on Sunday morning, 12 November. We had heard that the *Tirpitz* had been moved to Tromsø, but we didn't know her exact whereabouts. No one briefed us on the battleship. We had merely made an intermediate stopover to reorganise the squadron and to train the newcomers,' says Schultze.

*

While Ehrler and his pilots were working up the FW 190s, the British were contemplating renewed attacks on the *Tirpitz*. Bomber Command's planning staff had been deeply disappointed at the failure of the two Tallboy attacks to sink the battleship. They were acutely aware that on 27 November the sun would dip below the horizon, not to return for several months, so they had to act quickly. The aircrews shared the planners' disappointment, though for a different reason. They hated the thought of a new operation in the Arctic. It would entail fourteen hours' flying and impose heavy demands on both pilots and navigators. On the sleep-inducing return flight across the endless waste of sea between the island of Senja and Scotland, some of the pilots had resorted to banging their heads against the instrument panel to keep awake. On 5 November the crews were put on standby, but a report of bad weather over the target led to cancellation of the operation. Some days later, however, the meteorologists forecast cold weather and clear skies in the Tromsø area, and late in the evening of Saturday 11 November a third raid was launched. The Lancasters took off from their bases in Scotland and set a course that would take them diagonally across the North Sea. Dawn broke as they reached the Norwegian coast.

'The terrain below was bleak, precipitous and barren, and at the same time magnificent. . . . I have never felt so completely alone in my life,' wrote Flying Officer J.H. Leavitt in his logbook.

*

The bombers were sighted by observation posts in the next county to the south, Nordland, at 07.39 on Sunday morning. Twenty minutes later *Leutnant* Beniers at Bardufoss was informed that three Lancasters had passed over the small town of Mosjoen, flying east. A fourth aircraft had been observed not far from Bodø, heading in the same direction. Bodø was 1,000 kilometres south of Tromsø and no one in the Air Surveillance Service connected the two observations with an attack on the *Tirpitz*. Most of those involved assumed that the aircraft were crossing Sweden en route to the Soviet Union.

But when, shortly afterwards, *Kapitänleutnant* Fassbender received Beniers' report, he found it rather disturbing. The temperature was -8°C and there wasn't a breath of wind. The night sky was clear; only a streak of red above the snow-capped mountains in the south revealed that day was breaking.

'I immediately grabbed the phone and rang *Hauptflugwache Tromsø*. I wanted to make sure that the duty officer was aware that an attack might be impending. The circumstances were very similar to those of fourteen days earlier. It was Sunday morning, the weather was fine, and on that occasion the enemy aircraft had come in from Sweden,' Fassbender later explained.

The duty officer in Tromsø was 23-year-old *Leutnant* Ewald Hamschmidt from Paderborn. Hamschmidt was not rated very highly by his superiors, being characterised as thick-skinned, unreliable and somewhat immature. 'However, he has shown that he can do good work when under the supervision of a person of higher rank,' said one character assessment.

Hamschmidt saw no cause for alarm when he received the report from the *Tirpitz*. It was early in the morning and a few enemy aircraft had been observed far to the south; that was all. He saw no reason to alert Bardufoss.

At 08.25 the *Tirpitz* received a report to say that a further four Lancasters had overflown Mosjøen. Willi Müller ordered Fassbender to ring Härer, who outranked Hamschmidt, direct. 'I urged that enquiries be made as far south as Trondheim to find out where the planes had disappeared to. I said that the least we could do was to make sure that the fighters were standing by ready for take-off and that Bardufoss was kept abreast of developments.'

Premierleutnant Walter Härer had taken part in the discussions about the *Tirpitz* that had been held earlier that week. The *Luftwaffe* regarded him as a promising officer with a quick mind but, quick mind or not, he failed to respond. And at Air Surveillance headquarters in Tromsø no one thought it necessary to alert the satellite centre at Bardufoss of the *Tirpitz*'s repeated requests for action.

*

As a matter of routine, Beniers had in the meantime reported the observations of aircraft over Nordland on the internal network. But no one at Bardufoss, either, thought enemy air activity south of Bodø was anything to get excited about. To make matters worse, a sleepy corporal made a fateful error. He misread the coordinates and plotted the aircraft as being over Hammerfest, *500 kilometres to the north*, for which reason Ehrler and his fellow pilots, who had just got up, were not alerted. Nor, as Tromsø had failed to respond to the urgings of the *Tirpitz*, were they informed that a total of eight Lancaster bombers had been observed heading for Sweden. 'We hadn't been in battle for nearly three weeks and were dying for another crack at the enemy. But no one warned us about the threat to the *Tirpitz*. All that concerned us was getting away to Alta,' Schultze says.

On board the *Tirpitz* Fassbender and Hellendoorn discussed what to do. No further reports on the enemy aircraft had been received and the horizon was clear. 'We didn't feel unduly alarmed. We had warned the fighters via the proper channels and naturally assumed that they were standing by, ready to take to the air if anything should happen,' says Hellendoorn.

Observers attached to a gun battery on the coast sighted something they thought looked like a Boston bomber, a type of aircraft often used for reconnaissance. 'It was an uncertain observation,' Hellendoorn says, 'but we were not prepared to risk an attack from two sides, so we sounded the alarm.'

At 08.55 alarm bells jangled throughout the battleship and the blue-and-white flag signalling an impending air raid was hoisted. Seven minutes later the men were at their action stations and all watertight doors had been closed. A further seven minutes passed before the Würzburg radar picked up the first echoes, 120 kilometres to the south-east. Fassbender immediately sent a report to *Hauptflugwache Tromsø*: 'Enemy formation approaching from south.' Shortly afterwards the second wave of bombers was detected, prompting Fassbender to report: 'Second wave approaching from south. Height 3,500 metres. Distance about 100 kilometres.'

At last the alarm was sounded at Bardufoss airfield too. By then the time was 09.14.

'I was in a barrack hut not far from the base when, to my surprise, the sirens began to wail. I dropped what I was doing and hurried across to the Operations Room,' says Schultze.

In the Operations Room confusion reigned. The sergeant and corporal manning the plotting table had not received any of the early reports the *Tirpitz* had sent to *Hauptflugwache Tromsø*. Fassbender's first report *had* been recorded, as had his second, which was more detailed; but the latter had been misinterpreted, the corporal having logged it as: 'A new wave from south. Position unknown.'

At that moment Fassbender again phoned from the *Tirpitz*, where the lookouts could see the bombers fast approaching. 'Have the fighters taken off?'

he asked. Hamschmidt immediately called up Bardufoss and relayed Fassbender's query. 'Are the fighters ready to take off?' the corporal asked of no one in particular. A voice replied that they were, and the corporal informed Hamschmidt accordingly.

From 08.50 onwards *Major* Ehrler stayed close to the Operations Room in the expectation that his aircraft was being readied for his flight to Alta. The previous evening he had ordered three minutes' readiness for his seasoned pilots and ten minutes for the new arrivals, but that morning he had heard nothing about the *Tirpitz*'s fear of an impending attack. Only when, at 09.15, he chanced to look in at the Operations Room and was told of the reports from Tromsø, did he realise that the battleship might be in danger. Even then the information he was given – 'Noise of aircraft engines. Position and height not known' – was still very vague.

Ehrler was a man of action, and his reponse was immediate. At 09.18 he put his pilots on instant readiness and demanded more information from Beniers and his staff. All they could tell him was that aircraft engines had been heard. That was enough for the major, who was eager to bring his score up to 200. At 09.23 he ordered the squadron to scramble, while he himself sprinted down the runway and climbed into his Me Bf 109. Two minutes later he was airborne. When he looked down from an altitude of 2,000 metres, it was to see all the squadron's serviceable aircraft, their propellers spinning, still on the ground. Then he discovered that his wireless set wasn't working and that he thus had no means of contacting the Operations Room or his fellow pilots. 'For that reason I decided to carry on alone in the hope of finding the enemy formation and adding to my score,' he later explained.

While Ehrler was tearing down the runway at 09.25, a desperate call for help was received from the *Tirpitz*: 'The Captain orders the fighters to take off immediately.' At that, the men on the ground sprang into action, but by an unfortunate coincidence a Ju 88 came in to land just after Ehrler had taken off. Because of the resultant delay, *Premierleutnant* Gayko's flight didn't get off the ground until 09.30, and *Hauptmann* Dörr, *Leutnant* Schultze and the rest of the squadron were later still. More valuable time was lost when an erroneous report claimed that the bombers were heading for Bardufoss. Not until 09.36 did the last of the fighters take off.

'When I took off, one of the last to do so, I heard "Anti-aircraft fire over Tromsø!" in my earphones,' says Schulze.

*

On board the *Tirpitz* the atmosphere had changed from one of keen anticipation to anger and disappointment. For an hour and a half *Kapitänleutnant* Fassbender had been begging for fighter support, but his pleas had apparently not got through to Bardufoss. At 09.27, by which time the approaching bombers were only 40 kilometres away, they were visible to the naked eye. Bo'sun Theo Kunzmann was on duty in 'A' turret, whose heavy 38cm guns were swung round towards the bombers.

Suddenly there was a shout in my earphones that one of the planes was on fire. Then there was a second cry: another was burning! I sincerely hoped that our Arctic fighters were in action, and asked to be allowed to have a look through the viewfinder. I realised straightaway that somebody's nerves had got the better of them. There wasn't a sign of our fighters, but in the south a blazing, blood-red sun was rising into the blue-black sky. It lit up the fresh snow on the mountain tops and was reflected in the Plexiglas [actually Perspex] of the bombers' cockpit windscreens. The reports were the result of an optical illusion. What had been seen weren't flames, only the reflected rays of the sun.

Weber, Müller and the rest of the battleship's senior officers were gathered in the Command Centre with the armoured door bolted behind them. From their platform at the top of the turret Fassbender and Hellendoorn continued to search the sky for the fighters they were expecting.

We were angry and despairing. We kept on asking for fighter support, but it didn't seem to do any good. The silhouettes of the approaching bombers grew ever more distinct in the light of the low sun. Conditions were perfect for an attack. Without smoke generators we must have been visible for miles around. I never felt frightened, though. I was young. I remember that I asked Fassbender for permission to fetch my camera. He looked at me and shook his head. 'I don't think that's a very good idea,' he said.

At 09.38 Weber gave permission to open fire. The first shells screamed into the sky and exploded, but the barrage was too low. Flying in formation, the thirty-one Lancasters never wavered, but flew remorsely on towards their target. A bare three minutes later the lookouts saw the bomb-bay doors open and watched spellbound as the gigantic bombs came hurtling towards them.

*

Ehrler's tragedy was that he could find neither the *Tirpitz* nor the enemy bombers. He had been airborne for a quarter of an hour and could have reached Tromsø, if not before, at least at the same time as, the enemy bombers. But he had not been informed of where the battleship lay, and for that reason headed for Balsfjord. From there he flew north towards the island of Arnøy, turned and flew back south along the coast at an altitude of 6,000 metres.

'I stayed at that altitude as I assumed that the British would attack from a great height because of the fine weather, but I never saw a thing.' Only when he was about to give up did he see a trace of smoke on the horizon. When he reached the spot, there was no sign of either the *Tirpitz* or the bombers. After a further frustrating search Ehrler broke off and made for Alta, where he landed late that morning.

Dörr and Gayko's groups had not reached Tromsø in time either. All they found when they did get there was an enormous pall of smoke that blotted out the basin between Tromsø and Håkøy. Schultze got back to Bardufoss a little after ten. 'I was bitterly disappointed. Like the others, I had hoped that Ehrler had found the enemy and brought his score up to two hundred. Only when we reached our dispersal points did we learn of the disaster.'

*

The end had come with astonishing speed. Two of the very first bombs struck the *Tirpitz* amidships on the port side, causing catastrophic damage. The battleship took in vast quantities of water and immediately developed a list of nearly 20 degrees. Many of her guns jammed and men found it difficult to remain upright on the steeply sloping decks. At 09.45, by which time the list had increased to 40 degrees, *Kapitän-zur-See* Weber gave the order to evacuate the decks below the armour.

Many men never received their captain's order. One was Adolf Flauger, who was on duty on the lowest platform deck. Finding his phone dead, he climbed up into 'B' turret, only to find it deserted. 'I tried to open the hatch leading to the deck, but it was jammed tight. The ship was fast listing to port. I was struck on the head by some falling object and didn't come to until I found myself up to my waist in water. The emergency lighting was working, but I was completely alone and covered in blood. It gradually dawned on me that I was a prisoner in the turret.'

Some horrific scenes were now enacted on board the stricken ship. Nearly 1,000 men were trapped inside it. The armoured door to the Command Centre had jammed and *Kapitän-zur-See* Weber and the rest of the battleship's senior officers were unable to make their escape. In the long passageways below deck men fought to make their way to freedom, battling against leaking oil and water pouring in through gaping holes in the hull.

Five minutes later a violent shudder passed through the ship and a tongue of flame leapt high into the air. A magazine had exploded. 'C' turret, which weighed over 1,000 tons, was lifted high off its bearings. From that moment it took only a few seconds for the *Tirpitz* to turn turtle and come to rest, bottom up, on the seabed.

'I clung on to the platform as the ship slowly heeled over. There was no longer any question of firing our guns. I gave the order to put on life jackets. I didn't have mine with me, but I was a strong swimmer,' says Hellendoorn.

One man, a non-swimmer, panicked and jumped overboard.

'I had no choice, I jumped in after him. His panic gave him incredible strength, but after a violent struggle I eventually managed to get us both ashore. For me, the worst thing was the oil. It got into my eyes and blinded me,' Hellendoorn says.

Werner Hirsch, who had been operating the Würzburg radar amidships, had got out through the hatch in the armoured dome. Unable to keep his balance on the sloping deck, he slid off into the water. 'I saw the nets some distance away and started to swim towards them. Suddenly there was a violent explosion and everything went black. Only by expending my last ounce of strength did I succeed in reaching the surface and grabbing hold of a buoy. "C" turret had blown up.'

Horrified onlookers ashore and on board the flakships *Thetis* and *Nymphe* watched aghast as the steel colossus began to heel over and, a bare ten minutes later, capsized. A general alarm was sounded in Tromsø. Every available vessel raced to the rescue, and in the course of the next few hours several hundred men from the stricken battleship were rescued from the sea and taken off from the shore of Håkøy Island. The air temperature was -8°C and the water ice-cold, with the result that many men were badly frostbitten. The first would-be rescuers to reach the wreck could hear the sound of hammering from inside the hull. Hundreds of men were trapped in air pockets and were desperately appealing for help. One of them was Adolf Flauger:

I found a crowbar that someone had cast aside and started a rhythmical banging on the hull. I'd probably been at it for two or three hours when a hatch opened. A further sixteen men had crawled through a conduit into the compartment in which I was trapped. By then my arms were aching badly and I was very glad to have someone else take over. I remember that I had seventeen cigarettes left in a packet. That was one for each of us.

Leutnant Walter Sommer, a turbine engineer, took command of the rescue work and requisitioned oxygen cylinders and cutting torches from Tromsø and the repair ship *Neumark*. Clinging to the slippery hull, the men set to work with a will; but the armour was incredibly thick and work proceeded all too slowly. Not until eight o'clock in the evening, more than ten hours after the battleship had capsized, were Flauger and his sixteen companions able to climb out of their steel tomb to freedom. All attempts at rescue were abandoned four days later, by which time eighty-seven survivors had been released from the wreck.

The destruction of the *Tirpitz* was the death knell of the *Kriegsmarine*. The year before it had lost the *Scharnhorst*, along with nearly 2,000 men, off the North Cape. Now the *Tirpitz* had gone. No one knew how many of her crew had died, but it was estimated that between 900 and 1,000 men had been drowned or died of suffocation when the battleship turned over. Says Hein Hellendoorn:

For all of us who had served on board the *Tirpitz*, her capsizing was a terrible blow. It all happened so quickly, we hardly had time to react. One moment we were on board, the next we were fighting for our lives in the icy water. And at the same time we were haunted by the thought that it had all been quite unnecessary. Where were the Arctic fighters? Why hadn't they come over from Bardufoss, which was only ten minutes' flying time away? We had been promised support. In the event, as always in the past, we were left to fend for ourselves.

*

Hellendoorn wasn't the only one to pose such questions. When the admirals in Berlin realised the scale of the disaster, they began to look for scapegoats. All through the war there had been friction and head-on clashes between the *Luftwaffe* and the *Kriegsmarine*, the latter accusing the former of not providing support in the shape of reconnaissance planes or fighters when it was needed. The absence of the celebrated Arctic Squadron over Tromsø when fighter cover was so urgently required was cited as yet another instance of Air Force incompetence and failure to respond. As early as Sunday evening, 12 November, while Sommer and his men were still struggling to extricate the last survivors from the wreck, on direct orders from Berlin the first enquiries into the fighters' failure to show up were set in motion at Bardufoss.

To begin with Ehrler and those closest to him refused to take the allegations seriously: 'I tried to explain what had happened, but Ehrler, Dörr and the other pilots harboured a low opinion of the "paper generals" asking the questions. Ehrler maintained that they would never understand what it meant to be in the front line anyway, and said that if they were dissatisfied, they could come and take over the controls themselves.'

After a while, however, it was brought home to the major and his fellow pilots that the enquiry was far from being a joke. On the contrary, it was deadly serious. The accusations levelled against him, Dörr, Beniers, Hamschmidt and a number of others were very grave indeed. Things looked blackest for Ehrler himself. As Commander, he was accused of dereliction of duty on a number of counts. It was asserted that he should have controlled the fighters from the ground instead of racing off on his own – not to defend the *Tirpitz*, but to bring his score of victories up to 200. However, even after a long and detailed investigation it proved difficult to find concrete evidence of wrongdoing on the part of Ehrler or any of the others involved. But a vaguely worded directive issued by Göring a few months earlier had laid down that there should always be an officer present in the Operations Room. No account was taken of the fact that Ehrler had only been in transit at Bardufoss and had been told nothing about the plight of the *Tirpitz*. It was averred that a sergeant and a corporal were insufficient: an officer should have been there to deal with the confusing reports from Tromsø.

Leutnant Schultze, Ehrler's adjutant, accompanied his commanding officer to Oslo. 'The court martial was a farce from beginning to end,' he says. 'Judgement had been passed before it started. But they all knew that they would never get anywhere by trying to find Ehrler, war hero as he was, guilty of dereliction of duty and cowardice in the face of the enemy. He had shot down nearly two hundred enemy aircraft and had daily proved his mettle through four long years of war.'

But no such arguments could prevail against the judges, who had been appointed by Hitler himself. On the other hand, as they were well aware, to have sentenced Ehrler to death would have created a furore among the many pilots who admired him. Instead, he was stripped of his rank of major and sentenced to three years in prison. 'It didn't take long for Ehrler to realise what had happened – that he had been sacrificed to shield the men responsible for leaving the *Tirpitz* up there in the north without adequate defence. From that time on he was a broken man.'

CHAPTER EIGHTEEN

Peace

NORWAY AND GERMANY, POSTWAR

Many of the people forcibly evacuated from the still-smoking ruins of Finnmark were in Tromsø on Sunday 12 November and so witnessed the destruction of the *Tirpitz* at first hand. Wrote one of them: 'We were lying at anchor in the harbour when the guns opened up. I couldn't suppress a sense of elation when I heard the news that the *Tirpitz* had been sunk. I felt that it was just retribution for the destruction wrought by the Germans in Finnmark.'

The razing of the country's northernmost county and the battleship's destruction marked the end of the most dramatic epoch in Norway's recent history. Two great political systems, Nazism and Stalinism, had there fought a bloody war that had claimed tens of thousands of human lives. Hitler's navy had met defeat in the Norwegian fjords and his Mountain Army had been decimated on the rocky banks of the River Litza. Large tracts of the north lay desolate. Eduard Dietl, the hero of Narvik, had come to bring the blessings of National Socialism to the people of the Arctic; instead, his mission had ended in disaster.

The lives of all who were caught up in the maelstrom had been disrupted, and in many cases changed for ever.

In Jena, fourteen-year-old Inge waited in vain for the father she was expecting home for Christmas. 'I received my last letter from him in December. He wrote about the bombing. That frightened me and I longed for him to come home and comfort me. But in November Mother had had a dream. She dreamed that Father had been lost. When the [official] letter arrived, we found out what had happened. My father was still on board the *Tirpitz* when it capsized. His body was never found. It was a cruel blow, one it took me many years to recover from. I miss him still,' says Inge, who was trapped in East Germany when the Iron Curtain came down after the war. Only in recent years has she been able to visit the site of her father's watery grave.

The *Tirpitz*'s two carpenters, Karl Heinz Lohse and Werner Brand, were more fortunate. They were eventually granted leave and left for home – Karl Heinz in September 1944, Werner in October. Says Werner:

I left on a fishing boat after the last attack in the Kå fjord. They were cutting down on engine-room staff and I was able to journey back to Wilster, where Regina was waiting for me. I had scraped together a little money and as a wedding present had bought her a blue-fox fur coat. She borrowed a white veil and looked very beautiful in church. They were sad times, but we loved each other and spent some wonderful days together.

When their leave was up and the time came to return to Norway, the two had got as far as Copenhagen and were waiting for a ship to take them the rest of the way, when the terrible news came through that the *Tirpitz* had been sunk. Men who were fit for active service were then transferred to the army and thrown into the last desperate battles in defence of Berlin. Werner was wounded in the head by a shell splinter, but survived. He got back to Wilster in 1946 and found work as an engine-driver with the *Bundesbahn*. In 2004 he and Regina, who had first met at the Kå fjord in 1943 and married the year after, celebrated their diamond wedding in Hamburg, where they have lived for many years.

Karl Lausch was also one of the lucky ones. His Solveig was evacuated from Talvik to Oslo, where, after some hasty paperwork, the couple were given permission to marry as soon as the war was over. She accompanied him back to Germany, where they set up house in his home town of Salzgitter. But the Norwegian government has a long memory. Girls who consorted with German soldiers during the war were zealously persecuted. Solveig was deprived of her Norwegian citizenship and formally deported. When she died in 1999, she had still not got it back.

'She tried to, for many years, as she felt herself to be both Norwegian and German. But all her efforts were in vain. Even when she died and was buried in the town of her birth, there was no question of forgiveness – even though we loved each other and had married as soon as we were able,' Karl Lausch says.

Following destruction of the *Tirpitz*, Hein Hellendoorn was sent home to Bad Bentheim to recuperate. He still had splinters in his back from the bombing attack in the spring of 1944 and had been further incapacitated by his enforced swim to the safety of Håkøy Island in November. But he had little time to enjoy his well-earned sick leave, as early in 1945 he was summoned to the *Kriegsmarine*'s headquarters outside Berlin: 'It was Dönitz himself who wanted to see me. He had a special assignment lined up for me. There was a U-boat ready and waiting to transport arms and vital raw materials to Japan. I was to go with it and see what I could learn of the Japanese way of waging war.'

The U-boat, *U-864*, left Bergen in April 1945 with a cargo of uranium and a number of high-ranking German and Japanese officers on board. It had only got as far as the middle of the Atlantic when Germany capitulated. The captain surrendered to the US Navy and Hellendoorn finished the war as a prisoner of the Americans. On his return to Germany in 1946 he resigned his commission and eventually became a dentist in his home town.

In Norway, the two wireless operators captured by the Germans, Erling Duklæt and Aksel Bogdanoff, continued to transmit under German control, the former to London, the latter to Murmansk. But both the British and the Russians had learned their lesson, and it wasn't long before they realized that they were being hoodwinked.

'We succeeded in making contact with the base in Murmansk and achieved a certain measure of success to start with,' *SS-Obersturmbannführer* Kurt Karstens explained after the war. Thirty-three-year-old Karstens, the son of a clergyman from Schleswig, was Bogdanoff's controller. 'The Russians saw through our attempt to elicit information and broke off contact. After trying in vain for a few more months, we finally gave up and Bogdanoff was transferred to a prisoner-of-war camp.'

The *Gestapo* and *Abwehr* officers kept their word and no more agents were executed. Duklæt survived the war to return to his former calling and sail the seas as a ship's engineer. Bogdanoff moved to a town in western Norway.

In Iceland, Ib Arnasson Riis likewise continued transmitting spurious messages to Germany, in his case right up to the end of the war in 1945. 'I was demobbed and handed a ticket on a boat to Copenhagen. Beyond that I received nothing – no pay, no offer of a job, no recognition of any kind. The British simply turned their backs on me,' he says. He is now living in retirement in California, where, after the war, he worked as a watchman on board a museum ship.

After having spent the rest of the war in Germany as POWs, all six British survivors of the midget-submarine attack returned safely to England, where they were welcomed as heroes. Some of them went back to civilian life, working in industry, while others stayed on in the service.

'I never looked upon myself as a hero. I did what was expected of me and never had the feeling that I was engaged in anything special. It was wartime, and we all had to do our bit,' says Robert Aitken, who became manager of an engineering company after the war. In 2003 he returned to the Kå fjord to see where he had once been trapped in a 15-metre-long steel cylinder that very nearly became his coffin.

The Norwegian agents who had worked for the Russians had a harder time. When the Cold War broke out, they soon found themselves under suspicion. Many felt themselves hounded by the Norwegian Secret Service, and they were also embittered by the fact that they never received any token of appreciation for the sacrifices they had made.

Åge Halvari's confession to *Premierleutnant* Pardon had included a detailed description of the Soviet intelligence set-up in the north, and for many years after the war this was a key source of information for the Norwegian Security Service. After having been turned by the *Abwehr*, Halvari vanished without a trace. It is rumoured that he was among those killed when the ammunition train blew up in Rovaniemi in October 1944.

In 1944 young Leif Falck Utne, who had allowed himself to be persuaded into becoming a double agent, was despatched to the German meteorological station on Bear Island. One day he rowed out to sea in a rubber dinghy, never to return.

Heinrich Ehrler, who was made the scapegoat for Germany's military defeat in the north, never served his prison sentence. The Third Reich was nearing its end and Hitler needed all the men he could muster in the final phase. Although Ehrler was a broken man, he was still a first-class pilot. In his Me-262 he subsequently shot down eight Allied bombers, and with his 207 victories entered the annals of the air war as one of Germany's greatest aces.

Legend has it that in late April 1945, shortly after shooting down his last two Liberators over Berlin, Ehrler ran out of ammunition. A fighter to the last, before ramming a third bomber and plunging to earth in a sea of flame, he switched on his wireless set for the last time. 'Farewell, comrades,' he cried. 'See you in Valhalla!' The official (American) report says that he was shot down when he tangled with five P-51 Mustangs – which seems rather strange, as he was flying an Me 262 jet fighter, whose greater speed would normally have enabled him to make his escape. Perhaps, with his will to live gone, he did indeed choose to die in combat. Whatever the truth of the matter, there is no denying that he was a brilliant pilot who died fighting for his country in a cause that was unworthy of his valour.

Premierleutnant Fritz Pardon was arrested in Narvik and taken to Oslo for interrogation concerning his role in the destruction of the agent network in eastern Finnmark and his part in the execution of the men taken prisoner. For some unaccountable reason the British, who were responsible for questioning him, found no reason to condemn his actions. Pardon was released and allowed to return to his wife and two children in Germany. The concluding report summed up the bloody drama that had unfolded in the north in 1943 and 1944 as follows:

Hptm. PARDON is an exceptionally intelligent and educated man. He admits having believed in the ideas of National Socialism, but there is no doubt that he now fully understands the consequences of the Third Reich's disastrous policy. He is also aware that the whole system was rotten to the core, and that GERMANY's future can only be saved by the exclusion of nationalistic and militaristic ideas. There is no reason to doubt his sincerity, and it is thought that he will make a very good citizen of a democratic GERMANY.

Epilogue

News of the Norwegian divers' find in the Kå fjord spread rapidly throughout the world, where interest in the fate of the *Tirpitz* is still very much alive. In the winter of 2004 BBC *Timewatch* entered into a co-production agreement with the TV company for which I was working at the time, the Norwegian Broadcasting Corporation (NRK), the aim of which was to try to solve the mystery once and for all and also make a TV documentary about the X-craft attack.

When the BBC team reached Alta in March 2004, they brought with them Stuart Usher, who had long been engaged in an attempt to resolve the riddle of *X5*; he had, in fact, taken part in the 1974 expedition to the Kå fjord. Usher had with him a set of the original drawings from Vickers, the company that had built the first six midget submarines. We, for our part, had leased an ROV from the Alta-based ocean-survey company GeoFinnmark. This enabled us to relay a stream of images from the seabed to monitors on board the surface vessel.

With the aid of Usher's accurate drawings and sharp and detailed images from the wreck, for the first time we were able to study the tortured wreckage from every angle. The result was, to say the least, surprising. On the seabed, at the spot where the Germans claimed to have sunk *X5*, is a wreck closely resembling that of a midget submarine, a small craft, complete with hatches and ventilators, that has been cleft in two amidships. In all probability, though, it is *not* the missing *X5* – that we were able to determine from the drawings of the six midget submarines' hatches. The hatches on the wreck appear to be more strongly built and also differ in other respects from the open hatch on the wreckage forty metres down in the Kå fjord. 'It is very odd that there is a wreck in the *X5* position which has many similarities to a small underwater vessel.

However, in all probability it is not the X5, because I cannot see the two large hatches that were unique to the X-craft,' Usher said.

On the other hand our investigations revealed that the metal object lying some three hundred metres from the wreck really was an unexploded 2.5-ton side-charge, one of those transported at such great risk to the Kå fjord in September 1943 by Claud Barry's midget submarines. The films we made and the metal fragments recovered proved that beyond doubt – and that, sixty years later, the explosive it contained was most probably still intact. But which of the three X-craft had carried it to the spot where it was found: X5, X6 or X7?

As far as we could ascertain, there was nothing on the casing to identify it; nor did analysis of the metal provide conclusive proof of where it came from. An attempt by Norwegian naval divers to prise loose the timer proved unsuccessful. However, Stuart Usher plotted the position of the charge on an aerial photograph taken of the *Tirpitz* the day *after* the attack, Thursday 23 September, to show that the charge had settled on the bottom ninety metres *outside* the battleship's net cage.

'All the record books say that the four charges that were laid, were all laid inside the confines of the net. X6 dropped two charges under the port bow of the *Tirpitz*; X7 dropped one under the midship section and one under the stern. So if we have got four charges going off inside the net, and one lying outside unexploded, it can only have come from X5,' said Usher in the documentary *Lost Heroes*, which was screened in Britain in October 2004 and in Norway in January 2005. He thinks this gives added substance to the family's demand for a reassessment of Lieutenant Henty Henty-Creer's role in the attack.

His evidence affords *indirect* proof that X5 really did carry out its attack and will most probably lead to renewed controversy – until the charge is brought ashore and conclusively identified. But the crux of the matter is still unresolved. What became of X5, the last confirmed sighting of which was south-west of Sørøy Island two days before the attack was launched? And which small craft found a watery grave in almost the very same spot as Henty-Creer and his crew disappeared?

I have continued to devote a good deal of time and thought to the matter since the intensive investigations of 2003 and 2004, but the eye-witness accounts I have assembled are not altogether trustworthy, and in some cases they actually contradict one another. Among the testimonies of the British survivors, John Lorimer's is the most convincing. He was standing on the deck of the *Tirpitz* that dramatic September morning sixty years ago and saw X5 disappear amid the smoke and spray thrown up by exploding shells. 'I was never in doubt about what I had seen, as I also informed the Admiralty on my return home after having been a prisoner of war. I believe that *X5* was sunk in the Kå fjord, and that the wreck must still be there on the bottom. I can't identify the pieces of wreckage I have seen with 100 per cent certainty, but I think the find is very encouraging and that the wreck merits a full investigation,' he says.

On the German side, accounts are more at variance. It has proved impossible to trace the men who saw a midget submarine 500 to 700 metres away from the battleship and fired at it. The most reliable witness is *Leutnant* Eberhard Schmölder, who at the time was in a launch to the north of the battleship and reported seeing a midget submarine being heavily shelled, though he was unable to determine the direction the vessel was taking or observe any hits. He dropped five depth charges, the last but one of which left a strong swirl of foam on the water and brought oil to the surface. This induced Schmölder to claim that in all probability the submarine had been destroyed. But when, following the attack, two tugs, the *Arngast* and *Bardenfleth*, trawled the area in search of the submarine, they found nothing.

On board the *Stamsund*, a Norwegian cargo vessel lying at anchor some 400 metres north-east of the *Tirpitz*, Captain Sven Hertzberg and his crew were very close to the spot where *X5* was last seen. Interviewed in 1946, he explained that he had seen *several* midget submarines, 'one of them passing so near us that we could estimate her length to be about 30 feet'. As his attention had been caught by shouts and gunfire from the *Tirpitz* just after 09.00, it is unlikely that what he had seen was *X6* or *X7*, as by then they were both inside the nets. Thus it may well have been *X5* that the men on the deck of the *Stamsund* saw.

I am far more sceptical of the information provided by Mathis Sarilla when, in 1950, he went to visit Eulalia Henty-Creer at the inn. In his statement the veteran captain claimed to have seen a submerged German U-boat in the *First World War*, so, he said, he knew what a periscope looked like. But the midget submarines were much smaller than First World War U-boats and looked quite different. In my opinion little weight can be attached to Sarilla's experience on the fishing banks off the coast of Finnmark thirty years earlier; if anything, the reverse. I am in no doubt that he saw *something* in the sea off Mount Bossekop, but the question is, what was it? His sighting was made on the morning of Thursday 23 September 1943 – twenty-four hours after the attack. This presupposes that *X5* had survived Schmölder's depth charging and that Henty-Creer had then sailed his little craft *out of* the Kå fjord and *into* the shallows off Mount Bossekop – to a place close to German dockside installations. With luck, a submarine can survive heavy depth charging, as witness the Soviet submarine *M-105*, which emerged virtually unscathed from a vicious German attack in the Sylte fjord. To my mind it is by no means inconceivable that Henty-Creer could have succeeded in inching his way past the German destroyers and guardships that blocked the exit from the Kå fjord. But if he did so, why should he then have chosen to spend the night on the bottom in a part of the fjord where German surface traffic was at its heaviest and risk of discovery consequently very great?

According to Sarilla, the periscope was also seen by a number of German soldiers, who shouted 'British submarine' and raised the alarm. But on that Thursday morning the whole Alta region was still very much on the alert. The fjord had been sealed off, there were roadblocks everywhere and additional submarine chasers and guardships had been brought in from round about. The Germans were bent on revenge. They were determined not to allow any of the attackers to escape and were especially keen to study the technical specifications of the midget submarines. Beyond doubt, an alarm given in Bossekop would have resulted in a massive submarine hunt on the part of the Germans. But nothing appears to have happened. Even Sarilla had to admit that the Germans made no effort to intercept and destroy the submarine so boldly making its way out of the fjord at periscope depth in mid-morning.

I have spent a great deal of time perusing the relevant German war diaries, both those of the ships of the 1st Battle Group and those of the 230th Division, which was responsible for the security of the naval base. In none of them is there a word about Sarilla's alleged sighting; and there is no reference in the German records of a U-boat alarm from Bossekop. As far as I am concerned, that settles the matter. That Thursday morning the atmosphere in the Kå fjord was tense. The *Kriegsmarine* had suffered a humiliating blow. The British had succeeded in penetrating northern Europe's most closely guarded naval base. Someone must have been asleep at their post and there was every reason to fear Hitler's wrath. That being so, would any responsible officer have omitted to log such a significant observation as that reputedly made by Sarilla and the Germans soldiers who shared it with him? Would the local commanders merely have shrugged their shoulders and neglected to take appropriate action? No, not in my opinion. I believe that all available resources would have been called upon if, that fateful Thursday, something resembling a British submarine really had been seen off Mount Bossekop. Submarine chasers would immediately have been directed to the spot and the entire fjord would have been peppered with depth charges until the Germans felt sure that their quarry was no more. This prompts me to conclude that Sarilla must have been mistaken. He undoubtedly saw something but, whatever it was, it was *not* a midget submarine.

I am glad that we succeeded in proving that there is an unexploded side-charge, the only such in the world, at the bottom of the Kå fjord. But I am nevertheless disappointed at our inability to determine the identity of the wreck lying on the seabed right where X5 was last seen. Having spent so long investigating the matter, I have never quite been able to let it go, and every now and again have resumed my probing to see if a little more light can be shed on the matter. And in the summer of 2005 I was lucky! After exhaustive enquiries I finally managed to trace Hugo Leifert. Leifert, who is now in his eighties and still living in Germany, is probably the last survivor of the five sailors who were in the launch with *Leutnant-zur-Zee* Schmölder and therefore the very last witness I can ever hope to interview.

I visited him at his home and showed him Schmölder's report. He gave a nod of recognition.

'It is a morning I shall never forget,' he said. 'Schmölder had toothache and had asked me – I was in charge of the launch – to take him across to the dentist on the *Tirpitz*. Then things got so hectic that I think he forgot his toothache altogether!'

More than sixty years after the dramatic events of that day Leifert was no longer able to recall the details, but after having read the report he remarked: 'Schmölder was a conscientious young man. You may rest assured that when he wrote this it was correct.'

I also wrote a letter to Robert Aitken, X7's diver, a highly judicious man who had always been most forthcoming and eager to help us in our investigation.

When I went back over my records I found some notes in the *Tirpitz* war diary which, to me now, seem a bit puzzling – hence this letter to you. At about 10.30 in the morning of the attack – local time and after the explosion – Godfrey Place was taken on board the *Tirpitz* and interrogated by the ship's intelligence officer, *Korvettenkapitän* Woychechowsky-Emden.

At 10.51 the following note was made in the war diary, obviously on the basis of a statement by Lt Place: 'According to a statement from the prisoner taken from the second midget submarine (X7 – my comment) the boat laid both its mines *outside* the net (my italics). The timer can be set from ½ hour to 24 hours.'

When I read this earlier, I thought that Mr Place told the Germans a lie to keep them off balance. However, after seeing Mr Usher's calculations . . . which put the unexploded side-charge well outside the net, I have started to wonder. I know, of course, that you were fighting another battle when Lt Place spoke to the German intelligence interrogator, but I still need to ask the question: Have you any recollection that Mr Place after the events or during the years in captivity mentioned that he may have laid one of the charges outside the net, and not inside? I am sure you see the implications if the undetonated mine belongs to the X7 and not the X5, and I beg forgiveness for asking. But my business is facts – and I sincerely look forward to receiving any comments and thoughts you may have on the matter.

Aitken wrote back, enclosing a copy of Place's original report. He added:

Turning to the reason for writing your letter I am absolutely confident Godfrey Place did not make the statement attributed to him unless he was, as you suggested, trying to mislead the Germans. . . . I have highlighted relevant lines quoted from Godfrey's report, which I believe is the one he made to the Admiralty shortly after he returned to the UK from our POW camp in Germany [the report stating that both side-charges were laid under the keel of the *Tirpitz*]. I can confirm that the report accurately summarises my understanding of X7's attack based on comments made during the attack by Godfrey Place, who was the only one able to use both periscopes. Nothing Godfrey said to me whilst we were in Marlag POW camp modified the statements made in his report.

Aitken's letter and Leifert's words took a load off my mind, as they supported our finds – both on the seabed and in the many archives we had combed. There *had* been a third midget submarine in the Kå fjord on Wednesday 22 September 1943, and it can only have been that commanded by Henty-Creer, who, for reasons unknown, had been compelled to release one of his side-charges outside the *Tirpitz*'s net enclosure. He and his men had carried out their attack and were therefore entitled to full redress.

I had reached the end of the road. There was no more I could do. During the war, the Kå fjord had been the site of northern Europe's biggest naval base. For more than two years the attention of the principal warring powers had been directed towards the sounds and fjords of western Finnmark. The presence of the German fleet, and the attempts by the British to destroy it, undoubtedly constitute the most important chapter in the history of the war in Scandinavia. To my mind this also says something of no little relevance to the present day, namely that the Arctic regions and the seas round about were of immeasurable strategic importance – and still are. I am therefore of the opinion that the charge and the mysterious, submarine-like wreck on the bottom of the Kå fjord should be salvaged, as their recovery may help to resolve one of the war's greatest mysteries. But it will be of interest for other reasons too. It will help to draw attention to the importance of the northern regions to naval operations. This is a chapter in the history of northern Europe that must not be forgotten – not out of regard for the past, but with an eye to the future.

Notes

THE MYSTERY OF X5

p. 2 *We had no idea* To a great extent this account is based on interviews undertaken by the author in Germany in the spring and summer of 2003 with the following officers and men who served on board the *Tirpitz*: Hein Hellendoorn, Karl Heinz Lohse, Werner Brand, Helmut Simon, Hans Thomalia and Alfred Zuba. From some of them I have since received supplementary letters and personal anecdotes. On the British side I have interviewed the three survivors of the midget-submarine attack: John Lorimer, Robert Kendall and Robert Aitken. On the German side the key documents are the war diaries of the *Tirpitz* (RM 92/5201 ff, hereafter KTB Tirpitz) and the 1st Battle Group (RM 50/184, hereafter KTB 1st Battle Group), both of which are in Militärarchiv/Bundesarchiv in Freiburg (hereafter MA). The central British document is *Battle Summary No. 29: The Attack on the Tirpitz by Midget Submarines*, which was published as a supplement to the *London Gazette* on 10 February 1948 and which is in the National Archives (hereafter TNA) in London as ADM 1/20026. The report is in three parts. The first part is dated 8 November 1943 and is based on aerial photographs, intelligence sources and the debriefing of Lieutenant Kenneth Hudspeth, who was forced to abort his attack in *X10* as he neared the entrance to the Kå fjord. After spending a day submerged only a few kilometres from the German naval base that was his objective, Hudspeth succeeded in taking his damaged craft back to the seaward side of Sørøy, where, one week later, he and his crew were picked up by the *Stubborn*. The second part, dated 2 February 1944, is based on, among other sources, information obtained from the thirty-six men who survived the sinking of the German battlecruiser *Scharnhorst*. An important source in this regard was Able-Seaman Max Krause, who was on the staff of *Admiral* Oscar Kummetz and served on board the *Tirpitz* before being transferred to the *Scharnhorst* on Christmas Eve 1943, two days before she was sunk. His testimony is contained in *Draft Interrogation Report on Prisoners of War from the Scharnhorst*, Director of Naval Intelligence, 23 February 1944 (ADM 199/913). The Battle Summary was last updated on 26 July 1945, when the six survivors of X6 and X7 were debriefed on their return to England after having spent the rest of the war in prison camps in Germany. The attack by the midget submarines has been the subject of a number of books. Those on which I have drawn are C.E.T. Warren and James Benson: *Above Us the Waves* (London, 1953), Léonce Peillard: *Sink the Tirpitz* (London, 1968), Thomas Gallagher: *Against all Odds* (London, 1971), Pamela Mellor and Frank Walker: *The Mystery of X5* (London, 1986), Pamela Mitchell: *The Tip of the Spear* (Huddersfield, 1993) and Paul Kemp: *Underwater Warriors* (London, 1996).

p. 7 *On board the SS Stamsund* Captain Sven Hertzberg and several of the men on board the *Stamsund* were questioned by the Norwegian police on 4 February 1946. This quotation, in common with subsequent quotations relating to the *Stamsund*, stems from these interviews.

THE WRECKAGE IN THE KÅ FJORD

p. 13 *A few days later* Besides Jon Røkenes, two other divers, Kåre Bakkland and Terje Johansen, took part in the search for *X5*.

p. 15 *Deirdre Henty-Creer, who is now in her eighties* I interviewed Deirdre Henty-Creer in London on 22 July 2003 and have since spoken with her and her sister, Pamela Mellor, on a number of occasions on the telephone. The quotations from their mother's letter are from Pamela Mellor's book *The Mystery of X5*, p. 214 f.

FROM FORGOTTEN OUTPOST TO THEATRE OF WAR

p. 17 *I decide who* This quotation is from the Austrian historian Roland Kaltenegger's authoritative work *Krieg am Eismeer: Gebirgsjäger im Kampf um Narvik, Murmansk und die Murmanbahn* (Graz, 1999) and *Krieg in der Arktis: Der Operationen der Lappland-Armee 1942–45* (Graz, 2003), on which my account is largely based. A number of other books have also been published on the same subject, among them Mathias Kräutler and Karl Springenschmid: *Es war ein Edelweiss* (Graz, 1962), Werner Girbig: *Jagdgeschwader 5 'Eismeerjäger': Eine Chronik aus Dokumenten und Berichten 1941–1945* (Stuttgart, 1976), Werner Fehse: *Die Chronik der 1. Staffel (F) Aufklärungsgruppe 124* (privately published, 1999), Alfred Steurich: *Gebirgsjäger im Bild: 6. SS-Gebirgsdivision Nord 1940–1945* (Osnabrück, 1976) and Lars Gyllenhaal and James F. Gebhardt: *Slaget om Nordkalotten: Sveriges roll i tyske och allierade operationer i norr* (Lund, 2001). Unless otherwise stated in the text, the quotations in this chapter are from Kaltenegger, who has also written biographies of two of the foremost German generals who served in the north, Eduard Dietl and Ferdinand Schörner.

p. 19 *It wasn't the first time* For more about the Kå fjord and the history of Alta, see Jens Petter Nielsen: *Altas historie*, vol. 2.

p. 20 *The Germans were able* Little attention has been devoted in the literature to the consequences for the northern regions of the alliance between Hitler and Stalin. In the National Archives in Washington I have found two reports (DNI 45-1839) relating to the establishment of a German naval base on the Kola Peninsula: *The Arctic Sea Route* and *Basis Nord*. Both are dated December 1945.

p. 21 *Pressure on the civilian population* The story of the mass flight of the people of Kiberg eastwards and Norwegian partisan activities behind the German lines is recounted in a number of books, among them Hans Kr. Eriksen: *Partisaner i nord* (Oslo, 1979), Kjell Fjørtoft: *Lille Moskva* (Oslo, 1983) and *De som tapte krigen* (Oslo, 1979), and Morten Jentoft: *De som dro østover: Kola-nordmennenes historie* (Oslo, 2001). The central documents, on which Fjørtoft, in particular, appears to have drawn, are the war diaries (KTB = *Kriegstagebücher*) of the 210th Infantry Division, which was also responsible for the security of the eastern border regions. The war diaries of the Intelligence Section (Ic) have for the most part been preserved and contain a detailed description of the German offensive against the partisans, including transcripts of the interrogations of those taken prisoner in summer 1943 and of the indictments placed before the courts that same autumn. Åge Halvari was interrogated on 27 October and 1 November 1943 by the 210th Division's intelligence officer, *Premierleutnant* Fritz Pardon, a district stipendiary magistrate in civilian life, who was responsible for hunting down the partisans. The war diaries of the 210th Division are available both on microfilm in the National Archives, Washington (the most interesting part on Roll T315/1621), and in the original in MA, Freiburg (RH 26/210-23).

p. 23 *There was nothing there* I interviewed Hans Moos on several occasions in 2002 and 2003, both in Norway and in Germany.

p. 23 *Some days later* Information relating to the raid on the Soviet consulate is taken from Tore Pryser: *Hitlers hemmelige agenter: Tysk etterretning i Norge 1939–1945* (Oslo, 2001), p. 74 ff. Some interesting information on the German direction-finding stations in Kirkenes is contained in Heinz Bonath: *Seekrieg im Äther: Die Leistungen der Marine-Funkaufklärung 1939–1945* (Herford, 1981).

p. 23 *In Central Europe* Finland's dramatic war history is far more complex and voluminous than there is space for in this book. It is difficult to find relevant accounts that are wholly unbiased, but Allan Sandström: *Krieg unter der Mitternachtssonne* (Graz, 1996) and Olli Vehviläinen: *Finland in the Second World War: Between Germany and Russia* (Basingstoke, 2002) both provide a good overall picture of the situation.

p. 25 *One of the SS soldiers* These letters are quoted from Gyltenhaal and Gebhardt, p. 46 ff.

p. 27 *At about the same time* The German reports on the sinking of the *Donau* and *Bahia Laura* are in the archives left behind by AOK Nord-Norwegen. Microfilm no. T314/1556, National Archives, Washington.

p. 29 *Kurt Schultze, a former major* In 2003 I corresponded and several times spoke on the telephone with Schultze, who is now retired and resident in California. My thanks are due to the driving force behind the Tirpitz Museum in Tromsø, former Captain Leif Arneberg, who gave me Schultze's address.

THE JOURNEY TO FINNMARK

p. 31 *The first thing to greet* In July 2003 my wife and I spent a most interesting Sunday afternoon and evening in the company of Deirdre Henty-Creer and were enabled to peruse her large collection of photographs, documents and newspaper cuttings.

p. 37 *Meanwhile, another witness* The police interrogation of Lars Sarilla is dated 5 July 1950 and took place at the inn in Bossekop. A copy of his statement was given to me by Deirdre Henty-Creer.

THE KEY THEATRE IN THE NORTH

p. 41 *Ib Riis had first gone to sea* Information on the Icelander's recruitment as a double agent by the British and his part in the PQ17 deception was not released by MI5 and entrusted to the National Archives (ref. KV2/1137) until spring 2003, nearly sixty years after the end of the war. This illustrates with all desirable clarity how sensitive the matter was considered to be by the British. Ib Riis is still alive and is resident in California. I interviewed him several times by telephone in the summer of 2003 and also received from him a number of relevant documents.

p. 44 *Latchmere House was the site* For further details regarding Camp 020 see, for example, Nigel West: *MI5: British Security Operations 1909–1945* (London, 1981).

p. 46 *What a cargo for the Russians* Quoted from David Irving: *The Destruction of Convoy PQ.17* (London, 1985), p. 74 f. Controversial though the author may be, this book is still considered to be the best account of this ill-starred convoy, and all the quotations in this chapter are taken from it.

p. 46 *Why were the British* For more about the *Tirpitz*, see Jochen Brennecke: *Schlachtschiff Tirpitz* (Hamburg, 1975).

p. 48 *The situation was still unresolved* Michael Salewski's three-volume work *Die deutsche Seekriegsleitung 1935–1945* (Frankfurt, 1970–75) is still the best overall account of the strained relations between Hitler and the German Naval High Command. See vol. 2, p. 8 ff.

p. 49 *What Schörner found* The inhuman conditions prevailing on the Litza front have been described in many memoirs, among them Alex Buchner: *Vom Eismeer bis zum Kaukasus* (Utting, 1988).

p. 52 *The entry of the United States* I have based my account on Richard Woodman: *Arctic Convoys 1941–1945* (London, 1994).

p. 55 *By this time Tovey* See Henry Denham's autobiography: *Inside the Nazi Ring: A Naval Attaché in Sweden 1940-1945* (London, 1984), p. 86 ff. For an account of Swedish signal intelligence, see C.G. McKay and Bengt Beckman: *Swedish Signal Intelligence 1900–1945* (London, 2003).

p. 56 *Early in the afternoon* Douglas Fairbanks Jr is quoted from Irving, p. 74.

THE SEARCH

p. 61 *Quite by chance* Quoted from Pamela Mellor and Frank Walker: *The Mystery of X5* (London, 1986), p. 185. I have also spoken several times with Mrs Mellor on the subject.

p. 62 *The Germans kept the prisoners* Quoted from a letter to the editor that appeared in the Oslo daily newspaper *Aftenposten* shortly after the war. Not a few of the assertions made in this letter seem quite nonsensical. Regrettably, some of the other information given to the Henty-Creer family would also appear to lack credibility on a number of important points. I received a copy of the letter, which is undated, from Deirdre Henty-Creer.

p. 63 *I dived six times around the fjord* Quoted from Peter Cornish's 1975 report, which appeared in *After the Battle* no. 17.

IN LOVE AND WAR

p. 67 *August is a grim month* See Werner Girbig: *Jagdegeschwader 5 'Eismeerjäger'* (Stuttgart, 1976), p. 112 ff.

p. 68 *Undetected, a Soviet reconnaissance patrol* Quoted from Franz Kurowski: *Generaloberst Dietl: Deutscher Heerführer am Polarkreis* (Landsberg, 1990), p. 193 ff.

p. 70 *The diesel engine was* Interrogation of Harald Utne on 29 September 1943 by *Premierleutnant* Pardon, KTB 210th Division.

p. 72 *Whenever she had to go to Hammerfest* I interviewed Regina and Werner Brand for the first time in Heiligenhafen in May 2003 and subsequently visited them at their home in Hamburg, where Regina generously placed her wartime letters and photographs at my disposal. For more details of the German fish-filleting factory in Hammerfest and the forced workers from the Ukraine, see my book *Fra brent jord til Klondyke* (Oslo, 1996), p. 21 ff.

p. 73 *The new installations* The story of Karl and Solveig Lausch was told in an exemplary manner by the documentary film-maker Torill Svaar in her television film *Krigsbrudene* [The War Brides], which was shown by the Norwegian Broadcasting Corporation (NRK) in 1999. I have since talked to Karl Lausch on several occasions.

THE DIVERS RETURN

p. 75 *Our three week stay* Quoted from *The Kaafjord Expedition Report* (1975). Other information on this subject derives from the newspaper *Finnmark Dagblad*, Pamela Mellor and Deirdre Henty-Creer.

WAITING

p. 83 *The location really was* Lieutenant Ivor Jarvis in Pamela Mitchell: *The Tip of the Spear* (London, 1993), p. 60 ff. The account of the preparations for the attack, as well as the quotations, are from this book, which is not widely known but which was written by the daughter of one of the men who built the midget submarines, and from *Sink the Tirpitz* by Léonce Peillard, who interviewed some of the British survivors on their return from captivity in Germany. The quotations from Cameron's journal are likewise from Peillard. My account is similarly based on conversations I had with Aitken, Lorimer and Kendall in the spring and summer of 2003.

p. 86 *With nose tightly clipped* Quoted from *Underwater Warriors*, p. 117.

p. 87 *With special training* Frank Walker in *The Mystery of X5*, p. 152.

p. 88 *Two months had gone by* The never-to-be-completed memoirs left behind by Henty Henty-Creer make up the first half of *The Mystery of X5*. They take the story of the midget submarines up to the point when they set out for Alta.

p. 91 *Lieutenant Donald* Readers with specialist knowledge will know that there is no prehistoric fish named Pdinichthys. The true name of this fish is Dinichthys. Place added the initial 'P' to bring the name of his craft into line with the others.

p. 91 *On board the Tirpitz* The description of the situation on board the *Tirpitz* is based on my interviews with survivors, together with the war diaries of the Naval High Command (SKL), the 1st Battle Group, *Admiral Nordmeer, Tirpitz, Lützow, Scharnhorst,* 4th, 5th and 6th Destroyer Flotillas, *Z27, Z29* and Erich Steinbrink, as well as those of *Gruppe Nord,* Kiel, and the 230th Division. Together with the British sources referred to earlier in these notes, these sources combine to make up a mosaic which, in my opinion, provides a new – and correct – picture of the events in question.

p. 95 *One of the men who toiled* I am very grateful to Inge Ehrhardt for sharing with me her recollections and her father's letters. Although they were written as late as 1944, the letters afford an authentic insight into what service on board the *Tirpitz* was like. I have also been allowed access by *Riksarkivet* (The Norwegian National Archives) to documents relating to the Carl Zeiss branch office in Horten.

p. 97 *It emerged from the discussion* The transcript of the conversation between Menke and Kummetz is in KTB 1st Battle Group.

p. 97 *Fear of sabotage* My account is based on careful study of documents in KTB 210th Division (Ic). All quotations are from interrogations and reports compiled by *Premierleutnant* Fritz Pardon in the summer and autumn of 1943. The original text (here in translation) of these documents has never before been published.

p. 100 *While Pardon was in Kirkenes* I base myself here on the definitive German work *Von Nanok bis Eismitte: Meteorologische Unternehmungen in der Arktis 1940–1945* by the historian Franz Selinger (Bremerhaven, 2001). No equivalent Norwegian work exists, apart from a book by Thoralv Lund, a journalist, *Kalde krigsår: Svalbard 1940–1945* (Oslo, 1990). Lund, who was in the army, was serving in Spitsbergen in 1943 when the attack took place; the quotations in this chapter and later in the book are from his account.

THE PASSAGE

p. 103 *It was nearing four o'clock* This account is based on that in the *London Gazette* and on eye-witness accounts quoted in *The Tip of the Spear,* p. 70 ff, as well as my own interviews with Aitken, Lorimer and Kendall.

p. 107 *In the meantime MI6* These signals are in the *Upsilon* file in the Norwegian Resistance Museum in Oslo. See also Ragnar Ulstein: *Etterretningstjenesten på Norge 1940–1945* (Oslo, 1989–1992).

p. 109 *When that Spitfire flew* This account is based in its entirety on contemporary reports contained in KTB Tirpitz, KTB Scharnhorst and KTB 4th Destroyer Flotilla.

p. 112 *The destruction made* I interviewed *U-716*'s wireless operator, Peter Junker, in Cuxhaven in the summer of 2002.

p. 115 *The infantrymen were lined up* From Toralv Lunde: *Iskalde år,* p. 76 ff.

APPROACHING THE TARGET

p. 120 *Twelve hours after setting out* This account is based on *The Tip of the Spear*, *The Mystery of X5* and *Sink the Tirpitz*.

p. 123 *In the Kå fjord, autumn* I interviewed Hein Hellendoorn in his home early in July 2003. Supplementary information is from the relevant war diaries.

p. 128 *A strongly built man* This description is based on my interviews with Lohse himself and the Brand family, as well as the letters I have so kindly been given access to.

p. 130 *At his provisional headquarters* Detailed documentation is contained in KTB 210th Division (Ic). The same applies to transcripts of wireless signals passing between Finnmark and Murmansk. Reference has also been had to Fjørtoft: *De som tapte krigen*, p. 143 ff. From the point of view of military history, there is still much to be done in regard to partisan operations behind the German lines in Finnmark. This is because, sixty years after the war, the Russians have still not opened their archives on these operations, which were run partly by the Northern Fleet, partly by the NKVD. Looking back, it seems very strange that the Soviet commanders should have placed three groups of agents in the same area, all with more or less the same assignments, as this dramatically increased the risks to which those involved were exposed. It is also unclear what results were actually achieved. Many different figures have been adduced relating to the number of ships sunk on the basis of information radioed by the partisans to Murmansk, but most of them are far too high. Figures arrived at by Erling Skjold reveal that only nine vessels were irretrievably lost as a result of torpedo attacks between Makkaur and Vardø between April 1942 and September 1943 – six merchantmen, one guardship and two submarine chasers. The available figures suggest that the success of the Soviet Russians left much to be desired, despite the courage of the agents concerned and the great sacrifices they made. A final and objective assessment will have to wait until Moscow is more forthcoming.

THE ATTACK

p. 145 *Everybody's nerves were* See Peillard, p. 213 ff. The quotations in what follows are taken from Cameron's journal, interviews undertaken by Peillard, the *London Gazette* and my own interviews with the survivors. The description of the situation on the German side is from KTB Tirpitz and KTB 1st Battle Group.

p. 158 *On board the Tirpitz* Bo'sun Hans Schmidt was interviewed by History Films, Munich, in 1999.

p. 162 *In the Admiral's quarters* Max Krause's testimony is contained in the report of the interrogations of the thirty-six men who survived the sinking of the *Scharnhorst*; see note to p. 2.

p. 166 *In the fire-control centre* All the quotations that follow in this chapter are from the war diaries and reports in MA, Freiburg.

p. 167 *Not long after breakfast* Captain Hertzberg and the crew of the *Stamsund* were questioned in 1946, though I have been unable to discover why.

p. 172 *It was reaching to our knees* Aitken's statement to the author, summer 2003.

AFTER THE ATTACK

p. 177 *Everyone was deeply moved* See Peillard, p. 273 ff.

p. 178 *The immediate crisis had passed* All the following quotations are from KTB Tirpitz and other war diaries.

p. 183 *The man in charge of the shipyard workers* KTB 1st Battle Group, 28 November 1943.

p. 183 *In the meantime, Operation Tundra* KTB 210th Division (Ic).

p. 186 *But Pardon and the German naval officers* This is the first time the fate of the Soviet submarine has been disclosed, largely thanks to the work done by the Russian historian Miroslav Morozov, who was allowed access to the relevant archives. I wish to thank Captain Erling Skjold of the Royal Norwegian Air Force for putting me in touch with Morozov. Skjold is a leading authority on the naval aspects of the war in Norway. His database, *Norsk Skipsvrakarkiv*, is an invaluable source of information.

THE SEARCH

p. 193 *I spent much of the summer* References to sources are contained in the text. I wish nonetheless to point out that I have checked the testimonies of those involved against the war diaries and other documents.

ATTACK FROM THE AIR

p. 199 *The air-raid alarm sounded* This chapter is based on the war diaries of the *Tirpitz*, 4th Destroyer Flotilla and other vessels in the Kå fjord at the time, together with my interviews with Hellendoorn, Brand, Lohse and others. See also John Sweetman: *Hunting the Beast* (London, 2001), p. 50 ff.

p. 209 *'They were armour-piercing bullets* Hein Hellendoorn in an interview with the author in July 2003.

THE KÅ FJORD IS ABANDONED

p. 213 *A Luftwaffe NCO* For more details, see the report in KTB Tirpitz.

p. 214 *In late 1942 many of the nation's* For an account of Finland's capitulation, see Sandström, p. 266 ff.

p. 217 *In Hammerfest there is* The relevant letters are in my possession.

p. 221 *Early in the morning of 6 June 1944* For a full account of the destruction of the Lyra and Ida networks, see my book *Scharnhorst* (Stroud, 2003), p. 267 ff.

p. 222 *One of the men Klötzer had* See KTB 210th Division, interrogation of Signe Bogdanoff.

DEFEAT

p. 225 *The room was still* The judgement handed down by those who tried Heinrich Ehrler and the other men accused with him on 20 December 1944 is an exceptionally valuable source of information for an understanding of the final attack on, and sinking of, the *Tirpitz*. I was given my annotated copy by Kurt Schultze, Ehrler's one-time adjutant, who was in the air over Tromsø on 12 November 1944. In other respects I have drawn on *Kapitänleutnant* Fassbender's report (KTB Tirpitz), as well as my interviews with Hellendoorn, who was Fassbender's second-in-command and survived the attack. Other quotations and testimonies are taken from *Der Scheinwerfer*, the newsletter published by the Tirpitz Veterans Association.

p. 229 *In northern Finland* See Alfred Steurich: *Gebirgsjäger im Bild*, p. 160 ff.

p. 230 *The storming of the fortified* For an account of the liberation of Finnmark, see Anders Ole Hauglid, Knut Erik Jensen and Harry Westrheim: *Til befolkningen*, p. 22 ff.

p. 233 *The first of the townspeople to return* Quoted from my book *Fra brent jord til Klondyke*, p. 28 ff.

p. 233 *Lie and Lippestad* For information on this incident I am indebted to Per Bjørgan and Harald Riesto, authors of two excellent books, *Krigsår i Vadsø* (Vadsø, 1995) and *Den lille byen og krigen* (Stamsund, 2000).

p. 234 *This brought the total number* This figure represents the number of kills claimed by the squadron's pilots and officially recognised by the *Luftwaffe*. The true figure of aircraft shot down is indisputably a good deal lower, as in combat the number of aircraft downed tended to be overestimated.

p. 247 *I tried to explain* Interview with Kurt Schultze in the summer of 2003.

PEACE

p. 249 *We were lying at anchor* This account was given to a member of my own family. Most of those forcibly evacuated from Finnmark at the end of October 1944, among them my mother and father, were in Tromsø on 12 November and witnessed the sinking of the *Tirpitz*.

p. 253 *Premierleutnant Fritz Pardon* Interrogation of Fritz Pardon on 28 March 1946 (PWIS Norway Report No. 97), Norwegian Resistance Museum, Oslo.

Bibliography

Barnett, Correlli. *Engage the Enemy More Closely*, London, Penguin, 2000

Beesly, Patrick. *Very Special Intelligence: The Story of the Admiralty's Operational Intelligence Centre 1939–45*, revd edn, London, Greenhill, 2000

—— *Very Special Admiral: The Life of Admiral J.H. Godfrey CB*, London, Hamish Hamilton, 1980

—— and Rohwer, Jürgen. 'Special Intelligence und die Vernichtung der Scharnhorst', *Marine Rundschau* 10/74

Bekker, Cajus. *Verdammte See: Ein Kriegstagebuch der deutschen Marine*, Oldenburg, Ullstein, 1975

—— *Das grosse Bildbuch der deutschen Kriegsmarine 1939–45*, Oldenburg, Ullstein, 1972

Bjørgan, Per and Pedersen, Torbjørn. *Krigsår i Vadsø*, Vadsø, Vadsø Turnforening, 1995

Blair, Clay. *Hitler's U-boat War: The Hunted 1942–1945*, London, Cassell, 2000

Boehm, Hermann. *Norwegen zwischen England und Deutschland*, Lippoldsberg, Klosterhaus, 1956

Bonatz, Heinz. *Seekrieg im Äther: Die Leistungen der Marine-Funkaufklärung 1939–1945*, Herford, Mittler, 1981

Bredemeier, Heinrich. *Schlachtschiff Scharnhorst*, Herford, Koehler, 1994

Brennecke, Jochen. *Schlachtschiff Tirpitz*, Hamburg, Kohler, 1995

Breyer, Siegfried. 'Schlachtschiff Tirpitz', reprint from *Marine-Arsenal*, Friedberg, 1993

—— 'Schlachtschiff Scharnhorst', reprint from *Marine-Arsenal*, Friedberg, 1987

Brünner, Adalbert. 'Schlachtschiff Tirpitz im Einsatz: Ein Seeoffizier berichtet', reprint from *Marine-Arsenal*, Friedberg, 1993

Buchner, Alex. *Vom Eismeer bis zum Kaukasus: Die deutsche Gebirgstruppe im Zweiten Weltkrieg 1941/42*, Utting, Dörfler, 1988

Burn, Alan. *The Fighting Commodores*, Annapolis, Naval Institute Press, 1999

Busch, Fritz-Otto. *Tragödie am Nordkap*, Hanover, Sponholtz, 1958

Denham, Henry. *Inside the Nazi Ring*, London, Murray, 1984

Der Scheinwerfer, Tirpitz Veterans Association Newsletter, various editions

Dönitz, Karl. *Memoirs: Ten Years and Twenty Days*, London, Cassell, 2000

Evans, Mark Llewellyn. *Great World War II Battles in the Arctic*, Westport, Greenwood Press, 1999

Fehse, Werner. *Die Chronik der 1. Staffel (F) Aufklärungsgruppe 124*, Bonn, priv. pub., 1999

Fjørtoft, Kjell. *Lille-Moskva*, Oslo, Gyldendal, 1983

—— *De som tapte krigen*, Oslo, Gyldendal, 1995

Fraser, Bruce. 'The Sinking of the German Battle-cruiser Scharnhorst on the 26th December 1943', *London Gazette*, 5 August 1947

Gallagher, Thomas. *Against All Odds*, London, Macdonald, 1971

Gamst, Thorbein. *Finnmark under hakekorset*, Arendal, Agdin, 1984

Girbig, Werner. *Jagdgeschwader 5 'Eismeerjäger': Eine Chronik aus Dokumenten und Berichten 1941–1945*, Stuttgart, Motorbuch Verlag, 1976

Golovko, Arseni. *Zwischen Spitzbergen und Tiksibucht*, Berlin, Militärverlag DDR, 1965

Gray, Edwyn. *Hitler's Battleships*, Barnsley, Leo Cooper, 1999

Gyllenhaal, Lars and Gebhardt, James. *Slagt om Nordkalotten*, Lund, Historiske Media, 2001

Hauglid, Anders O., Jensen, Knut E. and Westerheim, Harry. *Til befolkningen!*, Oslo, Universitetsforlaget, 1982

Hinsley, F.H. *British Intelligence in the Second World War*, 5 vols, London, HMSO, 1979–90

Humble, Richard. *Fraser of North Cape*, London, Routledge & Kegan Paul, 1983

Irving, David. *The Destruction of Convoy PQ.17*, London, Panther, 1985

Jentoft, Morten. *De som dro østover: Kola-nordmennenes historie*, Oslo, Gyldendal, 2001

Jessop, Keith. *Goldfinder*, London, Simon & Schuster UK, 1998

Jones, Geoffrey. *Under Three Flags: The Story of Nordmark and the Armed Supply Ships of the German Navy*, London, William Kimble, 1973

Kaltenegger, Roland. *Krieg am Eismeer. Gebirgsjäger im Kampf um Narvik, Murmansk und die Murmanbahn*, Graz, Leopold Stocker, 1999

Kemp, Paul. *U-boats Destroyed: German Submarine Losses in the World Wars*, London, Arms and Armour, 1999

—— *Underwater Warriors*, London, Cassell, 1996

Kennedy, Ludovic. *Menace: The Life and Death of the Tirpitz*, London, Sphere Books, 1981

Kolyshkin, I. *Russian Submarines in Arctic Waters*, New York, Bantam, 1985

Koop, Gerhard and Schmolke, Klaus-Peter. *Battleships of the Scharnhorst Class*, trans. Geoffrey Brooks, London, Greenhill Books, 1999

Kurowski, Franz. *Generaloberst Dietl: Deutscher Heerführer am Polarkreis*, Landsberg, 1990

McKay, C.G. and Beckman, Bengt. *Swedish Signal Intelligence*, London, Frank Cass, 2003

Mellor, Pamela and Walker, Frank. *The Mystery of X5*, London, William Kimber, 1988

Mitchell, Pamela. *The Tip of the Spear*, Huddersfield, Richard Netherwood, 1993

Nauroth, Holger. *Schlachtkreuzer Scharnhorst und Gneisenau: Die Bildchronic 1939–1945*, Stuttgart, Motorbuch Verlag, 2002

Nielsen, Jens Petter and Eikeset, Kjell Roger. *Altas historie*, 3 vols, Alta, Alta kommune, 1990–98

Nøkleby, Berit. *Pass godt på Tirpitz!*, Oslo, Gyldendal, 1988

Ogden, Michael. *The Battle of North Cape*, London, Kimber, 1962

'Operation Source', supplement to the *London Gazette*, 10 February 1948

Ost, Horst Gotthard. *U-boote im Eismeer*, Berlin, Franz Schneider Verlag, 1943

Padfield, Peter. *Dönitz: The Last Führer*, London, Cassell, 2000

Pedersen, Gunnar. *Militær motstand i nord, 1940–45*, Oslo, Gyldendal, 1982

Peillard, Léonce. *Sink the Tirpitz*, trans. Robert Laffont, London, Jonathan Cape, 1968

Penrose, Barrie. *Stalin's Gold*, London, Granada, 1982

Peter, Karl. *Schlachtkreuzer Scharnhorst: Kampf und Untergang*, Berlin, Mittler, 1951

Pitt, Barrie et al (eds). *The Battle of the Atlantic*, New York, Time-Life Books, 1977

Pope, Dudley. *73 North: The Defeat of Hitler's Navy*, Annapolis, Naval Institute Press, 1958

Pryser, Tore. *Hitlers hemmelige agenter*, Oslo, Universitetsforlaget, 2001

Riesto, Harald. *Den lille byen og krigen: Vadsø 1940–1945*, Stamsund, Orkana, 2000

—— *Frihetskjemperen Karl Halvdan Rasmussen og etterretningsgruppen Ida*, Vadsø, Vadsø bibliotek, 1995

Rohwer, J. and Hümmelchen, G. *Chronology of the War at Sea*, New York, Arco, 1971

Roskill, Stephen. *The War at Sea*, London, HMSO, 1974–81

Ruge, Friedrich. *Der Seekrieg 1939–45*, Stuttgart, Koehler, 1962

Rust, Eric C. *Naval Officers under Hitler: The Story of Crew 34*, New York, Greenwood, 1991

Rørholt, Bjørn. *Usynlige soldater*, Oslo, Aschehoug, 1990

Salewski, Michael. *Die deutsche Seekriegsleitung 1935–1945*, 3 vols, Frankfurt am Main/Munich, Bernard & Graefe, 1970–75

Sandström, Allan. *Krieg unter der Mitternachtssonen*, Graz, Leopold Stocker, 1996

Schofield, B.B. *The Russian Convoys*, London, Pan Books, 1971

Sebag-Montefiore, Hugh. *The Battle for the Code*, London, Weidenfeld & Nicolson, 2000

Selinger, Franz. *Von Nanok bis Eismitte: Meteorologische Unternehmungen in der Arktis 1940–1945*, Hamburg, Convent, 2001

Showell, Jak P. Mallmann. *German Navy Handbook 1939–45*, Stroud, Sutton, 1999

Skodvin, Magne (ed.). *Norge i krig*, 8 vols, Oslo, Aschehoug, 1984–87

Smith, Michael. *Station X: The Codebreakers at Bletchley Park*, London, Macmillan, 1998

Steurich, Alfred. *Gebirgsjäger im Bild: 6. SS-Gebirgsdivision Nord 1940–1945*, Osnabrück, Munin, 1976

Storheill, Skule. 'Senkningen av slagskipet Scharnhorst den 26. desember 1943', *Norsk Tidsskrift for Sjøvæsen*, 1946

Sweetman, John. *Tirpitz: Hunting the Beast*, Annapolis, Naval Institute Press, 2000

Toliver, Raymond F. and Constable, Trevor J. *Fighter Aces of the Luftwaffe*, Atglen, Schiffer, 1996

Ullstein, Ragnar. *Etterretningstjenesten i Norge 1940–45*, 3 vols, Oslo, Cappelen, 1989–92

Vehviläinen, Olli. *Finland in the Second World War*, New York, Palgrave, 2002

Warren, C.E.T and Benson, James. *Above Us the Waves*, London, Harrap, 1953

Watts, A.J. *The Loss of the Scharnhorst*, London, Ian Allan, 1970

West, Nigel. *MI5: British Security Operations 1909–1945*, London, Bodley Head, 1981

Whitley, M.J. *German Capital Ships of World War Two*, London, Cassell, 1989

Winton, John. *The Death of the Scharnhorst*, London, Panther, 1984

Woodman, Richard. *Arctic Convoys*, London, John Murray, 1994

Woodward, David. *The Tirpitz and the Battle for the North Atlantic*, New York, Berkley, 1953

Øyfolk 'Årbok for lokalhistorie og kultur i Hammerfest' (Yearbook of Local History and Culture in Hammerfest), various editions, 1990–99

Index

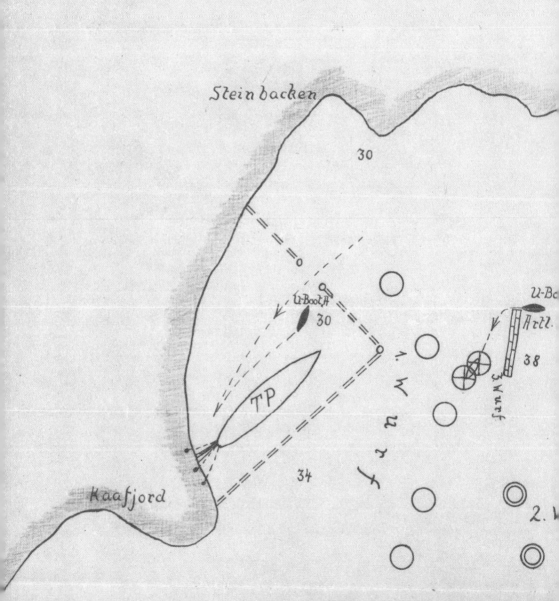

Skizze über U-Bootsbekämp[...]
durch
V-Boot „Z 29" am 22.9.1943.

Lage der Wasserbomben und sonstige
Entfernungen angenähert.

Steinbacken

30

U-Boot A
30

TP

1. Wurf

34

Kaafjord

U-Bo[...]
Artl.

38

Zwurf

2. [...]

25